## Grade 7

# Grammar Writing for

**Senior Series Consultant**

Beverly Ann Chin
Professor of English
University of Montana
Missoula, MT

**Series Consultant**

Frederick J. Panzer, Sr.
English Dept. Chair, Emeritus
Christopher Columbus High School
Miami, FL

**Series Consultant**

Anthony Bucco
Language Arts Literacy Teacher
Pierrepont Middle School
Rutherford, NJ

**Series Editor**

Phyllis Goldenberg

Sadlier

# Reviewers

# Acknowledgments

Every good faith effort has been made to locate the owners of copyrighted material to arrange permission to reprint selections. In several cases, this has proved impossible. Thanks to the following for permission to reprint copyrighted material.

From *A Place Called Ugly*, Copyright 1981 by Avi Wortis. Reprinted by permission of Brandt & Hochman Literary Agents, Inc. Used by permission of Brandt & Hochman Literary Agents, Inc. Any electronic copying or distribution of this text is expressly forbidden.

Excerpt from "Mrs Which" from A WRINKLE IN TIME by Madeleine L'Engle. Copyright © 1962, renewed 1990 by Madeleine L'Engle Franklin. Reprinted by permission of Farrar, Straus and Giroux, LLC.

Excerpt from *Across the Centuries*.

Copyright © 1999 by Houghton Mifflin Company.

*Call Me María* by Judith Ortiz Cofer. Copyright © 2004 by Judith Ortiz Cofer. All rights reserved. Published by Orchard Books, an imprint of Scholastic Inc.

Excerpt from *City of Beasts* by Isabel Allende. Copyright © 2002 by Isabel Allende. Published by HarperCollins Publishers.

*Esperanza Rising* by Pam Muñoz Ryan. Copyright © 2000 by Pam Muñoz Ryan. All rights reserved. Published by Scholastic Press, a division of Scholastic Inc.

Excerpt from *I'm a Stranger Here Myself*. Copyright © 1999 by Bill Bryson. All rights reserved. Published by Broadway Books, a division of Random House.

Excerpt from SOMETHING WICKED'S IN THOSE WOODS, copyright © 2000 by Marisa Montes, reprinted by permission of Houghton Mifflin Harcourt Publishing Company.

Excerpt from TANGERINE, copyright © 1997 by Edward Bloor, reprinted by permission of Houghton Mifflin Harcourt Publishing Company.

Excerpt from "Negro" from THE BIG SEA by Langston Hughes. Copyright © 1940 by Langston Hughes. Copyright renewed 1968 by Arna Bontemps and George Houston Bass. Reprinted by permission of Hill and Wang, a division of Farrar, Straus and Giroux, LLC.

*The Pigman & Me* by Paul Zindel. Copyright © 1991 by Paul Zindel. First appeared in *The Pigman and*

*Me*, published by HarperCollins Children's Books. Reprinted by permission of Curtis Brown, Ltd.

From *The Skin I'm In* by Sharon G. Flake. Copyright © 1998 by Sharon Flake. Reprinted by permissions of Disney • Hyperion Books, an imprint of Disney Book Group, LLC. All rights reserved.

Excerpt from *Where Will This Shoe Take You?* Copyright © 1996 by Laurie Lawlor. Published by Walker Publishing Company.

# Credits

**For additional online resources, go to www.grammarforwriting.com and enter the Teacher Access Code: instruction**

# CONTENTS

Introduction to *Grammar for Writing* . . . . . . . . . . . . . . . . T12–T13

Standards and Correlations . . . . . . . . . . . . . . . . . . . . . . . T14–T15

Five Ways to Use *Grammar for Writing* . . . . . . . . . . . . . . . . T16

Program Components—Print . . . . . . . . . . . . . . . . . . . . . . T17

Program Components—Online . . . . . . . . . . . . . . . . . . . . . T18

Writing Workshops and Writing Applications . . . . . . . . . . . . T19–T20

Steps to Finalize Writing . . . . . . . . . . . . . . . . . . . . . . . . . T21

Integrating Grammar and Writing . . . . . . . . . . . . . . . . . . . T22–T23

"Engaging Middle School Students in Writing and
Grammar Instruction" by Beverly Ann Chin, Ph.D. . . . . . . . . . T24–T27

Differentiating Instruction . . . . . . . . . . . . . . . . . . . . . . . . T28

Differentiating Instruction Charts . . . . . . . . . . . . . . . . . . . T29–T40

**ONLINE COMPONENTS**
www.grammarforwriting.com

**Available at www.grammarforwriting.com:**

**For Teachers**

✔ password-protected supplemental Answer Keys

✔ full-length research-based article by Beverly Ann Chin, Ph.D.

✔ writing rubrics

✔ professional development videos

✔ planning and pacing guide

✔ Answer Key to Student Test Booklet

**For Students**

✔ additional practice for grammar lessons

✔ work-in-progress writing models for each step of the writing process

✔ full-length writing models for each writing workshop

✔ step-by-step writing models

✔ peer review form

For more information about *Grammar for Writing* Online Components, see page T18.

# Introduction to *Grammar for Writing*

A strong English Language Arts curriculum covers five major strands: Reading, Writing, Speaking and Listening, Language, and Media and Technology. Each strand presents its own clear and consistent framework. Taken together, the five strands represent an integrated model of literacy for the twenty-first century.

***Grammar for Writing*** is designed as an effective tool to address the grade-specific goals of the writing component and language conventions of the standards. ***Grammar for Writing*** weaves the study of language conventions into a range of writing applications, including meeting the critical goal of writing to sources.

***Grammar for Writing,*** Grade 7, focuses students on using precise language, appropriate vocabulary and style, and effective transitions for their purpose and audience to

- produce *arguments* that support claims with strong reasons and relevant evidence to persuade a target audience;
- write *informative/explanatory* passages that introduce and convey ideas in an organized manner to develop a topic using germane facts, concrete details, and examples;
- compose *narratives* about real or imagined experiences using key narrative techniques to develop events and engage readers.

***Grammar for Writing,*** Grade 7, develops grammar skills by helping students
- demonstrate command of standard English grammar and usage;
- exhibit command of standard English capitalization, punctuation, and spelling;
- apply knowledge of language to use precise language when expressing ideas and to eliminate wordiness and redundancy.

Grammar Lessons provide instruction in key grammar, usage, and mechanics skills.

Exercises provide targeted practice for each skill.

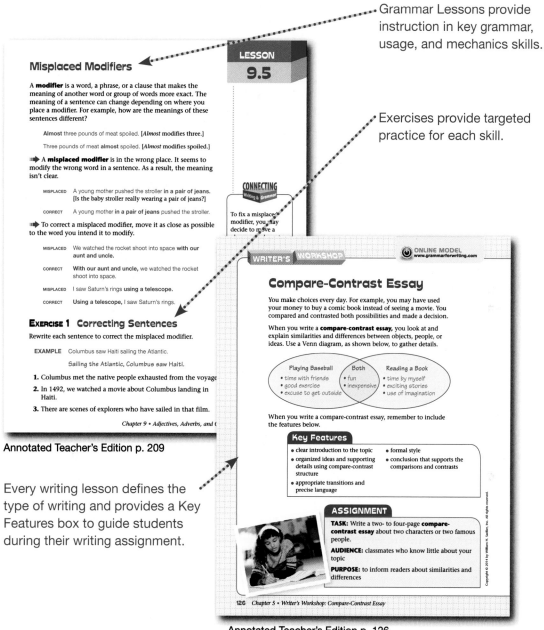

**Misplaced Modifiers**

LESSON
9.5

A **modifier** is a word, a phrase, or a clause that makes the meaning of another word or group of words more exact. The meaning of a sentence can change depending on where you place a modifier. For example, how are the meanings of these sentences different?

**Almost** three pounds of meat spoiled. [*Almost* modifies three.]

Three pounds of meat **almost** spoiled. [*Almost* modifies spoiled.]

➡ A **misplaced modifier** is in the wrong place. It seems to modify the wrong word in a sentence. As a result, the meaning isn't clear.

MISPLACED   A young mother pushed the stroller **in a pair of jeans**. [Is the baby stroller really wearing a pair of jeans?]

CORRECT   A young mother **in a pair of jeans** pushed the stroller.

➡ To correct a misplaced modifier, move it as close as possible to the word you intend it to modify.

MISPLACED   We watched the rocket shoot into space **with our aunt and uncle**.

CORRECT   **With our aunt and uncle**, we watched the rocket shoot into space.

MISPLACED   I saw Saturn's rings **using a telescope**.

CORRECT   **Using a telescope**, I saw Saturn's rings.

CONNECTING
Writing & Grammar

To fix a misplaced modifier, you may decide to move a

**EXERCISE 1  Correcting Sentences**

Rewrite each sentence to correct the misplaced modifier.

EXAMPLE   Columbus saw Haiti sailing the Atlantic.

Sailing the Atlantic, Columbus saw Haiti.

1. Columbus met the native people exhausted from the voyage
2. In 1492, we watched a movie about Columbus landing in Haiti.
3. There are scenes of explorers who have sailed in that film.

*Chapter 9 • Adjectives, Adverbs, and C*

Annotated Teacher's Edition p. 209

Every writing lesson defines the type of writing and provides a Key Features box to guide students during their writing assignment.

WRITER'S WORKSHOP

ONLINE MODEL
www.grammarforwriting.com

**Compare-Contrast Essay**

You make choices every day. For example, you may have used your money to buy a comic book instead of seeing a movie. You compared and contrasted both possibilities and made a decision.

When you write a **compare-contrast essay**, you look at and explain similarities and differences between objects, people, or ideas. Use a Venn diagram, as shown below, to gather details.

Playing Baseball
• time with friends
• good exercise
• excuse to get outside

Both
• fun
• inexpensive

Reading a Book
• time by myself
• exciting stories
• use of imagination

When you write a compare-contrast essay, remember to include the features below.

**Key Features**

• clear introduction to the topic
• organized ideas and supporting details using compare-contrast structure
• appropriate transitions and precise language
• formal style
• conclusion that supports the comparisons and contrasts

**ASSIGNMENT**

**TASK:** Write a two- to four-page **compare-contrast essay** about two characters or two famous people.

**AUDIENCE:** classmates who know little about your topic

**PURPOSE:** to inform readers about similarities and differences

126   Chapter 5 • Writer's Workshop: Compare-Contrast Essay

Annotated Teacher's Edition p. 126

The following table shows the text of generic Grade 7 writing and language conventions standards addressed in ***Grammar for Writing***. The left-hand column shows where each standard is covered in the program.

# WRITING STANDARDS

## Text Types and Purposes

Chapter and Lesson
(See key below.)

| | |
|---|---|
| **Write arguments** in a variety of forms; support claims with clear, logical reasons and relevant evidence. | WA2, 4.5, CR4, WW7, WW9 |
| Introduce claim(s), acknowledge alternate or opposing claims, and use organizational structures to present reasons and evidence clearly. | WA2, 4.3, 5.2, 5.3, 5.4, CR5, WW7, CR7, WW9 |
| Support claim(s) with clear, logical reasons and relevant evidence; use accurate and credible sources to demonstrate understanding of the topic or text. | WA2, 5.4, CR5, WW7, WW9 |
| Use effective transition words, phrases, and clauses to create cohesion and clarify relationships among claim(s), reasons, and evidence. | WA2, 4.3, 5.4, CR5, WW7, WW9 |
| Establish and maintain a consistent style and tone appropriate to purpose and audience. | WA2, WW7, WW9 |
| Present a concluding statement or section that follows from and supports the argument presented. | WA2, 5.5, CR5, WW7, WW9 |
| **Write informative/explanatory texts** in a variety of forms; examine a topic and convey ideas, concepts, and information through the selection, organization, and analysis of relevant content. | CR4, WW5, WA6, WA10, 11.8, WW11 |
| Introduce a topic; preview content to come; use organizational structures to present ideas, concepts, and information; use appropriate strategies such as definition, classification, comparison/contrast, and cause/effect; include formatting (e.g., headings), graphics (e.g., charts, tables), and multimedia when useful to support comprehension. | 4.3, 5.2, 5.3, 5.4, WW5, CR5, WA8 |
| Develop a topic with relevant facts, definitions, concrete details, quotations, or other information and examples from a variety of sources when appropriate. | 4.1, WW5, CR5, WA8 |
| Use effective transition words, phrases, and clauses to create cohesion and clarify the relationships among ideas and concepts. | 4.3, 4.4, 5.4, WW5, CR5, WA8 |
| Choose language and content-specific vocabulary to express ideas about a topic precisely. | WW5, WA8, WA12 |
| Establish and maintain a consistent style and tone appropriate to purpose and audience. | WW5, WA12 |
| Present a concluding statement or section that follows from and supports the information or explanation provided. | 5.5, WW5, CR5, WA12 |
| **Write narratives** in a variety of forms; develop actual or imagined experiences or events; use effective technique, relevant descriptive details, and clear sequences. | WW1, WW3, CR4 |
| Engage and orient the reader by establishing context and point of view; introduce a narrator and/or characters; organize events in a sequence that unfolds naturally and logically. | WW1, WW3 |
| Use narrative techniques, such as dialogue, pacing, and description, to develop experiences, events, and/or characters. | WW1, WW3, WA4, 11.6 |
| Use effective transition words, phrases, and clauses to convey sequence and signal shifts from one time frame or setting to another. | WW1, WW3, 4.4, WA4 |
| Choose precise words and phrases, relevant descriptive details, and sensory language to express the action and convey experiences and events. | WW1, WW3, 2.3, WA4 |
| Present a conclusion that follows from and reflects on the narrated experiences or events. | WW1, WW3 |

## Production and Distribution of Writing

| | |
|---|---|
| Produce texts whose development, organization, and style are appropriate to audience, purpose, and task. | 1.2, WW1, WA2, WW3, WA4, WW5, WA6, 7.5, WW7, WA8, WW9, WA10, WW11, WA12 |
| With some guidance and support from peers and adults, develop and strengthen writing as needed by planning, revising, editing, rewriting, or trying a new approach, with attention on how well purpose and audience are addressed. | 1.1, 1.3, 1.4, WW1, WW3, WW5, WW7, WW9, WW11 |
| Use technology to interact and collaborate with others to generate, produce, and publish writing and link to cited sources. | 1.5, WW3, WW5, WW9, WW11 |

**WW** Writer's Workshop   **WA** Writing Application   **CR** Chapter Review

## Research to Build and Present Knowledge

| | |
|---|---|
| Conduct research projects to answer a research question; draw information from multiple sources; redirect the inquiry when appropriate; develop additional questions for further inquiry. | WW11 |
| Gather relevant information from several print and digital sources; evaluate the credibility and accuracy of each source; quote or paraphrase the work of others while avoiding plagiarism; use a standard citation format. | WW11 |
| Draw evidence from literary or informational texts to support analysis, reflection, and research. | WW11 |
| Apply grade-level Reading standards to literature (e.g., "Compare and contrast a fictional portrayal of a time, place, or character and a historical account of the same period in order to understand how fiction writers use or alter history). | WA10 |
| Apply grade-level Reading standards to literary nonfiction (e.g., "Identify and evaluate the argument and claims in a text, assessing whether the reasoning is valid and the evidence is relevant and sufficient to support the claims"). | WA6 |
| Write regularly to produce text over extended time frames (time for research, reflection, and revision) and to produce text in shorter time frames (a single sitting or a day or two) for a variety of content-specific tasks, purposes, and audiences. | WW1, 2.1, 2.5, 2.6, 2.7, WA2, 3.1, 3.2, 3.3, 3.4, WW3, 4.2, 4.4, 4.5, WA4, 5.3, 5.5, WW5, 6.1, 6.2, 6.4, 6.6, WA6, 7.1, 7.5, WW7, 8.1, 8.2, 8.3, 8.5, WA8, 9.1, 9.2, 9.3, 9.4, 9.7, WW9, 10.2, 10.4, 10.5, WA10, CR10, 11.1, 11.2, 11.4, 11.6, 11.7, 11.8, WW11, 12.2, WA12 |

# LANGUAGE STANDARDS

## Conventions of Standard English

| | |
|---|---|
| Demonstrate command of the conventions of standard English grammar and usage when writing or speaking. | CR1, 2.1, 2.2, 2.4, 2.7, CR2, 3.1, 3.3, CR3, CR5, 6.1, 6.2, 6.3, 6.4, 6.5, 6.6, CR6, 7.1, 7.2, 7.3, 7.4, 7.5, 7.6, CR7, 8.1, 8.2, 8.3, 8.4, 8.6, CR8, 9.1, 9.2, 9.3, 9.4, 9.7, 10.1, 10.2, 10.3, 10.4, 10.5, CR10, 12.5 |
| Demonstrate understanding of the function of phrases and clauses in general and their function in specific sentences. | 3.4, 3.7, 8.6, CR8, 9.6, 10.2 |
| Choose among simple, compound, complex, and compound-complex sentences to show differing relationships among ideas. | 3.5, 3.6 |
| Place phrases and clauses within a sentence, identifying and correcting misplaced and dangling modifiers. | 3.7, 9.5, WW9, CR9 |
| Demonstrate command of the conventions of standard English capitalization, punctuation, and spelling when writing. | CR1, 2.1, 2.2, 2.4, CR2, 3.1, 3.3, 3.4, 3.6, CR3, 4.4, 5.5, 6.1, 7.1, 7.2, CR7, 9.1, 9.7, CR9, 11.1, 11.2, 11.3, 11.4, 11.5, 11.6, 11.7, 11.8, CR11, 12.1, 12.2, 12.3, 12.5, WA12, CR12 |
| Use a comma to separate coordinate adjectives (e.g. *It was a quick, drenching rain,* but not *They saw a tiny, baby chick.*) | 11.3 |
| Spell words correctly. | WW7, 8.2, 8.3, 9.2, WW9, 12.4, CR12 |

## Knowledge of Language

| | |
|---|---|
| Demonstrate knowledge of language and its conventions when writing, speaking, reading, or listening. | 2.3, 2.4, 2.7, CR2, 3.2, 3.3, 4.2, 5.3, 8.5, WA8, CR8 |
| Express ideas precisely and concisely, identifying and eliminating wordiness and redundancy. | 2.5, 2.6, CR2, 10.3, WA12 |

WW Writer's Workshop    WA Writing Application    CR Chapter Review

# Five Ways to Use *Grammar for Writing*

Flexible and versatile, *Grammar for Writing* can facilitate a variety of instructional purposes. Teachers may opt to use the program as the core vehicle for delivering language arts instruction, or they may choose to use it as a supplement to meet specific curricular goals and students' needs.

| Instructional Use | Key Features and Support |
|---|---|
| 1. **Complete Course** | • Comprehensive coverage of writing and language conventions<br>• Research-based instructional approaches<br>• Thorough explanations and abundant examples<br>• Instruction, practice, assessment, and reteaching<br>• Full array of components |
| 2. **Reference Tool** | • Easy two-part organization of chapters and lessons<br>• Complete index of grammar and writing concepts<br>• List of Frequently Misspelled Words<br>• List of Commonly Confused Words<br>• Online reference tools |
| 3. **Guide for Independent and/or Small Group Learning** | • Clarification of lesson topics<br>• Explanatory charts and graphic organizers<br>• Annotated Literary Models and Writing Models<br>• Activities for Working Together<br>• Strategic hints, tips, and reminders |
| 4. **Source of Review and Practice** | • Engaging and effective exercises for every lesson<br>• Meaningful student-centered online practice<br>• Writing Workshops<br>• Writing Applications<br>• Chapter Review activities |
| 5. **Test Preparations** | • Tests in standardized test formats<br>• Practice Test in every Chapter Review<br>• Additional assessment online and in Test Booklet<br>• Test-taking Tips<br>• Writing applications to practice for writing tests |

# Program Components—Print

### Student Edition

The Student Edition of this comprehensive grammar and writing program helps all learners meet rigorous expectations for English Language Arts. Its chapters provide an organized path to help students master increasingly sophisticated core skills in grammar, usage, punctuation, capitalization, and spelling—all in service to effective written communication.

### Key features of the print edition include:
- Teaching of the fundamental steps of the Writing Process
- Varied Writer's Workshop Assignments that clearly define task, audience, and purpose
- Sidebar tips, graphic organizers, and Key Features charts
- Frequent assessment options to evaluate ongoing progress via Chapter Review exercises

### Annotated Teacher Edition

The Annotated Teacher Edition that accompanies the program is a rich source for instruction, convenient on-page answers and annotations, as well as helpful tips and strategies for efficient lesson planning, classroom management, and assessment.

### Key elements of the ATE include:
- Targeted instructional notes
- Writing Process guidelines
- Support for English Language Learners and Striving Learners

### Test Booklet (separate purchase)

The Test Booklet extends testing and assessment opportunities that parallel the chapters in the Student Edition. It includes comprehensive chapter tests that follow typical standardized test formats: error recognition and correction. A Diagnostic Test helps teachers identify problem areas and address individual needs; a Mastery Test augments the assessments found in the Student Edition. A separate Test Book Answer Key is provided online for ease of scoring.

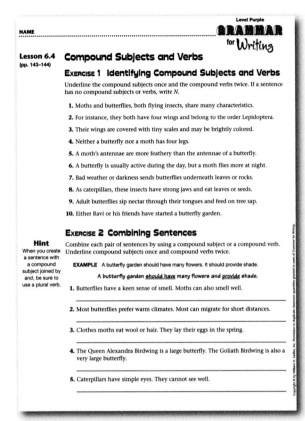

Extra Practice
Exercises,
Lesson 6.4

**Extra Practice Exercise Pages** present lesson-by-lesson exercises similar to those that appear in the print version. Teachers may assign these to individuals or groups as needed for practice, homework, or assessment.

**Student Edition Answer Keys** exist for each chapter. In cases where answers may vary, full sample answers or written responses appear.

**Writing Rubrics** are checklists specific to different text types and purposes: *expository, persuasive, narrative,* and *informative* writing. Each rubric presents three sets of specific evaluations characteristic of writing ranked as *excellent, average,* or *poor.* Teachers and students benefit from discussing a rubric <u>before</u> writing to clarify expectations and specify clear goals.

**Writing Workshops** illustrate the writing process. Multi-step "work in progress" pages model prewriting, drafting, revising, editing and proofreading, and publishing and presenting. In addition, full-length examples of Story, Comparison-Contrast Essay, Persuasive Essay, Book Review, Research Paper, and Autobiographical Incident demonstrate the features of each type of writing and encourage students to evaluate the strengths and weaknesses of each model essay.

The **Online Peer Review Form** is a set of ten questions that serves as a logical guide for students to use as they evaluate each other's drafts. Sidebar tips suggest ways to make specific, objective comments.

The **Pacing Guide** offers teachers a plan for using *Grammar for Writing* as a complete course in Language Arts.

# Writing Workshops and Writing Applications

Writing Workshops and Writing Applications at the end of each chapter cover:

- writing modes and forms, such as autobiographical incidents, compare-contrast essays, persuasive essays, book reviews, and research reports

- writing purposes, such as to describe, to entertain, to explain, and to persuade

Writing Workshops guide students through each step of the writing process, offering step-by-step instruction, Writing Models, tips, Revising checklists, and Editing and Proofreading checklists.

Each page in a Writing Workshop is dedicated to a different **step of the writing process**.

A **Writing Hint** addresses features of the text type.

**Visuals, such as graphic organizers and charts,** provide effective models for students.

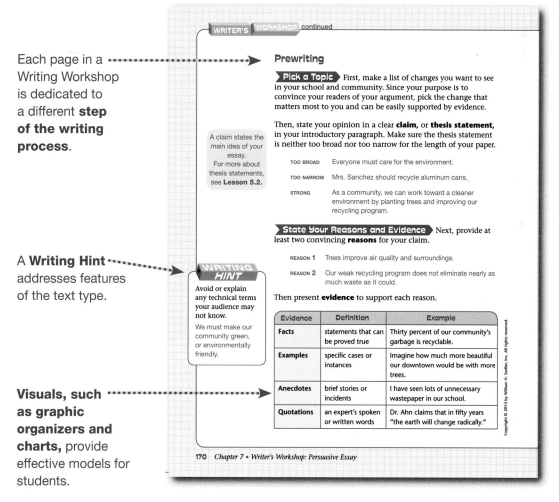

**WRITER'S WORKSHOP** continued

### Prewriting

**Pick a Topic** First, make a list of changes you want to see in your school and community. Since your purpose is to convince your readers of your argument, pick the change that matters most to you and can be easily supported by evidence.

Then, state your opinion in a clear **claim,** or **thesis statement,** in your introductory paragraph. Make sure the thesis statement is neither too broad nor too narrow for the length of your paper.

> A claim states the main idea of your essay.
> For more about thesis statements, see **Lesson 5.2.**

| TOO BROAD | Everyone must care for the environment. |
| TOO NARROW | Mrs. Sanchez should recycle aluminum cans. |
| STRONG | As a community, we can work toward a cleaner environment by planting trees and improving our recycling program. |

**State Your Reasons and Evidence** Next, provide at least two convincing **reasons** for your claim.

| REASON 1 | Trees improve air quality and surroundings. |
| REASON 2 | Our weak recycling program does not eliminate nearly as much waste as it could. |

**WRITING HINT**

Avoid or explain any technical terms your audience may not know.

We must make our community green, or environmentally friendly.

Then present **evidence** to support each reason.

| Evidence | Definition | Example |
|---|---|---|
| Facts | statements that can be proved true | Thirty percent of our community's garbage is recyclable. |
| Examples | specific cases or instances | Imagine how much more beautiful our downtown would be with more trees. |
| Anecdotes | brief stories or incidents | I have seen lots of unnecessary wastepaper in our school. |
| Quotations | an expert's spoken or written words | Dr. Ahn claims that in fifty years "the earth will change radically." |

170    *Chapter 7 • Writer's Workshop: Persuasive Essay*

Annotated Teacher's Edition p. 170

**Specific Revising Suggestions** help students evaluate their drafts.

**Looking Back** directs students to an earlier lesson.

**Annotated Writing Models** demonstrate effective ways to improve writing.

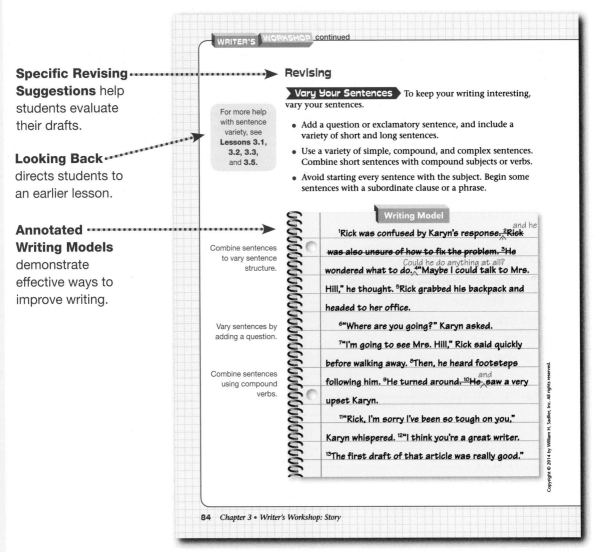

WRITER'S WORKSHOP continued

## Revising

**Vary Your Sentences** To keep your writing interesting, vary your sentences.

For more help with sentence variety, see **Lessons 3.1, 3.2, 3.3,** and **3.5.**

- Add a question or exclamatory sentence, and include a variety of short and long sentences.
- Use a variety of simple, compound, and complex sentences. Combine short sentences with compound subjects or verbs.
- Avoid starting every sentence with the subject. Begin some sentences with a subordinate clause or a phrase.

### Writing Model

Combine sentences to vary sentence structure.

Vary sentences by adding a question.

Combine sentences using compound verbs.

¹Rick was confused by Karyn's response. ²Rick ~~was also unsure of how to fix the problem.~~ ³He *and he* wondered what to do, *Could he do anything at all?* ⁴"Maybe I could talk to Mrs. Hill," he thought. ⁵Rick grabbed his backpack and headed to her office.

⁶"Where are you going?" Karyn asked.

⁷"I'm going to see Mrs. Hill," Rick said quickly before walking away. ⁸Then, he heard footsteps following him. ⁹He turned around. ¹⁰He *and* saw a very upset Karyn.

¹¹"Rick, I'm sorry I've been so tough on you," Karyn whispered. ¹²"I think you're a great writer. ¹³The first draft of that article was really good."

84 *Chapter 3 • Writer's Workshop: Story*

Annotated Teacher's Edition p. 84

Writing Applications are short, step-by-step lessons for crafting writing pieces, such as persuasive speeches, descriptive paragraphs, summaries, and business letters.

# Steps to Finalize Writing

*Grammar for Writing* provides several teaching and practice opportunities for students to finalize their writing.

## 1. Revising Questions

Revising Questions in the Writing Process Chapter and in each Writing Workshop help students focus on improving their drafts by using five of the six traits of good writing. (The sixth trait, conventions, is taught in the Editing and Proofreading lesson and in each workshop.)

## 2. Peer Review Form

Peer Review guidelines and tips are taught in the Writing Process chapter and in several Writing Workshops. An online Peer Review Form provides specific questions peers may ask each other in an easy-to-use format.

## 3. Publishing

Publishing tips are provided in the Writing Process chapter and in every Writing Workshop.

## 4. Presenting

A variety of tips and guidelines for presenting are provided in the Writing Process chapter and in every Writing Workshop. Suggestions are based on listening and speaking standards.

### Revising Questions

❑ How clear is my use of spatial order?
❑ Where can I add figurative language and imagery?
❑ How effective is my use of sensory details?
❑ How clearly have I expressed my feelings about the place?
❑ H

### Peer Review Questions

Peer Reviewer's Name: _____
Writer's Name: _____

1. Are the ideas in the paper easy to understand?
_____
_____

2. Does the writer include enough details?
_____

- Submit your work to a school or local newspaper.
- Send it to friends or family in an e-mail.
- Read your work aloud to several classmates. Discuss their reactions and questions.
- Add photos or illustrations, and display your writing in your class or at the school library.
- Share it as part of a formal or informal oral presentation or speech to another class.
- Post it on a blog, or send it to a Web site that publishes student writing.

### Publishing and Presenting

Choose one of these ways to share your personal response.

- **Collect it.** With your classmates, create a booklet of responses for the school library.
- **Talk about it.** Turn your paper into an oral presentation for the class or for your family. Include visual aids when appropriate.
- **Add it to your portfolio.** Keep a writing portfolio to track how you've grown as a writer throughout the year. To decide whether to add a piece to your portfolio, ask yourself, "Why is this one of my best pieces of writing?"

### Remember

When you make a presentation, follow these tips:

- Speak loudly so that everyone can hear you.
- Look at your audience as you speak to them.
- Practice several times beforehand.

# Integrating Grammar and Writing

Teachers know that knowledge of grammar is essential to improve their students' writing and communication skills.

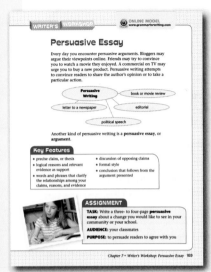

Annotated
Teacher's Edition
p. 169

## Why is grammar integral to instruction in writing?

- Grammar helps students construct and vary sentences.
- Grammar helps students write correctly and effectively.
- Grammar provides rules of standard English usage.

## Why is writing integral to instruction in grammar?

- Writing personalizes grammar and makes it meaningful through opportunities for students' own expression.
- Writing provides immediate application of grammar topics.
- Writing provides the practice that helps students master grammar skills.

## How does *Grammar for Writing* integrate grammar and writing?

- Every chapter culminates in a Writing Workshop or Writing Application, each with grammar features and organized teaching points.
- Connecting Grammar and Writing features integrate grammar tips into writing lessons.
- In the grammar chapters, diverse writing exercises allow students to apply grammar rules to their writing.

## Part 1: Composition Overview

The lessons in Part 1 focus on:

- the writing process
- writing effective sentences and word choice
- sentence variety and structure
- writing effective paragraphs
- writing effective essays

Writing Workshops and Applications cover descriptive, narrative, expository, persuasive, and real-world writing.

## Part 2: Grammar Overview

The lessons in Part 2 focus on:

- parts of a sentence
- parts of speech
- subject-verb agreement
- punctuation
- capitalization and spelling

Lessons focus on core **grammar topics**.

Boldface **lesson vocabulary** defines key academic terms.

**Step by Step** guidance helps students master difficult grammar topics.

**Sidebar features** offer tips and cross-reference related lessons.

Annotated Teacher's Edition p. 229

**Real-world formats** connect grammar topics to students' lives.

**Write What You Think** integrates grammar and writing and asks students to write and support brief passages.

Annotated Teacher's Edition p. 252

# Engaging Middle School Students in Writing and Grammar Instruction

**By Beverly Ann Chin, Ph.D.**

As teachers seek to balance instruction in the development and organization of ideas with choices in language fluency and correctness, they often ask, "What is the relationship between writing instruction and grammar?" Teachers also wonder, "What strategies help students in their understanding and mastery of conventions of standard written English? How can teachers make grammar instruction meaningful and enjoyable?" A review of the research provides answers to these important questions.

## What is the relationship between writing instruction and grammar?

Based on its own review of the research in writing and grammar instruction, the National Council of Teachers of English (NCTE) asserts: "Language skills and conventions (grammar, punctuation, spelling) are most successfully learned with a combination of carefully targeted lessons applied within the context of meaningful writing" (*http://www.ncte.org/library/ NCTEFiles/Resources/Positions/KnowAboutWriting.pdf*).

As middle school students read more diverse and sophisticated texts, teachers can help students observe how writers make choices in ideas, organization, language, and conventions of standard English to create an effect on readers. Teachers can also encourage students to reflect on how their writing choices affect their communication purpose and audience. By analyzing the conventions used by published authors as well as classmates, middle school students discover how grammar, usage, and mechanics are tools that clarify meaning.

## What strategies help students in their understanding and mastery of standard written English?

Based on an extensive review of the research on instructional methods, Graham and Perin (2007) identified eleven instructional practices that improve secondary students' writing skills. Their findings are published in *Writing Next: Effective strategies to improve writing of adolescents in middle and high school*. Among the recommended instructional practices are the following:

- **Writing Strategies:** Teaching students strategies for planning, revising, and editing their compositions

- **Collaborative Writing:** Grouping students to work together to plan, draft, revise, and edit their compositions

- **Sentence Combining:** Teaching students to construct more complex, sophisticated sentences

- **Study of Models:** Providing students with opportunities to read, analyze, and emulate models of good writing

Teachers who integrate grammar into their writing instruction during the revising and editing stages enable students to learn the conventions of standard written English in meaningful ways. Keeping in mind the recommendations of *Writing Next*, let's look at two strategies that help students understand and apply the rules of grammar, usage, and mechanics in their own writing.

## Sentence Combining

Sentence combining is a strategy in which students combine short, choppy sentences into longer, more fluent ones. As students experiment with different ways to combine their sentences, they discover how sentence beginnings, lengths, and complexities relate to the meaning and overall effect of the message. Through oral and written sentence combining activities, students learn to experiment with language and to make choices about language fluency.

Sentence combining is most effective when it is presented to students during the revising and editing stages of the writing process. Because sentence combining is based on students' own drafts, students do not need to focus on generating or organizing ideas. Teachers can use examples of sentences from students' writing to create sentence-combining activities. During the editing stage, teachers can use sentence combining to discuss punctuation rules—especially those related to commas, apostrophes, parentheses, dashes, and semicolons. By using students' new sentence combinations, teachers can also provide instruction in grammar concepts, such as independent and dependent clauses, phrases, subject-verb agreement, correct pronoun use, antecedents, active and passive voice, and parallel structure.

### Study of Models

Sentence imitation is a strategy that uses the study of good models. When students imitate sentences, they replicate the syntax of a model text, but use their own words and ideas. Teachers usually begin by showing a well-crafted sentence or paragraph, often from a published author. The teacher helps the students analyze how the author used specific parts of speech to create the text. Then, using their own topics, ideas, and words, students create their own sentences as they imitate the syntax of the model text.

Through sentence imitation, students can also learn to identify important grammar concepts, such as independent and dependent clauses, phrases, and modifiers, and punctuation rules, such as commas, dashes, parentheses, and colons. Students can discuss how the author's use of grammar, usage, and mechanics affects their understanding of the text.

Teachers usually introduce sentence-imitation activities during the revising stage as students work on their sentence fluency and voice. When students imitate sentences with complex punctuation, parallel syntax, or sophisticated modification, they enter the editing stage of the writing process.

---

### Example of Modeling

#### Original Model

Unusual rock formations appear in the cliffs by the river and provide valuable specimens for geologists from scientific organizations and universities.

#### Sentence Imitations

Healthy young people exercise in many ways throughout the week and eat balanced meals with varieties of green vegetables and fruits.

Majestic bald eagles soar in the sky above the mountains and cast dark shadows over lakes of deep blue and aquamarine.

---

# How can teachers make grammar instruction meaningful and enjoyable?

When middle school students value their writing purpose and audience, they discover how conventions affect the clarity and impact of their message. Here are four teaching suggestions that can help students enjoy learning grammar.

1. **Emphasize the positive.** Look for what students are doing effectively in their writing. By pointing out students' correct use of conventions, you reinforce the importance of grammar, usage, and mechanics as tools that help readers understand the written message.

2. **Keep the grammar lesson focused.** Prioritize and select the one or two important concepts to address in each lesson. Introducing too many concepts at the same time overwhelms many students.

3. **Show examples of grammar concepts in different texts and genres.** Create a bulletin board that displays the ways in which grammar, usage, and mechanics are used in various publications, such as magazines, poetry, and graphic novels. Cartoons and newspaper headlines offer creative opportunities to examine punctuation and word choice. Encourage students to contribute to the display.

4. **Make grammar lively.** Show examples from print and non-print media that use language in creative and unusual ways. Have students look for examples of humor and ambiguity in written language. Jokes, puns, and misplaced modifiers offer opportunities to discuss grammar.

During the middle school years, students are discovering the power of their voices in written communication. They are learning how purpose and audience influence the selection and organization of ideas. Students are also learning how word choice and sentence variety contribute to the written message. Furthermore, they are learning how the conventions of standard written English—grammar, usage, and mechanics—help their readers focus on the content and intent of this message.

*A more comprehensive discussion of current research in grammar and writing instruction, as well as suggestions for classroom practices that reflect that research, can be found in the Sadlier-Oxford Professional Development paper "Effective Strategies for Engaging Middle School Students in Writing and Grammar Instruction," by Beverly Ann Chin, Ph.D. For more information, visit www.grammarforwriting.com.*

# Differentiating Instruction

To support students whose first language is not English, teachers must often differentiate instruction. Similarly, teachers may need to accommodate native English speakers as they strive for mastery. Both groups respond well to many of the same techniques, such as consistent modeling, extended repetition, and a slower pace. Research supports the specific methods shown below for helping English learners succeed.

## Develop Vocabulary

- Model correct pronunciation that students echo.
- Invite students to point to examples.
- Vary activities to increase exposure to new words.
- Encourage students to use new vocabulary in conversation.

## Flash Card Games

- Bingo
- Definition Challenge
- Part of Speech Match
- Find Your Partner

## Model Concepts

- Use and expand lesson **EXAMPLES** to reinforce key points.
- Model out loud to demonstrate sensible and logical strategies.
- Use gestures, pictures, diagrams, and graphic organizers.

## Incorporate Other Strategies

- Say **Yes,** not **No,** to model and support understanding and correct usage for English learners and striving students. For example, "Yes, Juana, a conjunction joins sentences."
- Form pairs and small groups to increase students' comfort level when they respond aloud. Encourage them to discuss and complete tasks together.
- Invite students to use their broad experiences and knowledge to act as peer teachers. Have them write on the board, demonstrate or provide examples, explain a concept, or describe a strategy or process.

## Chapter 1

| Lesson | English Learners | Striving Learners |
|---|---|---|
| **Lesson 1.1** | To explain the concept of narrowing, use an Inverted Pyramid to narrow a topic. | Give students practice organizing details. Have them complete a Sequence Organizer about their day. |
| **Lesson 1.2** | Have partners use the Do & Don't chart to quiz each other's understanding of the drafting stage. | In Exercise 1, model creating an outline. Explain that outlines should include the 3 parts of an essay. |
| **Lesson 1.3** | Read aloud the checklist, and define each writing trait. To check students' understanding, have them suggest an additional question for each trait in the checklist. | Ask small groups to use the Revising Checklist to evaluate the Writing Model on page 16. Have them present positive feedback and suggestions for improvement. |
| **Lesson 1.4** | Read aloud the checklist, and define terms such as *fragment, subject*, and *verb*. | In Exercise 1, have students compare their answers with those of a partner. |
| **Lesson 1.5** | Explain the difference between *publishing* (making a written work public) and *presenting* (showing a work to an audience). | Have students review papers they've written recently for class, evaluating them based on the writing portfolio questions on page 21. |
| **Writer's Workshop: Autobiographical Writing** | Break down the word *autobiographical*. Explain that *auto* means "self," *bio* means "life," and *graph* means "to write." | To help students choose a topic and gather details, have small groups brainstorm topics and retell their experiences. |

### Chapter Vocabulary

- prewriting
- freewrite
- brainstorm
- narrow
- purpose
- audience
- organize details
- drafting
- introduction
- body
- conclusion
- writer's block
- revising
- traits of good writing
- peer review
- conventions
- editing and proofreading
- proofreading symbols
- publishing and presenting
- writing portfolio

## Chapter Vocabulary

- sentence fragment
- run-on sentence
- comma
- coordinating conjunction
- semicolon
- sensory details
- parallel structure (parallelism)
- wordiness
- concise
- passive voice
- active voice
- precise language
- clichés
- dictionary
- thesaurus
- synonyms
- formal English
- informal English

## Chapter 2

| Lesson | English Learners | Striving Learners |
|---|---|---|
| **Lesson 2.1** | Have students write a subject and verb on separate index cards. Have small groups use the cards to create complete sentences. | Define *subject* and *verb*. Have student volunteers give examples of subjects. For each subject, ask the class to add a verb and use both in a sentence. |
| **Lesson 2.2** | Give students practice pronouncing the chapter vocabulary. Model correct pronunciation, and have students repeat after you. | For Exercise 2, have students work in small groups to identify the run-on sentences before completing the exercise. |
| **Lesson 2.3** | Give an example of sensory details for each of the five senses. | Have volunteers share their revised sentences for Exercise 1. |
| **Lesson 2.4** | Note to Spanish-speaking students that *parallel* and *paralelo* are cognates. | Review compound subjects, gerund phrases, and subordinate clauses. |
| **Lesson 2.5** | Complete the first item in Exercise 1 together before students complete the exercise in pairs. | Have students give more examples of everyday wordy phrases and concise replacements for them. |
| **Lesson 2.6** | Define each cliché for students. Have them use a thesaurus to complete the exercises. | Show students how to use a thesaurus and dictionary to find synonyms. |
| **Lesson 2.7** | Read aloud the letter in Exercise 1. | Have students check each other's work for Exercise 2. |
| **Writing Application: Speech** | Read aloud and review the model speech on page 55. | Have students summarize each part of the Writing Application in their own words. |

**Chapter 3**

| Lesson | English Learners | Striving Learners |
|--------|------------------|-------------------|
| **Lesson 3.1** | Focus on the difference between declarative and imperative sentences. | Ask volunteers to give more examples of each type of sentence in the chart. |
| **Lesson 3.2** | Read aloud the first ORIGINAL example on page 63. Then read aloud the revision. Ask students which version they prefer. | Read aloud the Literary Model, and complete Exercise 1 together. |
| **Lesson 3.3** | Read aloud the Literary Model. | Have students complete the Exercises with a partner. |
| **Lesson 3.4** | Have students make flash cards with independent and subordinate clauses and use them to quiz a partner. | Give examples of independent and subordinate clauses, and have students identify the type of clause. |
| **Lesson 3.5** | Explain when to use *and, or, but,* or *so.* Review subordinate clauses. | Ask students to give additional examples of complex sentences. |
| **Lesson 3.6** | Review the Connecting Grammar & Writing feature on page 75. | Complete the first item in Exercise 1 as a class. |
| **Lesson 3.7** | Review the information in arrow 2 on page 77, and provide additional examples. | Have students underline the key words in Exercise 1 before combining the sentences. |
| **Writer's Workshop: Story** | Define each boldface term in the workshop. Ask students to write their story with a partner. | Have students share their stories in small groups and do a peer review. |

## Chapter Vocabulary

- declarative sentence
- imperative sentence
- interrogative sentence
- exclamatory sentence
- understood subject
- sentence variety
- variety of sentence beginnings
- clause
- independent (main) clause
- subordinate (dependent) clause
- sentence fragment
- subordinating conjunctions
- structure
- simple sentences
- compound sentences
- complex sentences
- compound subjects
- compound verbs
- coordinating conjunctions
- semicolon
- appositive phrase

## Chapter Vocabulary

- paragraphs
- main idea
- topic sentence
- imply
- implied main idea
- supporting details
- elaborate
- unity
- coherence
- chronological order
- spatial order
- order of importance
- logical order
- transitional words and phrases
- narrative paragraph
- descriptive paragraph
- sensory details
- expository paragraphs
- persuasive paragraphs

### Chapter 4

| Lesson | English Learners | Striving Learners |
|---|---|---|
| **Lesson 4.1** | Define the chapter vocabulary. Model correct pronunciation, and have students repeat after you. Read aloud the Literary Model. | For the second model on page 91, have students underline the details that support the implied main idea. |
| **Lesson 4.2** | Read aloud the paragraphs in Exercise 1. Ask students: *Which sentence seemed confusing because it was about a different topic?* | Have pairs read aloud the paragraphs they wrote for Exercise 2. Ask students to identify the topic sentence and note any problems with paragraph unity. |
| **Lesson 4.3** | Define *coherence.* To check students' understanding, have them explain each pattern of organization in their own words. | Ask students to say a short paragraph using one of the patterns of organization listed. |
| **Lesson 4.4** | Read aloud the passage in Exercise 1. Ask students to identify where transitions can be added. | Have students review their answers to Exercise 1, noting where commas should be added after transitions. |
| **Lesson 4.5** | Define *narrate, describe, inform,* and *persuade.* Give everyday examples of each purpose. | Tell students to keep their books closed as you read aloud each Writing Model. Ask them to identify the type of paragraph each model is. |
| **Writing Application: Descriptive Paragraph** | Spend time teaching sensory details and imagery. | Have volunteers share their paragraphs and read them aloud to the class. |

## Chapter 5

| Lesson | English Learners | Striving Learners |
|---|---|---|
| **Lesson 5.1** | Read aloud the essay on page 114. Then have students complete the exercise with a partner. | Ask students to explain their answers to the Exercise. Encourage them to use the chapter vocabulary as they explain their answers. |
| **Lesson 5.2** | Draw an Inverted Pyramid. Use it to explain the terms *broad* and *narrow*. | Have small groups brainstorm thesis statements for Exercise 2. |
| **Lesson 5.3** | Read aloud the models in Exercise 1. Discuss ways to improve the introductions before students revise them. | Ask students to explain what makes the Weak examples poor and the Revised example strong. |
| **Lesson 5.4** | Define and pronounce the chapter vocabulary. Then ask volunteers to define the terms in their own words. | Review *patterns of organization, transitions,* and *coherence.* |
| **Lesson 5.5** | Remind students that quotations should be set in quotation marks. | Have partners review magazine articles and identify the strategies used in the conclusion. |
| **Writer's Workshop: Compare-Contrast Essay** | Define *compare* and *contrast.* For practice comparing and contrasting, ask students to compare dogs and cats and then contrast them. | Focus on the two methods of organization listed on page 129. Encourage students to share their outlines and review them for consistent organization. |

## Chapter Vocabulary

- essay
- thesis statement
- claim (controlling idea)
- introduction
- body paragraphs
- unity
- topic sentence
- pattern of organization
- transitions
- coherence
- conclusion

## Chapter Vocabulary

- sentence
- complete subject
- complete predicate
- sentence fragment
- subordinate clause
- subject
- predicate
- simple subject
- verb
- verb phrase
- simple predicate
- understood subject
- inverted sentence
- compound subject
- compound verb
- direct object
- linking verb
- subject complement
- predicate nominative
- predicate adjective

## Chapter 6

| Lesson | English Learners | Striving Learners |
|---|---|---|
| Lesson 6.1 | Have students complete the exercises with a partner. | Ask small groups to discuss ways to fix the fragments they identified in Exercise 1. |
| Lesson 6.2 | Ask students to search a news article and find an example of each boldface term on page 139. | Encourage volunteers to give additional examples of verb phrases and use them in a sentence. |
| Lesson 6.3 | Focus on inverted sentences, providing additional examples and asking students to identify the subject. | Have students make their own chart based on the chart on page 141. Have them come up with new examples for each rule. |
| Lesson 6.4 | Complete item 1 in Exercise 2 as a class. Then have partners complete the exercise. | Focus on the Remember feature on page 143. Ask students to explain the subject-verb agreement in each example on the page. |
| Lesson 6.5 | Walk through the Step by Step feature. Have students follow each step as they complete Exercise 1. | Ask students to say a sentence that contains a direct object. Have other students identify the direct object. |
| Lesson 6.6 | Define and pronounce the chapter vocabulary. Give examples of each term. | Review *noun, pronoun,* and *adjective*. Ask students to give examples of each. |
| Writing Application: Summary | Encourage students to use a thesaurus as they draft their summaries. | Give students practice summarizing. Ask them to summarize a movie they've all seen. |

**Chapter 7**

| Lesson | English Learners | Striving Learners |
|---|---|---|
| Lesson 7.1 | Have small groups give examples of each type of noun by pointing to items in the classroom. | Have students use the images in their books to find one example of each type of noun. |
| Lesson 7.2 | Help students identify the plural and singular nouns in Exercise 1 before they complete the exercise. | Encourage pairs of students to exchange papers and compare their answers to Exercise 2. |
| Lesson 7.3 | Explain that *ante* means "before" and antecedents should come before a pronoun in order for the pronoun to make sense. | Have students read the lists on page 161 and use some of the indefinite and demonstrative pronouns in sentences. |
| Lesson 7.4 | Have volunteers use a personal pronoun in a sentence. Ask students to identify whether the pronoun functioned as the subject, predicate nominative, direct object, or object of a preposition. | Review predicate nominatives and linking verbs. In Exercise 1, encourage students to discuss the function of the pronoun in each sentence before selecting their answer choice. |
| Lesson 7.5 | Have students underline the antecedents in the Exercises. | Have small groups come up with additional examples for each arrow on page 165. |
| Lesson 7.6 | Discuss what makes each sentence in Exercise 1 confusing before having students fix it. | Ask students to do think-alouds for Exercise 1. Example: *Who forgot to turn off the light? Dad or Jim?* |
| Writer's Workshop: Persuasive Essay | Define and give examples of each persuasive technique on page 171. | Have students share their drafts with a partner and conduct a peer review. |

**Chapter Vocabulary**

- parts of speech
- noun
- common noun
- proper noun
- concrete noun
- abstract noun
- collective noun
- compound noun
- plural noun
- possessive noun
- pronouns
- antecedent
- personal pronouns
- possessive pronouns
- indefinite pronouns
- demonstrative pronouns
- subject pronoun
- predicate nominative
- object pronoun
- direct object
- object of a preposition

## Chapter Vocabulary

- verb
- action verbs
- linking verbs
- verb phrase
- main verb
- helping verb
- principal parts
- regular verb
- irregular verbs
- tense
- present
- past
- future
- present perfect
- past perfect
- future perfect
- active voice
- passive voice
- verbals
- participle
- participial phrase
- gerund
- gerund phrase
- infinitive
- infinitive phrase

### Chapter 8

| Lesson | English Learners | Striving Learners |
|---|---|---|
| **Lesson 8.1** | Explain that action verbs are usually verbs you can draw a picture of. | Read aloud the Literary Model. Have students identify each type of verb. |
| **Lesson 8.2** | Point out to Spanish-speaking students that *regular* and *irregular* are cognates. | Emphasize that participles always need a helping verb while present and past forms do not. |
| **Lesson 8.3** | Read aloud the chart as a group. Then say a verb, and have students give the four forms of it. | Have students use a dictionary to check their spelling of irregular verbs in both Exercises. |
| **Lesson 8.4** | Have students create and use flash cards that contain examples of each kind of tense. | Tell students to give an additional example for each tense listed on page 187. |
| **Lesson 8.5** | Explain *active* (taking action) and *passive* (allowing things to happen to you). | Have small groups identify the verbs in passive voice in Exercise 2 before they complete the Exercise. |
| **Lesson 8.6** | Define, pronounce, and give examples of each boldface term. | Complete Exercise 1 as a group, and discuss the reasoning for each answer. |
| **Writing Application: Instructions** | Make sure students understand chronological order (shown on page 195). | Have students switch drafts with a partner and ask their partner to point out any confusing steps. |

## Chapter 9

| Lesson | English Learners | Striving Learners |
|---|---|---|
| **Lesson 9.1** | Read aloud the paragraph in Exercise 1, and complete the Exercise together. | To complete Exercise 1, have students do think-alouds (asking *What kind?*, *Which one?*, *How much?*, and *How many?*). |
| **Lesson 9.2** | Pronounce each boldface term. Review syllables. | Have students read Lesson 12.4 for spelling rules. |
| **Lesson 9.3** | Review and give examples of nouns, pronouns, and verbs. | Tell students to first underline the words being modified in Exercises 1 and 2. |
| **Lesson 9.4** | Point out to Spanish-speaking students that *negative* and *negativo* are cognates. | Have students circle the negative words in Exercise 2 before they revise the passage. |
| **Lesson 9.5** | Read aloud Exercise 1. Work together to identify the modifiers first. | Have students do a think-aloud for each Exercise item. |
| **Lesson 9.6** | Define and pronounce each boldface term. | Read aloud the Literary Model, and discuss it. |
| **Lesson 9.7** | Focus on the difference between coordinating and correlative conjunctions. | Have pairs complete Exercise 1 together. |
| **Writer's Workshop: Book Review** | Use the organizer on page 217 to explain the parts of a book review. | Monitor the different steps of students' work. |

### Chapter Vocabulary

- adjective
- articles
- adverb
- degrees of comparison
- positive
- comparative
- superlative
- predicate adjectives
- double negative
- modifier
- misplaced modifier
- preposition
- prepositional phrase
- object of the preposition
- adverb phrase
- adjective phrase
- conjunction
- coordinating conjunctions
- correlative conjunctions
- interjection

## Chapter Vocabulary

- verb
- subject
- singular
- plural
- verb phrases
- prepositional phrase
- compound subject
- inverted sentence
- collective noun
- indefinite pronoun

### Chapter 10

| Lesson | English Learners | Striving Learners |
|---|---|---|
| **Lesson 10.1** | Point out to Spanish-speaking students that *singular* and *plural* are cognates. | For Exercise 1, tell students to first identify whether the subject they underlined is singular or plural. |
| **Lesson 10.2** | Tell students to cross out the prepositional phrases in Exercise 1 before they select their answer choice. | Have pairs check each other's answers to Exercise 1 and discuss any discrepancies. |
| **Lesson 10.3** | Give additional examples for the third arrow on page 231. | Tell students to underline the subject of each sentence in Exercise 1 before they combine the sentences. |
| **Lesson 10.4** | Have students complete the Exercises with a partner, explaining their work to each other. | Encourage pairs to exchange their responses to Exercise 3 and check each other's work. |
| **Lesson 10.5** | Define and pronounce the boldface terms. Give additional examples of each. Model correct agreement by using each example in a sentence. | Have pairs take turns generating sentences for each pronoun in the side column. Encourage them to check for correct agreement. |
| **Writing Application: Writing Prompt Response** | Have small groups brainstorm a poem to analyze and jot down possibilities. | Have students work in pairs to evaluate each other's thesis statement before they write their response. |

**Chapter 11**

| Lesson | English Learners | Striving Learners |
|---|---|---|
| **Lesson 11.1** | Have students make vocabulary flash cards and quiz each other. | Review the Remember feature, and ask students to provide more examples. |
| **Lesson 11.2** | Point out that *breve* means "short." | Have students read aloud the sentences in Exercise 1 before they punctuate them. |
| **Lesson 11.3** | Focus on the last arrow on page 249. Review adjectives. | Ask students to review their answers to the Exercises with those of a partner. |
| **Lesson 11.4** | Define, pronounce, and give examples of each boldface term. Focus on 2 rules in a single class period. | Tell students to put a check mark next to rules they understand. Focus on the rules they didn't mark. |
| **Lesson 11.5** | Have students complete Exercise 2 with a partner. | Review compound sentences and coordinating conjunctions. |
| **Lesson 11.6** | Provide an additional example for each chart item. | Have pairs read aloud the dialogue in Exercise 2. |
| **Lesson 11.7** | Review singular nouns, plural nouns, and indefinite pronouns. | Have students brainstorm additional examples of contractions. |
| **Lesson 11.8** | Point out that a dash is longer than a hyphen. | Emphasize the difference between using parentheses and using dashes. |
| **Writer's Workshop: Research Report** | Ask students to define *summary, paraphrase,* and *quotation* in their own words. | Check that students' outlines are clear and logical. |

**Chapter Vocabulary**

- period
- declarative sentence
- imperative sentences
- exclamation point
- exclamatory sentence
- question mark
- interrogative sentence
- abbreviation
- acronyms
- comma
- semicolons
- colons
- compound sentence
- quotation marks
- direct quotation
- apostrophes
- contraction
- parentheses
- hyphens
- dashes

## Chapter Vocabulary

- proper nouns
- proper adjectives
- prefix
- suffix
- plural nouns

### Chapter 12

| Lesson | English Learners | Striving Learners |
|---|---|---|
| **Lesson 12.1** | Define difficult vocabulary in the chart, such as *nationalities, continents, geographical,* and *celestial.* | Have small groups create their own capitalization charts, using their own wording for rules and giving new examples for each rule. |
| **Lesson 12.2** | Have students read aloud the items in Exercise 1 before they mark their answers. | Focus on one arrow in a single class period. Have students complete Exercise 1 during the first period. |
| **Lesson 12.3** | Ask students for additional examples of each rule in the chart. | Encourage students to consult a dictionary as needed when completing the Exercises. |
| **Lesson 12.4** | Have students put a check mark next to rules they know well. For unmarked rules, have them jot down additional examples of words that fit the rule. | Tell students to compare their answers to Exercises 1 and 2 with those of a partner. Have them discuss discrepancies and search for the rule that fits the word. |
| **Lesson 12.5** | Review *nouns, consonants, vowels* and *compound nouns.* | As a class, go over the answers to Exercise 1. |
| **Writing Application: Business Letter** | Encourage students to check their letters for errors in grammar, punctuation, and spelling. | Focus on the concept of paragraph unity on page 284. Discuss the model with students. |

Grade 7

# Grammar for Writing

### Senior Series Consultant

Beverly Ann Chin
Professor of English
University of Montana
Missoula, MT

### Series Consultant

Frederick J. Panzer, Sr.
English Dept. Chair, Emeritus
Christopher Columbus High School
Miami, FL

### Series Consultant

Anthony Bucco
Language Arts Literacy Teacher
Pierrepont Middle School
Rutherford, NJ

### Series Editor

Phyllis Goldenberg

 Sadlier

## Reviewers

**Maria Davis Baisier**
English Teacher
Holy Cross School
New Orleans, LA

**Joan Borrasso**
English Teacher
Aquinas Academy
Gibsonia, PA

**Melissa Churchwell**
Language Arts Teacher
Brooklawn Middle School
Parsippany, NJ

**Jay Falls**
Language Arts Teacher
Solon Middle School
Solon, OH

**Stephanie Jones**
Sixth Grade Teacher
Saint Francis of Assisi
Cordova, TN

**Sister Rita Ann Keller, IHM**
Language Arts Teacher
St. Gregory the Great
Virginia Beach, VA

**Cheryl Kordes**
Language Arts Teacher
St. Peter in Chains
Hamilton, OH

**John T. Ludwig**
Language Arts Teacher
Our Lady of Lourdes
Melbourne, FL

**Darbie Dallman Safford**
Language Arts Teacher
St. Monica School
Dallas, TX

**Joan Sieja**
Language Arts/Reading Teacher
Mary Queen of Heaven
Brooklyn, NY

**Sister June Clare Tracy, O.P., Ed.D.**
District Superintendent
Manhattan Catholic Schools
New York, NY

**Mollie Mumau Williams**
Language Arts Teacher
James W. Parker Middle School
Edinboro, PA

## Acknowledgments

Every good faith effort has been made to locate the owners of copyrighted material to arrange permission to reprint selections. In several cases this has proved impossible. Thanks to the following for permission to reprint copyrighted material.

From *A Place Called Ugly,* Copyright 1981 by Avi Wortis. Reprinted by permission of Brandt & Hochman Literary Agents, Inc. Used by permission of Brandt & Hochman Literary Agents, Inc. Any electronic copying or distribution of this text is expressly forbidden.

Excerpt from "Mrs Which" from A WRINKLE IN TIME by Madeleine L'Engle. Copyright © 1962, renewed 1990 by Madeleine L'Engle Franklin.

Reprinted by permission of Farrar, Straus and Giroux, LLC.

Excerpt from *Across the Centuries.* Copyright © 1999 by Houghton Mifflin Company.

*Call Me María* by Judith Ortiz Cofer. Copyright © 2004 by Judith Ortiz Cofer. All rights reserved. Published by Orchard Books, an imprint of Scholastic Inc.

Excerpt from *City of Beasts* by Isabel Allende. Copyright © 2002 by Isabel Allende. Published by HarperCollins Publishers.

*Esperanza Rising* by Pam Muñoz Ryan. Copyright © 2000 by Pam Muñoz Ryan. All rights reserved. Published by Scholastic Press, a division of Scholastic Inc.

Excerpt from *I'm a Stranger Here Myself.* Copyright © 1999 by Bill Bryson. All rights reserved. Published by Broadway Books, a division of Random House.

Excerpt from SOMETHING WICKED'S IN THOSE WOODS, copyright © 2000 by Marisa Montes, reprinted by permission of Houghton Mifflin Harcourt Publishing Company.

Excerpt from TANGERINE, copyright © 1997 by Edward Bloor, reprinted by permission of Houghton Mifflin Harcourt Publishing Company.

Excerpt from "Negro" from THE BIG SEA by Langston Hughes. Copyright © 1940 by Langston Hughes. Copyright renewed 1968 by Arna Bontemps and George Houston Bass.

Reprinted by permission of Hill and Wang, a division of Farrar, Straus and Giroux, LLC.

*The Pigman & Me* by Paul Zindel. Copyright © 1991 by Paul Zindel. First appeared in *The Pigman and Me,* published by HarperCollins Children's Books. Reprinted by permission of Curtis Brown, Ltd.

From *The Skin I'm In* by Sharon G. Flake. Copyright © 1998 by Sharon Flake. Reprinted by permissions of Disney • Hyperion Books, an imprint of Disney Book Group, LLC. All rights reserved.

Excerpt from *Where Will This Shoe Take You?* Copyright © 1996 by Laurie Lawlor. Published by Walker Publishing Company.

## Credits

**Cover Art and Design**
Quarasan, Inc.

**Interior Photos**
age fotostock/Jeff Greenberg: 180. Alamy/Tony Cortizas, Jr.: 8 background; Jim Lane: 226; Eddie Linssen: 136 bottom; James Nesterwitz: 8 bottom; ilian return: 272; Adrian Sherratt: 244. CartoonBank/© 2003 The New Yorker Collection from cartoonbank. com. All rights reserved.: 51; © 2008 Leo Cullum from cartoonbank. com. All rights reserved.: 205. CartoonStock/© Joel Mishon, www.CartoonStock.com: 49; © Richard Jolley, www.CartoonStock. com: 257; © Sidney Harris, www. CartoonStock.com: 184. Corbis/ Rubberball/Nicole Hill: 136 top;

Thinkstock: 200. Getty Images/ Ableimages: 156; FPG: 234; French School: 122; Lori Adamski Peek: 204; Rob Gage: 104; Roger-Viollet: 115; Ruby Washington: 164; Seth Joel: 22; Tim Graham: 103; Time & Life Pictures: 202. iStockphoto.com/Amy Stebbins: 169; APCortizasJr: 69; Cat London: 124; Chris Schmidt: 214; Chris Scredon: 48; Jacom Stephens: 187; Jim Jurica: 93; Miodrag Gajic: 68; Nicholas Monu: 63; Paul Kline: 20; Sasha Radosavljevic: 193; Sean Locke: 237, 246; Torjorn Lagerwall: 149; Wojciech Kopczyski: 215. Jupiter Images/BananaStock: 100, 232; Brand X Pictures: 37, 46, 52, 142, 168, 230; Comstock Images: 11, 40, 236; Creatas Images: 146; Photos.com: 19, 76, 144, 160; Pixland : 261; Thinkstock:

15, 41, 99, 126, 276. Library of Congress/Prints and Photographs Division, LC-H824-T01-0523: 274; LC-USZ62-119343 : 260; LC-USZ62-7862: 210; LC-USZC4-7214: 148. Punchstock/Corbis: 60; Image Source: 32 background, 60 background; Photodisc: 90; Stockbyte: 272 background; Tetra Images: 8 top. Used under license from Shutterstock.com/absolut : 78; Blend Images: 137; Christopher Meder - Photography: 79; David Lee: 226 background; Doug Raphael: 278; Franc Podgorsek: 90 background; Gelpi: 283; iofoto: 208; Ken Hurst: 32; Lorraine Swanson: 98; Matthew Jacques: 119; Morozova Oxana: 249; Thomas M. Perkins: 112; Tom Grundy: 182; Tony Campbell: 33; William Casey: 12. ZIGGY ©

1997 ZIGGY AND FRIENDS, INC. Reprinted with permission of UNIVERSAL PRESS SYNDICATE. All rights reserved.: 23. ZIGGY © 2000 ZIGGY AND FRIENDS, INC. Reprinted for permission of UNIVERSAL PRESS SYNDICATE. All rights reserved.: 282. Zits © Zits Partnership. King Features Syndicate.: 44.

Printed in the United States of America
Student Edition: ISBN: 978-1-4217-1107-2
7 8 9 10 LSCW 23 22 21 20

**A**s a student, you are constantly being challenged to write correctly and effectively in a variety of subjects. From homework to standardized tests, more and more assignments require that you write in a clear, correct, and interesting way.

*Grammar for Writing, Enriched Edition,* teaches you the writing and language skills you'll need to be an effective writer and speaker, and prepares you to build on those skills in high school, college, and beyond. The first half of the book focuses on writing. In this section, you'll learn how to write correct and effective sentences, choose the best words to get your message across, and write strong paragraphs and essays. The second half of the book presents grammar lessons in a clear and entertaining way. You'll learn how grammar is used in everyday writing and how grammar mistakes can lead to misinterpretations that you'll want to avoid. Also, **Writer's Workshops** show you how to craft different types of writing, such as essays and stories.

Writing and grammar are subjects that you use every day. Whether you are writing a paper for class or e-mailing your friend, you can express yourself best if you know how to write effectively. *Grammar for Writing* was created with you in mind, and it includes topics that will inspire you and spark your curiosity.

While no textbook can make writing easy, *Grammar for Writing* breaks down the essential steps of writing in a way that makes sense. Throughout the book, there is a **Write What You Think** feature that helps you think critically to develop clear arguments. **Literary Models** draw examples from popular literature. Exercises in each lesson are interesting and easy to understand. If you need help, **Hint** features point you in the right direction and ensure that you get the most out of the practice.

The point of *Grammar for Writing, Enriched Edition,* is to sharpen the way you speak and write. By explaining grammar rules and writing techniques in a simple way, this book will help you become a better writer and more successful student.

Good luck!
The Authors

# CONTENTS

## Part I: Composition

**Chapter 1**    **The Writing Process** . . . . . . . . . . . . . . . . . . . **8**

**Lesson 1.1**   Prewriting . . . . . . . . . . . . . . . . . . . . . . 9

**Lesson 1.2**   Drafting . . . . . . . . . . . . . . . . . . . . . . 12

**Lesson 1.3**   Revising . . . . . . . . . . . . . . . . . . . . . . 14

**Lesson 1.4**   Editing and Proofreading . . . . . . . . . . . 17

**Lesson 1.5**   Publishing and Presenting . . . . . . . . . . . 20

Narrative Writing    **Writer's Workshop: Autobiographical Writing** . . . . . . . . . . . 22

**Chapter Review** . . . . . . . . . . . . . . . . . . . . . . . . . . . 29

**Chapter 2**    **Effective Sentences and Word Choice** . . . . . . . . . . . . . . . . . . . **32**

**Lesson 2.1**   Correcting Sentence Fragments . . . . . . . . . . . 33

**Lesson 2.2**   Correcting Run-on Sentences . . . . . . . . . . . 36

**Lesson 2.3**   Adding Details . . . . . . . . . . . . . . . . . . . . . . 39

**Lesson 2.4**   Using Parallel Structure . . . . . . . . . . . . . . . 41

**Lesson 2.5**   Avoiding Wordiness . . . . . . . . . . . . . . . . . . 44

**Lesson 2.6**   Choosing the Right Word . . . . . . . . . . . . . . 47

**Lesson 2.7**   Using Formal and Informal English . . . . . . . . . . . 50

Persuasive Writing    **Writing Application: Speech** . . . . . . . . . . . . . . . . . . . 52

**Chapter Review** . . . . . . . . . . . . . . . . . . . . . . . . . . . 56

**Chapter 3**    **Sentence Variety and Structure** . . . . . **60**

**Lesson 3.1**   Kinds of Sentences . . . . . . . . . . . . . . . . . . . . 61

**Lesson 3.2**   Varying Sentence Length . . . . . . . . . . . . . . 63

**Lesson 3.3**   Varying Sentence Beginnings . . . . . . . . . . . . 66

**Lesson 3.4**   Independent and Subordinate Clauses . . . . . . . . . 69

**Lesson 3.5**   Varying Sentence Structure . . . . . . . . . . . . . . 72

**Lesson 3.6**   Combining Sentences: Compound Parts . . . . . . . 75

**Lesson 3.7**   Combining Sentences: Key Words and Phrases . . . 77

Narrative Writing    **Writer's Workshop: Story** . . . . . . . . . . . . . . . . . . . 79

**Chapter Review** . . . . . . . . . . . . . . . . . . . . . . . . . . . 86

**Chapter 4**     **Effective Paragraphs**..............**90**
   **Lesson 4.1**   Supporting the Main Idea ................ 91
   **Lesson 4.2**   Paragraph Unity......................... 94
   **Lesson 4.3**   Patterns of Organization ................. 96
   **Lesson 4.4**   Transitional Words and Phrases ........... 99
   **Lesson 4.5**   Types of Paragraphs..................... 101

Descriptive Writing

   **Writing Application: Descriptive Paragraph** ........... 104
   **Chapter Review** ...................................... 108

**Chapter 5**     **Writing an Essay** ...............**112**
   **Lesson 5.1**   Parts of an Essay ....................... 113
   **Lesson 5.2**   Thesis Statements ...................... 115
   **Lesson 5.3**   Introductions........................... 117
   **Lesson 5.4**   Body Paragraphs ....................... 120
   **Lesson 5.5**   Conclusions............................ 123

Expository Writing

   **Writer's Workshop: Compare-Contrast Essay** ........... 126
   **Chapter Review** ...................................... 133

# Part II: Grammar, Usage, and Mechanics

**Chapter 6**     **Parts of a Sentence**...............**136**
   **Lesson 6.1**   Sentences and Sentence Fragments........... 137
   **Lesson 6.2**   Subjects and Predicates ................... 139
   **Lesson 6.3**   Hard-to-Find Subjects ................... 141
   **Lesson 6.4**   Compound Subjects and Verbs ........... 143
   **Lesson 6.5**   Direct Objects ......................... 145
   **Lesson 6.6**   Subject Complements .................... 147

Expository Writing

   **Writing Application: Summary** ...................... 149
   **Chapter Review** ...................................... 153

**Chapter 7**  **Nouns and Pronouns** . . . . . . . . . . . . . . . .**156**

**Lesson 7.1**  Nouns. . . . . . . . . . . . . . . . . . . . . . . . . . . . . . . . . 157

**Lesson 7.2**  Plural and Possessive Nouns . . . . . . . . . . . . . . 159

**Lesson 7.3**  Pronouns . . . . . . . . . . . . . . . . . . . . . . . . . . . . . 161

**Lesson 7.4**  Subject and Object Pronouns . . . . . . . . . . . . . 163

**Lesson 7.5**  Pronoun Agreement . . . . . . . . . . . . . . . . . . . . . 165

**Lesson 7.6**  Clear Pronoun Reference. . . . . . . . . . . . . . . . . . 167

Persuasive Writing

**Writer's Workshop: Persuasive Essay** . . . . . . . . . . . . . . . . 169

**Chapter Review** . . . . . . . . . . . . . . . . . . . . . . . . . . . . . . . . . . 176


**Chapter 8**  **Verbs**. . . . . . . . . . . . . . . . . . . . . . . . . . . . . .**180**

**Lesson 8.1**  Verbs . . . . . . . . . . . . . . . . . . . . . . . . . . . . . . . . . 181

**Lesson 8.2**  Regular and Irregular Verbs. . . . . . . . . . . . . . . . 183

**Lesson 8.3**  More Irregular Verbs . . . . . . . . . . . . . . . . . . . . . 185

**Lesson 8.4**  Verb Tense . . . . . . . . . . . . . . . . . . . . . . . . . . . . . 187

**Lesson 8.5**  Active and Passive Voice . . . . . . . . . . . . . . . . . . 189

**Lesson 8.6**  Verbals and Verbal Phrases . . . . . . . . . . . . . . . . 191

Real-World Writing

**Writing Application: Instructions** . . . . . . . . . . . . . . . . . . . . 193

**Chapter Review** . . . . . . . . . . . . . . . . . . . . . . . . . . . . . . . . . . 197


**Chapter 9**  **Adjectives, Adverbs, and Other Parts of Speech** . . . . . . . . . . . . .**200**

**Lesson 9.1**  Adjectives and Adverbs . . . . . . . . . . . . . . . . . . . 201

**Lesson 9.2**  Comparing with Adjectives and Adverbs . . . . . . 203

**Lesson 9.3**  Adjective or Adverb? . . . . . . . . . . . . . . . . . . . . . 205

**Lesson 9.4**  Double Negatives. . . . . . . . . . . . . . . . . . . . . . . . 207

**Lesson 9.5**  Misplaced Modifiers . . . . . . . . . . . . . . . . . . . . . . 209

**Lesson 9.6**  Prepositions and Prepositional Phrases. . . . . . . . 211

**Lesson 9.7**  Conjunctions and Interjections . . . . . . . . . . . . . 213

Writing About Literature

**Writer's Workshop: Book Review**. . . . . . . . . . . . . . . . . . . . 215

**Chapter Review** . . . . . . . . . . . . . . . . . . . . . . . . . . . . . . . . . . 222

**Chapter 10**    **Subject-Verb Agreement** . . . . . . . . . . . **226**

  **Lesson 10.1**    Agreement of Subject and Verb . . . . . . . . . . . . . 227

  **Lesson 10.2**    Phrases Between Subject and Verb . . . . . . . . . . 229

  **Lesson 10.3**    Compound Subjects . . . . . . . . . . . . . . . . . . . . 231

  **Lesson 10.4**    Inverted Sentences. . . . . . . . . . . . . . . . . . . . . 233

  **Lesson 10.5**    Other Agreement Problems . . . . . . . . . . . . . . . 235

*Writing for Assessment*

  **Writing Application: Writing Prompt Response** . . . . . . . . . . 237

  **Chapter Review** . . . . . . . . . . . . . . . . . . . . . . . . . . . . . . . 241


**Chapter 11**    **Punctuation** . . . . . . . . . . . . . . . . . . . . . . . . **244**

  **Lesson 11.1**    End Marks . . . . . . . . . . . . . . . . . . . . . . . . . . . 245

  **Lesson 11.2**    Abbreviations. . . . . . . . . . . . . . . . . . . . . . . . . 247

  **Lesson 11.3**    Commas in Compound Sentences and Series. . . . 249

  **Lesson 11.4**    Other Comma Uses . . . . . . . . . . . . . . . . . . . . . 251

  **Lesson 11.5**    Semicolons and Colons . . . . . . . . . . . . . . . . . . 253

  **Lesson 11.6**    Quotation Marks . . . . . . . . . . . . . . . . . . . . . . 255

  **Lesson 11.7**    Apostrophes . . . . . . . . . . . . . . . . . . . . . . . . . 257

  **Lesson 11.8**    Other Marks of Punctuation . . . . . . . . . . . . . . 259

*Research Writing*

  **Writer's Workshop: Research Report** . . . . . . . . . . . . . . . . 261

  **Chapter Review** . . . . . . . . . . . . . . . . . . . . . . . . . . . . . . . 269


**Chapter 12**    **Capitalization and Spelling** . . . . . . . . . **272**

  **Lesson 12.1**    Proper Nouns and Proper Adjectives. . . . . . . . . 273

  **Lesson 12.2**    Quotations and Titles . . . . . . . . . . . . . . . . . . . 275

  **Lesson 12.3**    Other Capitalization Rules . . . . . . . . . . . . . . . 277

  **Lesson 12.4**    Spelling Rules. . . . . . . . . . . . . . . . . . . . . . . . . 279

  **Lesson 12.5**    Plural Nouns . . . . . . . . . . . . . . . . . . . . . . . . . 281

*Real-World Writing*

  **Writing Application: Business Letter** . . . . . . . . . . . . . . . . 283

  **Chapter Review** . . . . . . . . . . . . . . . . . . . . . . . . . . . . . . . 287


  Frequently Misspelled Words . . . . . . . . . . . . . . . . . . . . . . 291

  Commonly Confused Words . . . . . . . . . . . . . . . . . . . . . . . 293

  Index. . . . . . . . . . . . . . . . . . . . . . . . . . . . . . . . . . . . . . . 297

# The Writing Process

# Prewriting

Before you can begin writing, you need to plan. **Prewriting,** the first stage of the writing process, involves the steps below.

- finding possible topics to write about
- choosing and narrowing your topic
- deciding on your purpose and audience
- collecting and organizing details

➠ Use one of the techniques below to generate a topic.

1. **Freewrite** Start with a word or broad topic, or look at a photograph to generate ideas. For five minutes, write down every thought you have about it. Be specific.

2. **Brainstorm** Use one or two words to come up with more specific ideas. Instead of writing full sentences, make a list or jot down ideas in a Web.

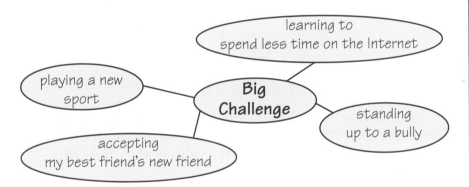

➠ Next, review your ideas, and **narrow** the topic you like best. Make sure your topic matches the length of the assignment.

TOO BROAD    the Internet
             [This is too much to cover in a short paper.]

TOO NARROW   checking e-mail last night
             [This is not broad enough to write about in
             three pages.]

GOOD TOPIC   spending less time on the Internet

**Remember**

The **writing process** consists of five stages.

| Prewriting |
| Drafting |
| Revising |
| Editing and Proofreading |
| Publishing and Presenting |

## TOPIC CHECKLIST

✔ How strongly do I feel about this topic?

✔ Is it narrow enough?

✔ Can I gather information about it?

▥➡ Choose your **purpose** for writing, and analyze your **audience.**

| Purpose | Audience |
|---|---|
| • Is my purpose to entertain, inform, persuade, or describe?<br>• What is the main thing I want my readers to learn?<br>• Why do I want to share this topic with others? | • Who will read my paper?<br>• How much does my audience already know?<br>• What are their interests? How can I help them connect to the topic? |

▥➡ Next, use a graphic organizer, such as the Sequence Organizer below, to help you collect and **organize details.**

- on Internet every day
- ignored chores and friends

→ parents and friends upset with me

→ • followed everyone's advice
- started other activities

→ • learned I had lots of other interests
- had fun offline

**Starter Words**

embarrassing
family
favorite
funny moments
happiness
hobbies
technology
wish

# EXERCISE 1  Generating Topics

Use the brainstorming technique to come up with a topic for a three-page paper. Pick a word or phrase from the list to the left, or choose one of your own. Write the word in the center of a Web. List related ideas.   Answers will vary.

**Inverted Pyramid**

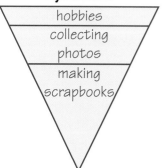

hobbies
collecting
photos
making
scrapbooks

# EXERCISE 2  Choosing a Topic

Review your Web from Exercise 1. Indicate the two topics you like best. Answers will vary. See www.grammarforwriting.com for writing models for each stage of the writing process.

1. Review those topics to see if you need to narrow them or expand on them. You can use the organizer shown to the left to narrow broad topics. Write the topic at the top. In the next line, write one smaller part of it. Keep making each part smaller until you find a good writing topic.

2. Use the Topic Checklist on the previous page to help you choose the best topic.

# EXERCISE 3 Choosing Your Purpose

Now, determine a purpose for the topic you chose. Write three different purposes for your topic. Choose the topic and purpose you know well and that you would most enjoy writing about. Put a check mark next to it. Answers will vary.

ENTERTAIN    share the time I won a scrapbook contest

EXPLAIN    explain how to make a scrapbook ✔

PERSUADE    convince readers that scrapbooks are fun to make

# EXERCISE 4 Analyzing Your Audience

Next, decide who your readers are and what background information they have. Make a chart like the one below.
Answers will vary.

My audience is teens who may have never made a scrapbook.

| What They Know | What They Need to Know |
|---|---|
| • what a scrapbook is<br>• some of the materials they'll need<br>• what a scrapbook is for | • where to find great pictures<br>• all the steps involved<br>• different types of scrapbooks |

# EXERCISE 5 Collecting Details

Finally, gather and organize details about your topic. Answers will vary.

For more on organizing ideas, see **Lesson 4.3.**

1. Review the topic, purpose, and audience you chose in the previous exercises.

2. Refresh your memory about your topic by doing research or talking to a peer or adult who knows about it.

3. Jot down a list of details, or complete a Sequence Organizer, such as the one shown on the previous page.

4. Include any specific details that you will want to add to your paper.

# Drafting

During the **drafting** stage, you turn your prewriting plan into complete sentences and paragraphs. Here are some guidelines about the drafting stage.

| Do | Don't |
|---|---|
| • Open up your mind, and let your ideas flow.<br>• Cross out ideas you don't like, and add new ones.<br>• Even if you're not sure how to spell some words, use them anyway.<br>• Jot notes in the margins about details you want to research more or things you want to check later.<br>• Be open to making changes to the plan you created during prewriting.<br>• Write legibly. | • Don't stop to wonder about whether you should include an idea.<br>• Don't expect your draft to be perfect.<br>• Don't write so messily that you can't read your own writing.<br>• Don't feel you must stick to every detail of your prewriting plan. Once you begin drafting, your plan may develop or change. |

➠ Organize your ideas into a strong **introduction** that grabs readers' attention, a **body** that supports the main point, and a **conclusion** that readers will remember.

➠ During drafting, you may encounter **writer's block,** or a mental block that keeps you from writing. Here are some tips for overcoming it.

**1.** Take a break. Let your mind rest and reenergize.

**2.** Discuss your paper with a teacher, parent, or friend. Talk about your topic, and ask for suggestions or ideas.

**3.** Refer to your prewriting notes.

**4.** Start freewriting. Write about anything related to your topic.

Read part of one writer's draft on the next page.

For more about writing the introduction, body, and conclusion of an essay, see the lessons in **Chapter 5.**

**Writing Model**

Knock! Knock! Knock! "Alicia, this is the third time Cindy has called you. Get off that computer!" I could hear Dad's shouting through my earphones. I swiftly clicked one button, and the computer was off—well, not completely off. What if someone sent me an e-mail? I always left my computer on, no matter what. What if the song I was downloading wasn't finished yet? That's why my parents are upset. ~~Don't get me wrong. That was a while ago.~~ ~~It took me a while to see that~~ I wasn't doing my work. My friends were getting tired of me ignoring their invitations. They wanted to go out. All I wanted was to be left alone on my computer.

Introduction catches readers' attention.

Arrow shows that a detail should be moved to clarify the organization.

Cross-outs show ideas the writer no longer wants to include.

# EXERCISE 1  Planning a Draft

Review and add to any notes, organizers, or lists you made during prewriting. Think more about your main points and how to organize them. Be sure you have at least three key ideas and two or more details that support each one. Students' notes will vary.

# EXERCISE 2  Writing a Draft

Now, on a separate sheet of paper, write a complete draft from beginning to end. Make sure to build on your prewriting ideas from the previous lesson and from Exercise 1.

Students' drafts will vary. See www.grammarforwriting.com for writing models for each stage of the writing process.

# Revising

Now that you have a first draft, the next step is to improve it. During the **revising** stage of the writing process, you evaluate your draft and decide what works and what doesn't.

➡️ Revising always entails looking at five of the six **traits of good writing.** Use the checklist below as you revise.

The sixth trait of good writing is **conventions**, or correctness in grammar, spelling, usage, punctuation, and mechanics. You will look for and correct these kinds of errors in the editing and proofreading stage of the writing process. See **Lesson 1.4.**

## REVISING CHECKLIST

### Ideas and Content
✔ How clearly did I express my ideas?
✔ Where should I add or delete details?

### Organization
✔ How clear is the order of details?
✔ Where should I add transitions to improve the connections between sentences and paragraphs?

### Sentence Fluency
✔ How smooth does the writing sound when I read it aloud?
✔ Which sentences seem choppy?
✔ How well have I varied sentence structures, sentence lengths, and sentence beginnings?

### Word Choice
✔ Which nouns, adjectives, adverbs, or verbs should be replaced with more precise words?
✔ Which words have I used too often?

### Voice
✔ How original and fresh is my writing?
✔ In which places does my writing sound forced or unnatural?

➡ Follow the tips below for revising your paper.

- Read your paper carefully several times. Focus on a different trait in the checklist each time you read.

- Make all the necessary changes, even if they're major. Do what it takes to improve the quality of your paper.

- Add, delete, or rearrange details as necessary.

➡ Do a **peer review.** Exchange drafts with a partner, and use the checklist on the previous page to check each other's work. Follow these guidelines as you review your partner's draft:

- Always start with positive feedback.

- Ask questions about things you don't understand.

- Offer specific suggestions. Both suggestions and positive feedback should always be specific enough so the writer understands your point.

The chart below highlights examples of specific feedback you might give to a partner during the revision stage.

**Real-World Writing**

Note how one author describes her response to the comments of reviewers and editors.

"They note what needs to be fixed, but it's up to me to do the repairs."

—Peg Kehret

| Vague | Specific |
|---|---|
| This needs work. | Maybe you could add some transitions. |
| Good stuff. | The details in this paragraph are really interesting, and they strongly support the main idea. |
| This doesn't make sense. | Can you help me understand your main idea? |
| Great essay! | Your introduction made me curious to read on, and your ideas were clear. |

The passage on the next page shows a revision of the draft from Lesson 1.2. How effective are the revisions? If you were a peer reviewer, what other revisions would you suggest?

**Writing Model**

Knock! Knock! Knock! "Alicia, this is the

third time Cindy has called you. Get off that

computer!" I could hear Dad's shouting through

*One swift click of a*

my earphones. ~~I swiftly clicked one button~~, and

the computer was off—well, not completely off.

What if someone sent me an e-mail? What if the

song I was downloading wasn't finished yet?

I always left my computer on, no matter what.

*have been disappointed*

That's why my parents ~~are upset~~. I wasn't doing

*homework or practicing the violin*

my ~~work~~. My friends were getting tired of me

ignoring their invitations. ~~They wanted to go out.~~

All I wanted was to be left alone on my computer.

*Vary sentence beginnings.*

*Use precise words, and add details.*

*Combine short sentences.*

**Working Together**

# EXERCISE 1  Doing a Peer Review

Exchange papers with a partner. Use the Revising Checklist and peer review tips to check each other's drafts. Include at least two positive comments, a question, and two suggestions. Talk with your partner about any suggestions you don't understand.
Answers will vary.

# EXERCISE 2  Revising Your Paper

Next, evaluate your paper on your own. Students' revisions will vary.
See www.grammarforwriting.com for writing models for each stage of the writing process.

1. Review your partner's suggestions from the peer review. Put a check mark next to changes you agree with.

2. Use the Revising Checklist to carefully review your draft.

3. Put together your ideas and your partner's feedback. Then revise your draft on a separate sheet of paper.

# Editing and Proofreading

Now that the content of your paper is solid, identify and fix any errors in the sixth writing trait, **conventions**: grammar, usage, spelling, mechanics, and punctuation.

➡ Follow these tips for **editing and proofreading:**

1. Use a checklist like the one below. Keep track of the common mistakes you make, and add them to the list.

2. Carefully read your draft several times. Each time, focus on a single item on the checklist. If you try to check too many things at one time, you are likely to miss some errors.

3. Focus on one line at a time.

4. Read your paper aloud sentence by sentence. This practice can help you catch any missing words or confusing sentences.

> **R**emember
>
> Ask for help. Exchange papers with a partner, and check each other's work. It's always helpful to have a second pair of eyes.

## Editing and Proofreading Checklist

❑ Are all words spelled correctly?

❑ Have I fixed all fragments and run-on sentences?

❑ Are any commas missing or unnecessary?

❑ Does every sentence end with the correct punctuation mark?

❑ Do all subjects and verbs agree?

❑ Have I capitalized the names of people and places?

❑ Did I mix up any easily confused words, such as <u>accept</u>/<u>except</u>?

❑ Did I indent the first line of each paragraph?

➡ Use **proofreading symbols** to mark any errors. In the margin on page 18, you'll find a list of commonly used symbols. Write your corrections neatly so you can easily read them later.

⫶▶ Even if you wrote your draft on a computer, take time to edit and proofread it. Here are some tips for editing and proofreading while using a computer.

- When you make a correction, reread it to make sure you typed it correctly.

- Use an online dictionary to check the spellings or definitions of any words you're not sure about.

- Use spell-check, but don't substitute it for your own review. Spell-check won't catch all errors, such as whether you used *their* instead of *there*.

Here is how one writer edited and proofread this paragraph.

## Proofreading Symbols

| | |
|--------|---------|
| ⍦ | Delete. |
| ∧ | Add. |
| ⊙ | Add a period. |
| ⋏ | Add a comma. |
| ⸯ | Add quotation marks. |
| / | Make lowercase. |
| ∿ | Switch order. |
| ≡ | Capitalize. |
| ¶ | Start a new paragraph. |

### Writing Model

My evening away from the computer finally came. Cindy was smiling and gig**g**ling as she led me out the front door and into her older sister's car. "You're going to have fun, I promise. you won't think about your stupid computer or online buddies at all," Cindy told me as we strapped on our seat belts. Immediately her older ~~S~~ister began telling funny stories about her new job. Cindy and I shared stories about things that happened at school. We talked and lau~~h~~ged all the way to the bowling alley. Soon all thoughts of my computer drifted away.

## EXERCISE 1 Proofreading a Draft

Practice using the proofreading tips you learned in this lesson to review the draft on the next page. Use the proofreading symbols to mark any mistakes you find.

[1]"Wow, I had totally forgotten how much I love batting cages," I shouted to no one in particular. [2]Cindy and her sister were buying tickets so we could play miniature golf next. [3]it dawned on me that playing real sports was more fun than playing them on the computer. [4]I felt as if someone had locked me up and kept me away from all real, fun things. [5]Then I realized that the person who locked me up was me! [6]I felt silly. [7]it's fun to play computer games online against teens from other country. [8]However, it doesn't compare to experiencing the crack of the bat as I slam a softball or sharing such moments with friends I can see and hear⊙

## EXERCISE 2 Checking Your Draft

Reread the tips on the first page of this lesson. Use them to edit and proofread the draft you wrote in the previous lesson.

1. Use the Editing and Proofreading Checklist to review your paper.
2. Use the proofreading symbols to mark your changes neatly.
3. Finally, create a clean copy of your paper.

Students' papers will vary. See www.grammarforwriting.com for writing models for each stage of the writing process.

## EXERCISE 3 Making Your Own Checklist

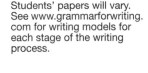

Now exchange papers with a classmate. Work together to proofread your papers one final time. Create a checklist of errors that you frequently make. Answers will vary.

# Publishing and Presenting

The last stage of the writing process is **publishing and presenting.**

1. Make a final error-free copy of your paper.

2. Share your paper with others, either through an oral presentation, a written paper, or a multimedia presentation.

▭▶ Before you turn in your final paper, proofread it one last time. Then check that you followed the format your teacher required.

▭▶ Be creative about the way you share your work with others. Try one of the ways below to present your work.

**WRITING HINT**

Be sure to give your paper a title. It's your first chance to grab your readers' attention and give them an idea of what your writing is about.

| Oral Presentation | • small-group presentation with a Question-and-Answer session<br>• speech to the class |
|---|---|
| Written Paper | • blog or e-mail<br>• school or community newspaper<br>• magazine for young writers<br>• online Web site for writers |
| Multimedia Presentation | • class presentation with pictures, graphics, and music<br>• slide presentation<br>• skit based on paper<br>• video recording |

▭▶ Make sure the type of presentation you choose matches the type of paper you wrote. Here are just a few examples of the types of presentations you can give.

| HOW-TO ESSAY | Give a demonstration for the class. |
|---|---|
| PERSUASIVE ESSAY | Make a speech to your audience. |
| POEM | Perform it at a poetry reading. |
| RESEARCH REPORT | Make a slide presentation with graphs and visuals to display data. |
| SHORT STORY | Read it to the class. |

⏭ Keep a **writing portfolio** throughout the school year. A writing portfolio is a collection of your best writing. It allows you to track your growth as a writer.

To choose whether to add a piece to your portfolio, ask yourself questions, such as the following:

- How does this piece reveal something new about my writing skills?

- How will this piece add something new to my portfolio?

- How does this paper compare to other papers I've written?

## Exercise 1 Choosing a Presentation

Make a presentation of the paper you wrote in the previous lessons. Choose one of the presentation techniques listed on the previous page. With a partner, elaborate on the idea you chose. Brainstorm further ways to make your presentation come alive, using suggestions like the ones below. Answers will vary.

- **Visuals,** such as photos and clip art, can liven up your paper or oral presentation. Post visuals on poster board or on the bulletin board, or insert them into your paper.

- **Graphics,** such as pie charts or bar graphs, can clarify complex information, such as statistics and other data.

- **Audio,** such as songs, narrations, or speeches, can add authority or interest to your presentation.

- **Costumes/Scenery** are important to skits. Even if you are doing an oral presentation, set the mood by wearing a costume. To create scenery, decorate a poster or bring in real objects.

**Remember**

Be sure to speak loudly and clearly so everyone can hear you. Stress key words and phrases to emphasize their importance.

## Exercise 2 Making a Presentation

Now gather the necessary materials, and prepare your presentation. Practice your presentation several times in front of a mirror. Then present your work to the class or to small groups.

Students' final presentations will vary. See www.grammarforwriting.com for writing models for each stage of the writing process.

# Autobiographical Writing

You share stories about your life often—in a letter, an essay, or an e-mail to a friend. When you write true stories, or narratives, about your life, you are writing autobiographically.

**Autobiographical writing** may tell the story of the author's entire life or focus on a significant period. Either way, this kind of writing shows how events and people shaped the author's life, such as this Timeline shows.

moved    had trouble    joined music    met my best    learned to like
         making friends      club          friend       my new home

When you write autobiographically, include the following features.

## Key Features

- natural and logical event sequence
- first-person point of view
- dialogue and descriptive details
- transition words to convey sequence

- precise words and sensory language
- resolution that concludes and reflects on the events

## ASSIGNMENT

**TASK:** Write a two- to three-page **autobiographical essay.** Tell about a challenge or experience with a person that caused a change in your life.

**AUDIENCE:** your teacher and classmates

**PURPOSE:** to tell the story of a meaningful experience and to entertain your readers

## Prewriting

**Pick a Topic** First, brainstorm ideas for a topic. Use a chart to jot down thoughts about people who have changed your life and challenges you have faced.

| Topics | How I Felt | What Happened | How I Changed |
|---|---|---|---|
| **Person** Ms. Wang, teacher | scared of speaking in public | the time she helped me practice | joined debate team, won first championship |
| **Event** sticking up for my brother | used to tease my little brother a lot | a bully picked on him at school | learned how to be a big brother |

Choose a topic that you feel strongly about and remember well. Take your audience into consideration. Which topic will readers find most interesting?

**Gather Details** List details about your topic. Be sure to include all of the information your readers will need to know.

INCOMPLETE    Someone picked on Lee.

COMPLETE    Bill, a bully at school, started picking on my little brother Lee.

**ZIGGY**                                                    **BY TOM WILSON**

## Prewriting

**What's the Trouble?** Some narratives revolve around a problem, or **conflict.** Conflicts can be internal or external.

INTERNAL  You struggle with yourself to make a decision or to change something you believe or feel or a way you act.

EXTERNAL  You struggle with someone or something else, such as a friend, rules at school, or an outside force, such as a storm.

Think about what conflict is involved in the change you are describing. Whom or what are you struggling against?

> **People Involved**
> my little brother, Bill, me

> **Conflict**
> younger brother getting picked on by bully (external)

> **Outcome**
> I learned how to be a good big brother.

**Put Details in Order** **Chronological order** is a type of organization often used in autobiographical writing. When you tell a story chronologically, you describe events in the order that they occurred in time.

List your details in order in a graphic organizer. Use a Timeline like the one on the first page of this workshop. Or create a Sequence Organizer like the one below.

| Lee starts going to my school. | → | I tease Lee. | → | Bill picks on Lee in school. | → | I stick up for Lee. |

# Drafting

**▶ Bring Your Story to Life ▶** **Dialogue** makes your story and your characters seem more real. Dialogue is different from description because it lets your characters speak for themselves.

DESCRIPTION    My brother was very angry, and he shouted.

DIALOGUE    "You shouldn't play tricks on other people," my brother shouted angrily.

Follow these tips for using dialogue:

**1.** Always make sure the reader knows who is speaking. Use **speech tags** before or after dialogue.

> **Bill explained**, "It was a joke. Get over it."

> "A joke is supposed to be funny. Yours wasn't," **Lee yelled**.

**2.** Avoid overusing the word *said*. Be specific. Did the character whisper, yell, mutter, or speak? Find synonyms in a thesaurus.

**▶ Make It Matter ▶** Explain your feelings about what happened. Consider what **impression** you want to leave on your readers. Also, do more than list facts. Stop and reflect on how those facts affected you, how you feel about them, and why they're important.

**CONNECTING**
*Writing & Grammar*

Add a comma after the speech tag if it comes before the dialogue. See **Lesson 11.6.**

I said**,** "I'm sorry."

Add a comma at the end of the dialogue if the speech tag follows.

"I forgive you**,**" Lee responded.

## Writing Model

¹Lee's <u>hands shook, and tears started to run down his</u> <u>face.</u> ²"You shouldn't pick on me," he shouted. ³That's when I raced over from the other side of the cafeteria. ⁴Sweat dripped from my forehead. ⁵I grabbed Lee by the hand and looked Bill Jackson in the eye.

⁶<u>"You leave my little brother alone!" I yelled.</u> ⁷As Bill backed away, I could feel Lee's hand tightly gripping mine. ⁸<u>I really was a big brother.</u>

Specific details

Dialogue

Writer's feelings

## Revising

As you revise, keep in mind the traits of good writing. See **Lesson 1.3.**

Now that you have written your draft, slowly reread your writing, and look for ways to improve your work. Begin by considering the overall structure and organization of your story. Ask yourself if the story would make sense to your readers. Use the Revising Questions below to help guide your revision.

### Revising Questions

❏ How clearly have I described the event or person that caused a change in my life?

❏ Where can I improve the chronological order?

❏ How well have I used first-person point of view?

❏ Where can I add dialogue?

❏ How clearly have I expressed my feelings?

**Work with a Peer** Often another person's opinion of your draft can give you valuable insights on how to improve it. In a **peer review,** a classmate or friend reads your work and offers suggestions.

**Remember**

When you offer feedback as a peer reviewer, be prepared to give examples to support your opinions.

Follow the guidelines below during a peer review.

1. **Do** give positive feedback. **Don't** focus entirely on what is not working.

2. **Do** ask precise questions about the writing. **Don't** rewrite entire sentences or paragraphs of the paper.

3. **Do** offer specific suggestions. **Don't** be overly critical.

# Revising

**Include Interesting Details** Your readers weren't present when the events you are describing occurred, so you have to help them imagine they were. You can do this by including **vivid details** that show, not tell, readers what happened.

See **Lesson 2.3** for help with adding details to your sentences.

TELLING    Lee was embarrassed.

SHOWING    Lee turned red in the face and started to stutter.

As you read the passage below, notice how the author uses vivid details.

### Literary Model

[1]I remember one summer a friend of my mother's in Kansas City sent her son to pass a few weeks with me at my grandmother's home in Lawrence. [2]But the little boy only stayed a few days, then wrote his mother that he wanted to leave, because we had nothing but salt pork and wild dandelions to eat. [3]The boy was right. [4]But being only eight or nine years old, I cried when he showed me the letter he was writing his mother. [5]And I never wanted my mother to invite any more little boys to stay with me at my grandmother's house.

[6]You see, my grandmother was very proud, and she would never beg or borrow anything from anybody.

—Excerpt from *The Big Sea* by Langston Hughes

**Reading as a Writer**    Answers will vary. Sample answers are shown.

1. **What specific details does the author use to show that the family is poor?** The author describes the family's meals (salt pork and wild dandelions).

2. **How do the vivid details shape your impression of the narrator?** The vivid details of the narrator's crying and never wanting another friend to visit give me the impression that he is lonely, sad, and embarrassed.

## Editing and Proofreading

Use this checklist to edit and proofread your draft.

### Editing and Proofreading Checklist

❑ Have I checked that all words are spelled correctly?
❑ Have I used quotation marks around dialogue?
❑ Have I correctly used commas with dialogue?
❑ Have I capitalized all proper nouns and the first word of every sentence?

**Proofreading Symbols**

⊙ Add a period.
⋏ Add a comma.
/ Make lowercase.
≡ Capitalize.

¹lee and I sat in the backyard talking about how scared Bill Jackson looked when I confronted him. ²Lee looked up to me as a Brother, and I was going to be a great big Brother, no matter what. ³"Come on, let's go inside" I suggested. ⁴when Lee took my hand, I realized how much I'd changed.

## Publishing and Presenting

Choose one of these ways to share your essay.

- Add photographs or other illustrations of the people and places described in your essay. Present your illustrated work to the class.

- Create a script from one part of your essay. Practice reading your script aloud with other members of your class. Then perform it for the group.

**R**eflect **O**n **Y**our **W**riting

- What do you like best about your autobiographical essay?
- What ideas, scenes, or people did you have the hardest time describing?

# Chapter Review

## A. Practice Test

In the passage below, there is a question *for each numbered item*. Read the passage carefully, and circle the best answer to each question.

### Stand Up for Your Lunchtime Rights

Millbrook High School needs to enact an open lunch policy. <u>Currently, we are forbidden to leave campus during lunchtime. This rule has a negative effect not only on our lives</u>**1** <u>but also on our self-esteem.</u>

Students are supposed to get privileges as they get older. <u>Privileges give them confidence. They teach them responsibility. They send a</u>**2** <u>message of trust.</u> The staff is worried we will abuse the open lunch privilege, but how can we prove ourselves if we never even get a chance to <u>earn the staff's trust.</u>**3**

Our country values its <u>citizens' rights live</u>**4** in a free society. Our school should be training us to be responsible members of that society—not second-class citizens. <u>So join us in tomorrow's demonstration march. Stand up for your rights!</u>**5**

1. What is the purpose and audience for this passage?
   A. persuade; school staff
   B. persuade; fellow students
   C. entertain; teacher
   D. describe; students' parents

2. What should the writer focus on in the underlined part?
   A. proofreading
   B. organizing ideas
   C. deleting details
   D. improving sentence fluency

3. What is the best replacement for the underlined section?
   A. NO CHANGE
   B. earn their trust.
   C. earn their faith in us.
   D. earn the staff's trust?

4. What is the best replacement for the underlined section?
   A. NO CHANGE
   B. citizens' Rights to live
   C. citizens' rights to live
   D. Citizens' rights live

5. What does the underlined part suggest would be the best presentation format for the passage?
   A. e-mail to education officials
   B. schoolwide newsletter
   C. story for neighbors
   D. speech to a group of students

## B. Evaluating Writing Tips

Read each tip about the five stages of the writing process. Is it a good tip to follow? Write *Y* for yes or *N* for no.

_N_ **1.** When you freewrite during the prewriting stage, don't try to make your ideas specific. It's better to stick to extremely broad topics.

_N_ **2.** During the drafting stage, the most important thing is to make sure you narrow your topic.

_Y_ **3.** During the revising stage, you should focus more on content and organization than on spelling and grammar.

_Y_ **4.** It's okay to use a computerized spell-check program during the editing and proofreading stage, as long as you do your own review as well.

_N_ **5.** During the publishing and presenting stage, ask a classmate to do a peer review of your writing.

## C. Matching Topics to Presentations

Match the topic in the first column with the most appropriate presentation format in the second column. Write the letter of your choice in the space provided. Then write one sentence to explain your choice.

Answers will vary. Sample answers are shown.

_d_ **1.** Profile of Student Basketball Player
A school newspaper article would help me reach the audience who would be interested in this topic.

_e_ **2.** Why We Need a Youth Center
An editorial in a local newspaper is appropriate for a topic that affects the community.

_b_ **3.** My Coin Collection
A blog is a good place to share details about a hobby.

_a_ **4.** Quilting Step-by-Step
Slides would help me show one step at a time.

_c_ **5.** Africa's Endangered Species
A presentation with visuals would help me show the different endangered species and their populations.

**a.** slides

**b.** blog

**c.** class presentation including maps, charts, and graphs

**d.** article in a school newspaper

**e.** editorial in a local newspaper

## D. Proofreading Autobiographical Writing

Use proofreading symbols to correct any errors in the draft below.

| Proofreading Symbols | |
| --- | --- |
| ⨎ Delete. | ⌃ Add. |
| ⊙ Add a period. | ⌄ Add a comma. |
| / Make lowercase. | ☰ Capitalize. |
| ∩∪ Switch order. | ¶ Start a new paragraph. |

¹When the cast list was posted for the school musical, i̲ thought my life was over. ²I hadn't made the cut. ³Performing in the play was what I most wanted in all the wo(u)rld, Ør so I thought. ⁴I decided to give the director a piece of my mind. ⁵He listened calmly. ⁶Then he asked ᵢf I would be interested in helping build the sets. ⁷I was mad. ⁸I didn't want him to humor me. ⁹But I got over it. ¹⁰I ⨎ wanted to ᵇᵉ part of the Ρlay. ¹¹This was the only way.

¹²t̲h̲e first thing we painted was a mural of a forest. ¹³It turned out beautifully. ¹⁴ᴵWas excited. ¹⁵Next, I helped build the front of a cottage. ¹⁶I even made a door that the actors could walk through⊙ ¹⁷I discovered a talent I didn't know I had.¶ ¹⁸In the end, I learned ᵃⁿ important lesson. ¹⁹Sometimes, things can happen that seem bad at first, but they turn out ~~out~~ to be the best thing for you. ²⁰I've learned that working backstage can be as rewarding as performing onstage!

# Effective Sentences and Word Choice

# Correcting Sentence Fragments

A **sentence fragment** does not express a complete thought. It may lack a subject, a verb, or both.

▥➡ To correct sentence fragments, add what is missing so that the words make sense by themselves and express a complete thought.

FRAGMENT    The first people to live in North America.
[The verb is missing. *What* did these people do?]

SENTENCE    The first people to live in North America **came from Asia.**

FRAGMENT    Over hundreds of years, settled into a variety of tribes.
[The subject is missing. *Who* settled into tribes?]

SENTENCE    Over hundreds of years, **Native Americans** settled into tribes.

FRAGMENT    In North America during the 1500s.
[Both a subject and a verb are missing from this group of words.]

SENTENCE    **Europeans first settled** in North America during the 1500s.

▥➡ Some sentence fragments have a subject and a verb but do not express a complete thought. Correct these fragments by attaching the fragment to a sentence that comes before or after it.

FRAGMENT    Buffalo hide was used to cover tepees. Because it was strong and flexible.
[The second word group is a subordinate clause and does not express a complete thought.]

SENTENCE    Buffalo hide was used to cover tepees **because it was strong and flexible.**

**WRITING HINT**

Although you should use complete sentences in almost everything you write for school or business, you can use fragments to make written dialogue sound realistic.

"Sure," Maria agreed. "No problem."

For more about subordinate clauses, see **Lesson 3.4**.

*Chapter 2 • Effective Sentences and Word Choice*   **33**

## EXERCISE 1  Identifying Sentence Fragments

Read the sentences below. Write *SF* for a sentence fragment or *CS* for a complete sentence. Correct each fragment on a separate sheet of paper.  Answers will vary. Sample answers are shown.

**EXAMPLE**   <u>SF</u>  String instruments difficult to play.

String instruments are difficult to play.

_____SF_____ **1.** Even though drums are the coolest instruments. Even though drums are the coolest instruments, I prefer the trumpet.

_____CS_____ **2.** Symphony orchestras are located across the world.

_____SF_____ **3.** In huge concert halls with expensive sound systems. Many concerts are played in huge concert halls with expensive sound systems.

_____SF_____ **4.** The only time we went to the symphony. That was the only time we went to the symphony.

_____SF_____ **5.** The low notes of the cello. I heard the low notes of the cello.

## EXERCISE 2  Revising Sentence Fragments

Read each group of words below, and decide whether it contains a fragment.  Answers will vary. Sample answers are shown.

**1.** Write *C* for items that contain only complete sentences.

**2.** Revise each fragment on a separate sheet of paper. Add the missing part(s) (a subject, a verb, or both), or join the fragment to another sentence.

**3.** Then, explain how you fixed each fragment.

**EXAMPLE**   Included two drummers and one guitarist.

The band included two drummers and one guitarist. (I added a subject.)

**HINT**

As you revise, you may need to add, delete, or change words, punctuation, and capitalization.

**1.** The concert hall a converted movie theater. The concert hall was a converted movie theater. (I added a verb.)

**2.** When the opening band played too long. We yawned when the opening band played too long. (I added a subject and a verb.)

**3.** During the intermission at 8 o'clock. I bought a snack during the intermission at 8 o'clock. (I added a subject and a verb.)

**4.** Left for a moment and missed the best song!
I left for a moment and missed the best song! (I added a subject.)

**5.** The singer has a deep voice. He sounds sophisticated.
C

**6.** I was excited. When Tracy called.
I was excited when Tracy called. (I joined the fragment to a sentence.)

**7.** The last set was winding down.
C

**8.** On the way home in the car after the concert. We talked about music on the way home in the car after the concert. (I added a subject and a verb.)

**9.** I loved the guitar in the last few songs.
C

**10.** My sister asked me. If I liked the new CD.
My sister asked me if I liked the new CD. (I joined the fragment to a sentence.)

# EXERCISE 3 Revising a Draft

Read the concert review below.
Answers will vary. See sample answers in Answer Key at www.grammarforwriting.com.

**1.** Revise it to fix the fragments. Remember to check capitalization and punctuation.

**2.** Exchange papers with a partner, and review each other's work. Did you correct any fragments in different ways?

¹On Saturday evening, the concert hall was filled with eager teens. ²The opening band played. ³For forty minutes, even though they came on late. ⁴When the main act took the stage. ⁵Fans went wild! ⁶The audience applauded for an entire ten minutes. ⁷Some people even cried. ⁸The guitarist, who is often praised for his spontaneous solos. ⁹Only one song. ¹⁰The highlight of the night was when the drummer joined the singer at center stage for a duet. ¹¹A night to remember!

**Write What You Think** Answers will vary. See sample answers in Answer Key at www.grammarforwriting.com.

Respond to the prompt below in a short paragraph. Remember to check for and correct any sentence fragments.

How would your life be different if there were no music of any kind? Give two examples, and support each example with details.

# Correcting Run-on Sentences

If you run together two or more complete sentences as if they were a single sentence, you create a **run-on sentence.**

▮▶ Some run-on sentences have no punctuation mark between the two sentences.

> The eyewitness stared hard at the back of the speeding vehicle she could not see the license plate number.

In other run-on sentences, only a comma is used between the two sentences. However, a comma alone cannot join two complete sentences.

> Four police officers ran to the injured child**,** he was only six or seven years old.

▮▶ Run-on sentences can be confusing because a reader cannot tell where one idea ends and another one starts. You can correct a run-on sentence in several ways.

**1.** Rewrite a run-on sentence as two separate sentences.

> The eyewitness stared hard at the back of the speeding vehicle. **S**he could not see the license plate number.

**2.** Use a **comma** and a **coordinating conjunction** to join the two sentences. Coordinating conjunctions are the joining words *and, or, nor, but, for, so,* and *yet.*

> The eyewitness stared hard at the back of the speeding vehicle**,** **but** she could not see the license plate number.

**3.** Join the two sentences with a **semicolon (;)**. Use this method only if the sentences are closely related. Notice that the second part of the sentence does not begin with a capital letter.

> Four police officers ran to the injured child**; h**e was only six or seven years old.

**TEST-TAKING TIP**

Many tests ask you to correct run-on sentences. If you add a coordinating conjunction between the sentences, remember to use a comma before the conjunction. See item 4 in Section D on page 58 for an example.

# EXERCISE 1 Identifying Run-on Sentences

Read the sentences below, and identify whether or not they are run-ons. Students' revised sentences will vary. Sample answers are shown.

**HiNT**

Some of the numbered items run together three complete sentences.

1. If a sentence is a run-on, correct it by using one of the three ways discussed in this lesson. Write your revised sentences on a separate sheet of paper.

2. If the sentence is already correct, label it with a *C*.

**EXAMPLE**   My favorite season is winter I like bundling up to go outside.

*My favorite season is winter; I like bundling up to go outside.*

1. We had one snow day this year, I went sledding with my brother, my sister did not go. We had one snow day this year. I went sledding with my brother, but my sister did not go.

2. The best sledding hill in town, Art Hill, is located in front of the art museum.
C

3. Sometimes I ride down the hill I convince my brother to bring the sled back up.
Sometimes I ride down the hill, and I convince my brother to bring the sled back up.

4. The best kind of snow for sledding is powdery and soft the sled just glides right over it. The best kind of snow for sledding is powdery and soft. The sled just glides right over it.

5. Even though I love sledding, sometimes the lack of control scares me.
C

6. At the top of Art Hill, a man sells hot chocolate I bet he gets a lot of business on snowy days. At the top of Art Hill, a man sells hot chocolate; I bet he gets a lot of business on snowy days.

7. One thing I don't like about winter is the piercing wind, sometimes it is too cold to be outside. One thing I don't like about winter is the piercing wind. Sometimes it is too cold to be outside.

8. On those days, my mom and I stay in we read a book or watch a movie, sometimes we bake bread. On those days, my mom and I stay in. We read a book or watch a movie. Sometimes we bake bread.

9. If it is snowing hard, I have to shovel the driveway.
C

10. I walk around the neighborhood and shovel walkways, I always make a few extra dollars. I walk around the neighborhood and shovel walkways. I always make a few extra dollars.

11. One time, it snowed two feet, we couldn't even open the front door! One time, it snowed two feet, and we couldn't even open the front door!

Remember that some sentences have more than one verb.

Kristy **slammed** the door and **ran** down the steps.

This sentence has a compound verb and is not a run-on sentence. See **Lesson 6.4** for more about compound verbs.

**12.** Luckily, we had everything we needed we didn't leave the house all day long.
Luckily, we had everything we needed, so we didn't leave the house all day long.

**13.** We ate a lot of food and watched movies.
C

**14.** It took three days for the snow to melt, I couldn't wait to leave the house.
It took three days for the snow to melt; I couldn't wait to leave the house.

**15.** You can bundle up and play in the snow, you can ski or skate.
You can bundle up and play in the snow, or you can ski or skate.

# EXERCISE 2 Revising a Passage

Identify the run-ons. Revise the passage on a separate sheet of paper, eliminating the errors. Answers will vary. See sample answer in Answer Key at www.grammarforwriting.com.

[1]This story is good it is especially interesting because of the vivid details. [2]The story is about a girl who came home from school on a rainy day, her father said she must go to the post office to mail a letter. [3]The girl told her dad that she was tired and cold and that she didn't want to go outside he said he really needed the letter mailed. [4]She put her rain boots back on, grabbed the letter, and walked out the door. [5]On her way home, the sun came out, a rainbow appeared the girl had never seen a rainbow, she was overjoyed!

[6]I think this story does a good job of describing the situation and the emotions of the character, the plot itself failed to keep my attention it is not very exciting. [7]However, I am glad I read this story, and I might read more stories by the same author.

# Adding Details

Some sentences are ineffective because they repeat vague ideas or lack useful or interesting details.

➤ Replace repeated ideas with new information.

ORIGINAL    I liked all the songs and didn't dislike any.

REVISED    I liked all the songs, **especially the first one.**

➤ Add specific details to expand short sentences and express an idea more clearly and completely. The details can tell *who, what, when, where, why,* and *how.*

ORIGINAL    We went to a show.

REVISED    **Last Friday, Zach and I** went to a performance **in the Harris Theater.**

➤ Avoid sentences that simply express opinions. They leave the reader asking "Why?" Add facts, statistics, examples, and other reasons to support your opinion. Use **sensory details** to describe how something looks, sounds, smells, tastes, or feels.

ORIGINAL    The show was impressive.

REVISED    **The fast-paced rhyming lyrics and the pounding drumbeats made** the show impressive.

➤ Add details to various parts of your sentences.

ADD TO THE BEGINNING    **After the end of the last piece,** the audience cheered loudly.

ADD TO THE MIDDLE    The audience, **mostly teens, stood and** cheered loudly.

ADD TO THE END    The audience cheered loudly **for several minutes, hoping the group would perform one more piece.**

> **Real-World Writing**
>
> Details help writers show, not tell, readers what is happening.
>
> "Don't tell me the moon is shining; show me the glint of light on broken glass."
>
> —Anton Chekhov

# EXERCISE 1 Adding Details

Read the sentences below. On a separate sheet of paper, add specific details to support the main idea. Make each sentence more interesting and specific. Answers will vary. Sample answers are shown.

**EXAMPLE** Dolphins are animals that live in the ocean.

*Dolphins are aquatic mammals that live in the ocean and are often found in Florida.*

1. **Many animals are good swimmers.**
   Many dolphins swim quickly.
2. **Some creatures are really big.**
   Some mammals, such as blue whales, can weigh thousands of pounds.
3. **Dolphins are playful.**
   Dolphins like to play with seaweed and enjoy riding waves.
4. **The whale population is changing.**
   The whale population is rapidly declining to its lowest levels in years.
5. **Scientists use things to track ocean animals.**
   Scientists use tracking devices to learn the movements of whales and sharks.

# EXERCISE 2 Writing Sentences

Study the photo below. Answers will vary. Sample answers are shown.

1. On a separate sheet of paper, write five sentences about the photo using descriptive words and sensory details.

2. Exchange papers with a partner, and discuss the similarities and differences in your sentences.

1. The diver is wearing a large mask, a wet suit, and fins.
2. The sandy ocean bottom is dotted with small rocks and plants.
3. The diver's deep breaths interrupt the silence of the underwater scene.
4. A few small striped fish glide in and out of the jagged clump of coral.
5. The icy water makes the diver shiver as he watches the nearby stingrays.

# Using Parallel Structure

In **parallel structure,** or **parallelism,** two or more words, phrases, or clauses are written in the same grammatical form.

NOT PARALLEL    A chess champion needs to be **intelligent, patient,** and **using imagination.**
[two adjectives and a phrase]

PARALLEL    A chess champion needs to be **intelligent, patient,** and **imaginative.**
[three one-word adjectives]

PARALLEL    A chess champion needs to **have intelligence, show patience,** and **use imagination.**
[three phrases each made of a verb and a noun]

�)➤ When you combine sentences, check for parallel structure. Be sure to express similar ideas in the same way.

ORIGINAL    Playing chess relaxes my friend Natalie. She also relaxes when she listens to music.

NOT PARALLEL    **Playing chess** and **when she listens to music** relax my friend Natalie.
[compound subject made of one gerund phrase and one subordinate clause]

PARALLEL    **Playing chess** and **listening to music** relax my friend Natalie.
[compound subject made of two gerund phrases]

▸➤ Writers use parallel structure to create balance and rhythm in their sentences. As you read the passage on the next page, notice the parallel structure.

**CONNECTING**
Writing & Grammar

Remember to use a comma between items in a series of three of more. See **Lesson 11.3.**
You should plan each move, take your time, and have fun.

For more about subordinate clauses, see **Lesson 3.4.**

Review gerunds with students. Explain that gerunds are verb forms that act as nouns and end in -*ing*. See Lesson 8.6 for more information.

## HINT

Determine if a sentence is parallel by looking at the grammatical construction. For example, a verb should be matched with a verb, a noun with a noun, an adjective with an adjective, and a phrase with a phrase.

- had run and had won
- a shout, a whisper, and a cry
- loud and strong
- in the morning and at night

### Literary Model

¹When I awoke the next morning, I felt (stiff) and (dirty) from sleeping in my clothes. ²Worse, I had no idea what time it was. ³All I knew was that the house was full of (bright, white) light and the radio had nothing but static. ⁴I turned it off.
⁵For a long time I lay on the bed, (sorting) out my thoughts, (trying) to think what to do next, (reminding) myself that I had made the decision to stay. ⁶Though the sunlight made me feel better, I kept thinking about the way people were reacting: (Bill, Mr. Janick, Terri, the bottle throwers.) ⁷Just thinking about it brought back uneasy feelings.

—Excerpt from *A Place Called Ugly* by Avi

### Reading as a Writer

**1.** Circle words or phrases that are parallel.

**2.** Now continue the passage by writing two sentences of your own. Use parallel structure in both sentences. Answers will vary. Sample answer is shown. I was scared, worried, and confused. I listened to the barking dogs and the chirping birds.

## EXERCISE 1 Revising for Parallel Structure

Read the sentences below. On a separate sheet of paper, rewrite each sentence to make it parallel. You can add, delete, or rearrange words as needed.
Students' revisions may vary. Sample answers are shown.

**EXAMPLE**   In Greek mythology, Poseidon ruled the sea and was in control of earthquakes.

*In Greek mythology, Poseidon ruled the sea and controlled earthquakes.*

**1.** Dionysus took a risk, and he went down to the underworld, and was bringing his mother back to life.
Dionysus took a risk, went down to the underworld, and brought his mother back to life.

**2.** Other creatures in Greek myths were found living in the water, or they lived on a mountain.
Other creatures in Greek myths lived in the water or on a mountain.

**3.** Much of Greek mythology focuses on the births, dying, and special powers of gods and goddesses. Much of Greek mythology focuses on the births, deaths, and special powers of gods and goddesses.

4. Athena loved war and was always admiring of heroes.
   Athena loved war and admired heroes.
5. Reading myths and to study Greek culture interest me.
   Reading myths and studying Greek culture interest me.

# EXERCISE 2 Combining Sentences

Use parallel structure to combine the sentences in each of the examples below. Answers may vary. Sample answers are shown.

**EXAMPLE**   In my English class, we study ancient myths. We are also taking a test on Greece.

In English class, we are studying ancient myths and taking a test on Greece.

1. I like the story about Sisyphus. I also am enjoying the myth about Aphrodite.
   I like the story about Sisyphus and the myth about Aphrodite.
2. According to the *Odyssey,* Sisyphus was always rolling a huge boulder up a hill. The boulder always rolled back down.
   According to the *Odyssey*, Sisyphus always rolled a huge boulder up a hill, but the boulder always rolled back down.
3. Zeus was the king of the gods. He ruled from Mount Olympus.
   Zeus was the king of the gods and ruled from Mount Olympus.
4. Mount Olympus is tall. It is also cold.
   Mount Olympus is tall and cold.
5. Hera possessed courage. She was also strong.
   Hera possessed courage and strength.
6. Zeus controlled thunder. Lightning was also under his control.
   Zeus controlled thunder and lightning.
7. The god Apollo played music. He was also a poet.
   The god Apollo played music and wrote poetry.
8. Artemis was Apollo's twin sister. She was a goddess.
   Artemis was Apollo's twin sister and a goddess.
9. Artemis spent her time in forests. She also was in the mountains and was also spending time in marshes.
   Artemis spent her time in forests, mountains, and marshes.
10. Many Greek gods and goddesses were intelligent, brave, and have jealousy and not much patience.
    Many Greek gods and goddesses were intelligent, brave, jealous, and impatient.

# EXERCISE 3 Using Parallel Structure

Students' sentences will vary. Sample answer is shown.

Think of a talent you have. Write three sentences about your talent. At least two sentences should have parallel structure. Exchange sentences with a partner. Identify any sentences with errors in parallelism, and discuss how to fix them.

Working Together

I am a talented musician and singer. I can play the trumpet, read sheet music, and sing well. I've sung and played music since I was little.

# Avoiding Wordiness

As you revise, ask yourself, "Have I used more words than I need to make my meaning clear?" Use the tips below to avoid **wordiness** and to make your writing **concise.**

**1.** Avoid saying the same thing more than once.

It's a ~~true~~ fact that many Americans speak ~~or talk in~~ a language other than English at home.

**2.** Generally, avoid unnecessary repetition of words.

~~The language of~~ Mandarin is one of the world's most popular languages.

**3.** Replace a long clause with a phrase or a phrase with a single word or words.

My uncle, who is an architect, ~~with a lot of experience,~~ speaks ^experienced Mandarin, Spanish, Japanese, and English.

**4.** Cut out all empty words or phrases that add little or no meaning. To the left is a list of wordy phrases and ways to shorten them.

^Now ~~At this point in time,~~ Mandarin is the principal language ~~of the country~~ of China.

**5.** Change verbs in the **passive voice** to the **active voice.** In sentences with active verbs, the subject performs the action of the verb. The active voice uses fewer words.

^Mina speaks ~~Russian and Arabic are spoken by Mina~~.

[The subject (*Mina*) performs the action of the verb (*speaks*).]

## Wordy — Concise

as a matter → in fact
of fact

at a later → later
point

at this → now
point in
time

in the → if
event that

See **Lesson 8.5** for more information about active and passive voice.

MR. JEREMY DUNCAN
144 HUMMINGBIRD LANE

DEAR JEREMY
I AM WRITING TO CONFIRM THAT I WILL
PICK YOU UP IN FRONT OF THE SCHOOL
AT APPROXIMATELY FIVE-THIRTY P.M. AS WE
HAVE PREVIOUSLY DISCUSSED. IF THERE
ARE ANY CHANGES TO THIS SCHEDULE,
PLEASE NOTIFY ME IMMEDI--

Next          Options

I THINK THE IDEA OF TEXT MESSAGING IS TO BE BRIEF.

HANG ON— I'M ALMOST DONE.

Zits © Zits Partnership. King Features Syndicate.

# Exercise 1 Eliminating Wordiness

On a separate sheet of paper, rewrite the wordy sentences below. Use the tips from this lesson to eliminate wordiness.

Answers will vary. Sample answers are shown.

**EXAMPLE**    The community at this point in time needs to be strong and show its strength.

*The community now needs to remain strong.*

1. Community service is a really good thing to do for the community because it helps out the community and the people in it in many different ways.
Community service helps people in many ways.

2. One of the most popular and well-known community service organizations is Habitat for Humanity, which was started in 1976 to provide houses for needy people who cannot afford a home. One of the most popular community service organizations is Habitat for Humanity, which was started in 1976 to provide homes for needy people.

3. Volunteers are sent to building sites by the organization, and they usually are assigned jobs, such as hammering with a hammer or working on the floor, roof, and walls. Habitat for Humanity sends volunteers to building sites to do jobs, such as working on the floors, roof, and walls.

4. It is very important that you listen to the supervisor or the person who gives you directions to be sure that you don't hurt yourself and to ensure your safety.
It is very important to listen to the supervisor to ensure your safety.

5. Along with Habitat for Humanity, there are many nonprofit community service organizations and groups that improve society and the people in it.
Along with Habitat for Humanity, many nonprofit organizations help improve society.

6. Most community service is done and performed by schools, religious groups, and clubs.
Schools, religious groups, and clubs do the majority of community service.

7. If you are interested in the environment, there are lots of organizations that you can join that help clean up the community and make life better. If you are interested in the environment, you can join many organizations that work to clean up the community.

8. Community service many times helps to bring together and unite people of all races regardless of their race.
Community service often unites people of different races.

9. One fall, at a homeless shelter, Thanksgiving dinner was served by my sister and me to people who didn't have any food and who would have gone hungry.
My sister and I helped serve Thanksgiving dinner at a homeless shelter to people who would have gone hungry.

**10.** In the event that you are interested in volunteering to do community service, you can research events on the Internet or talk to people at school who have worked at and performed community service in your town.

If you want to do community service, research events on the Internet or talk to people at school who have done community service in your town.

## EXERCISE 2 Revising a Thank-you Note

Read and revise the thank-you note below to eliminate wordiness.

Answers will vary. See sample answer in Answer Key at www.grammarforwriting.com.

Dear Aunt Sally,

¹Thank you so much for the leather journal and the sketchbook that you gave me for my birthday! ²I am so excited to have a place to write down all my thoughts, due to the fact that often I want to write something down, and now I have somewhere to do so! ³At this point in time, I have been very interested in drawing, mostly cartoons, ever since I was about seven years old. ⁴I know I will use the sketchbook all the time or very often. ⁵I also plan to use it to explore new kinds of art. ⁶You always know as a matter of fact just what to get me for my birthday! ⁷Again, I thank you.

Love,

Charlie

## EXERCISE 3 Writing a Thank-you Note

Write a thank-you note on a separate sheet of paper. It can be to a relative or to a friend for a gift or for an act of kindness.

Answers will vary. See sample answer in Answer Key at www.grammarforwriting.com.

**1.** Read your note aloud to a partner, and listen for wordiness.

**2.** Work together to eliminate unnecessary words and passive verbs.

# Choosing the Right Word

Choose your words carefully. Using **precise language** helps you explain your ideas clearly and develop a lively, interesting writing style.

➤ As you revise, replace vague, general words with more specific ones. Ask yourself, "How can I create a more vivid picture in my readers' minds?"

| Original | As the woman went out of the building, she made the floor dirty. |
|---|---|
| Revised | As the **doctor hurried** out of the **hospital, her muddy boots left a trail of dark footprints on the white floor.** |

➤ Avoid using **clichés,** or overused expressions. Replace them with original words that convey more specific meaning.

| Clichés | Original Words |
|---|---|
| light as a feather | light as the whipped cream on strawberries |
| raining cats and dogs | a drenching, steady rain |
| beat around the bush | hesitated for five minutes |
| spill the beans | tell the secret |

➤ Use a **dictionary** or a **thesaurus** to help you select the word with the precise meaning you want. Even **synonyms,** or words with similar meanings, have slightly different shades of meaning. Consider, for example, these synonyms for *loud*.

| | | | |
|---|---|---|---|
| deafening | earsplitting | noisy | shrill |
| deep | blaring | piercing | thundering |

➤ Avoid using big words just to impress your readers.

ORIGINAL   The hero was smart, handsome, and dauntless.

REVISED   The hero was smart, handsome, and brave.

## Real-World Writing

Professional writers know that word choice is important.

"The difference between the right word and the almost right word is the difference between lightning and a lightning bug."

—Mark Twain

## EXERCISE 1  Revising Sentences

On a separate sheet of paper, rewrite the sentences below to make them more vivid and precise. Some sentences may need only a word or two changed. Others may take a different form completely. Answers will vary. See sample answers in Answer Key at www.grammarforwriting.com.

1. We went on a trip to a farm.

2. The farm was far away, so it took a while to get there.

3. However, I thought the ride was fun.

4. As we got farther from the city, we saw many new things.

5. When we got there, the man was waiting for us.

6. He talked to us about life there.

7. He said he gets up early to do chores and then goes to bed early, too.

8. Some people rode horses, but I was too scared.

9. The weather got bad after a while.

10. The chickens were behind the house.

11. I've never heard birds make so much noise!

12. The great thing about the trip was that I saw a peacock.

13. The pigs were dirty.

14. I didn't realize how much it takes to maintain a farm.

15. It seems as if the farmers take good care of the animals.

16. The wheat fields were big, and there weren't many cornstalks.

17. My mom grew up in the country, and she had animals, too.

18. For lunch, we had pancakes and a side dish.

19. When we left, I felt as if I had learned a lot about farming.

20. We're going somewhere new next time.

# EXERCISE 2 Using Synonyms

Choose two of the words listed below, and look them up in a thesaurus. Find five synonyms for each word. Then pick one synonym for each word, and use it in a sentence.
Answers will vary. See sample answers in Answer Key at www.grammarforwriting.com.

| | | |
|---|---|---|
| cold | scared | nice |
| happy | sad | bad |

# EXERCISE 3 Rewriting Clichés

Choose five clichés from the ten listed below. Come up with fresh expressions to use instead, and write them on a separate sheet of paper. Answers will vary. Sample answers are shown.

1. fresh as a daisy
   as fresh as a spring rain
2. in the nick of time
   slipping through the crack before the door closes
3. crystal clear
   as clear as the water in a still pond
4. as flat as a pancake
   as thin as paper
5. get the ball rolling
   take a deep breath and get started
6. blind as a bat
   as unaware as a newborn baby
7. cold as ice
   as frigid as a bitter wind
8. happy as a clam
   as cheerful as a puppy
9. break a leg
   be ready for an encore
10. easy as pie
    simple as counting to ten

"Who wants to get the ball rolling?"

http://www.CartoonStock.com

# EXERCISE 4 Writing a Journal Entry

Think about a memorable trip you took. Describe your trip in a journal entry on a separate sheet of paper. Write at least five sentences using precise language.
Answers will vary. See sample answers in Answer Key at www.grammarforwriting.com.

# Using Formal and Informal English

With writing—as with speaking—your choice of words depends on your purpose and audience. **Formal** and **informal English** are appropriate for different situations.

▥▶ Use formal English when your reader is in a position of authority and you want to discuss a subject in a serious way.

**R**emember

Slang is not appropriate in formal situations.

SLANG The speaker needs to **chill out** before he **splits**.

FORMAL The speaker needs to relax before he leaves.

## Formal English

| Types of Writing | Common Features | Example |
|---|---|---|
| business letters, business e-mails, news articles, speeches, reports, most school essays | advanced vocabulary, no slang, few (if any) contractions, longer and more complex sentences | Because the food was not cooked well and the service was disappointing, the critic gave the restaurant a poor review. |

▥▶ Use informal English if your reader is a friend or family member or if you want to convey a more casual, conversational style.

## Informal English

| Types of Writing | Common Features | Example |
|---|---|---|
| friendly letters or friendly e-mails, humorous writing, dialogue in stories and plays | everyday language, slang, contractions, shorter and simpler sentences | The food tasted yucky, and the service wasn't great. That's why the critic blasted the restaurant in the review. |

▥▶ Be consistent. Avoid jumping back and forth between formal and informal language within the same piece of writing. An abrupt change may distract the reader or sound awkward.

ORIGINAL    "Yikes!" Chris muttered. "There's no way I will be able to **commence my written composition** before Friday's deadline." [The formal phrase is out of place.]

REVISED    "Yikes!" Chris muttered. "There's no way I'll be able to **start my paper** before Friday's deadline." [The dialogue seems more realistic and natural and matches the rest of the sentence.]

*"Is everything all right, Jeffrey? You never call me 'dude' anymore."*

© 2003 The New Yorker Collection from cartoonbank.com. All Rights Reserved.

# EXERCISE 1  Revising Informal Language

On a separate sheet of paper, rewrite the letter below by making the language more formal and appropriate.

Answers will vary. See sample answer in Answer Key at www.grammarforwriting.com.

Hi Tim Chapin!

$^1$Thank you for getting with me to talk about that reporting gig. $^2$The newspaper seems to be a really great place to hang and work. $^3$I can't imagine a job that is better for me. $^4$The offices were super cool, and the workers seem with-it and hip. $^5$I hope to talk to you soon!

Thanks a bunch,

Candice

For information about writing business letters, see the writing application in **Chapter 12.**

# EXERCISE 2  Writing a Formal Letter

Write a letter to a potential employer about a job opportunity. Make sure you use formal language. Write your letter on a separate sheet of paper.

Answers will vary. See sample answer in Answer Key at www.grammarforwriting.com.

# Speech

Speaking to others is an important part of everyday life. You tell stories, share opinions, describe problems, and explain things. Knowing how to give an effective speech is a useful skill in school and in life. When you give a **persuasive speech,** you develop an **argument** in which you state your opinion, or claim, and support it with logical reasons and relevant evidence.

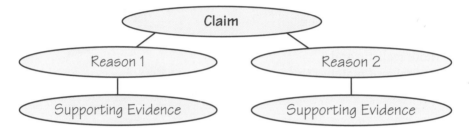

Claim

Reason 1

Reason 2

Supporting Evidence

Supporting Evidence

## Key Features

- precise opinion statement, or claim
- supporting reasons and relevant evidence
- words that connect your claim, reasons, and evidence
- formal style
- conclusion that supports the argument presented

## ASSIGNMENT

**TASK:** Does the Internet prevent students from spending valuable time with family? Write a **persuasive speech** to present an **argument** on this topic. Include two reasons and relevant evidence to support your claim.

**PURPOSE:** to persuade

**AUDIENCE:** your teacher, parents, and classmates

**KEY INSTRUCTIONS:** Make your speech one to two pages long.

**Take a Stand** First, focus on the topic. Then, figure out your **position,** or opinion, on the issue. Begin by asking yourself some questions.

1. What personal experiences have I had related to this topic?

2. What are other people's positions on this topic? Which position seems most reasonable to me?

3. Other than my personal experiences, what kinds of arguments and evidence can I add?

Then, write a sentence in which you state your opinion as clearly and strongly as you can.

> WEAK    Just because students are on the Internet, it doesn't mean they don't spend time with family.

> STRONG   The Internet does not take valuable family time away from students if families use the Internet as a tool to increase their time together.

**Support Your Claim** Support your position, or claim, with two clearly stated reasons. Use a variety of relevant facts, statistics, and expert opinions to support each reason, as shown in the chart below.

| Reason 1 | Students can play a variety of online games with their siblings and parents. |
|---|---|
| Evidence: Fact | There are hundreds of family-oriented games online. |
| Evidence: Expert Opinion | Doctors claim that families who play games together have better communication and a closer bond than families who do not play games. |
| Evidence: Statistic | About 52 percent of young people reported that they wished their families would participate in more family-oriented activities. |

**CONNECTING**
*Writing &* **Grammar**

As you write your speech, avoid fragments. A fragment may be missing a subject, a verb, or both. To fix a fragment, add the missing part. See **Lessons 2.1** and **6.1.**

FRAGMENT Using the Internet.
[missing a subject and verb]

COMPLETE Students enjoy using the Internet.

Copyright © 2014 by William H. Sadlier, Inc. All rights reserved.

## WRITING HiNT

Catch your audience's attention immediately by opening your speech in one of these ways.

- an interesting anecdote or story
- a challenging question
- an exciting or shocking example or fact
- a memorable quotation

For more help with parallel structure and precise language, see **Lessons 2.4** and **2.6**.

**Keep the Spotlight** The effectiveness of a speech depends on more than just ideas. It also depends on how the ideas are presented. Use a few of these common **persuasive techniques.**

| Technique | Definition | Example |
|---|---|---|
| **Parallel Structure** | the repetition of similar grammatical structures | The Internet **can bring families closer together** just as much as it **can keep families apart.** |
| **Repetition** | the reuse of key words and phrases | **The Internet** is interactive. **The Internet** connects people. |
| **Rhetorical Question** | a question asked for effect | Why don't we just all blame technology for keeping families apart? |

Also, make sure to use **precise language.** Using confusing or vague language may cause you to lose your audience's attention.

**VAGUE**      I think we can do more fun stuff together. There are a lot of cool things online.

**PRECISE**      Online games and movies, online books, and interactive Web sites are high-tech, exciting ways to unite families.

**Practice Your Speech** In a speech, how you say it is just as important as what you say. Avoid simply reading your speech aloud. Instead, keep these tips in mind:

1. **Connect.** Look at your audience, and maintain eye contact. Make everyone feel involved in your presentation.

2. **Keep a good pace.** Avoid speaking too quickly or too slowly. Use pauses to emphasize your main points.

3. **Move around.** Use your body and gestures as tools to emphasize your ideas.

4. **Monitor your voice.** Speak loudly enough so that everyone can hear you. Change your tone, or how high or low you say words, to match the content of your speech.

5. **Record it.** Try making a video or audio recording of your speech so you can play it back and find ways to improve it.

Use the Writing Checklist to check your speech one last time. The model below shows part of one student's speech.

## WRITING CHECKLIST
### Did you...

✔ state a strong position, or claim, two reasons, and evidence?

✔ use precise language and persuasive techniques?

✔ start with a strong opening?

✔ make your speech one to two pages long?

**Writing Model**

¹Many people are blaming the Internet for taking away valuable family time. ²However, it depends on how we use it. ³For example, if we choose to play a card game by ourselves, should we blame the deck of cards for keeping us away from our families? ⁴<u>The Internet does not take family time away if families use the Internet as a tool to increase their time together.</u>

⁵For instance, students can play a variety of online games with their siblings and parents. ⁶Hundreds of family-oriented online games can change the Internet experience from a solitary game to a group game. ⁷Also, doctors claim that families who play games together have better communication and achieve a closer bond.

Rhetorical question

Clear position, or claim

First reason

Evidence to support reason

# Chapter Review

## A. Practice Test

Read each sentence below carefully. If you find an error, choose the underlined part that must be changed to make the sentence correct.
Fill in the circle for the corresponding letter. If there is no error, fill in circle *E*.

EXAMPLE

Ⓐ Ⓑ Ⓒ Ⓓ Ⓔ      The Springfield Community <u>Theater's</u> production of <u>*Grease*</u>
                                  A                                B
     was <u>superb, the</u> actors did <u>an excellent</u> job.    <u>No error</u>
              C                       D             E

Ⓐ Ⓑ Ⓒ ⬤ Ⓔ    **1.** The <u>spirit of the Fifties</u> was shown in <u>the sets</u>, <u>the costumes</u>,
                             A                         B        C
      and <u>the way the actors' hair was styled</u>.    <u>No error</u>
                       D                    E

Ⓐ ⬤ Ⓒ Ⓓ Ⓔ    **2.** The men in the <u>cast wore</u> black leather <u>jackets the</u>
                            A                         B
      women wore <u>poodle skirts</u>.    <u>No error</u>
               C         D         E

Ⓐ Ⓑ ⬤ Ⓓ Ⓔ    **3.** <u>The best</u> number <u>in the show was</u> "Greased
                      A                 B
      <u>Lightning." Because</u> the dancing <u>was neat</u>.
                 C                    D
      <u>No error</u>
        E

⬤ Ⓑ Ⓒ Ⓓ Ⓔ    **4.** <u>Because of the fact that</u> the songs were great, many
                            A
      <u>audience members</u> were heard <u>humming the tunes</u> during
               B                        C
      the <u>intermission</u>.    <u>No error</u>
               D         E

Ⓐ Ⓑ Ⓒ Ⓓ ⬤    **5.** Tara O'Malley, <u>the actress</u> who <u>played Sandy</u>, <u>was convincing</u>
                             A                B              C
      in <u>her role</u>.    <u>No error</u>
          D        E

Ⓐ Ⓑ Ⓒ ● Ⓔ  **6.** Nick Rosenberg <u>lent his</u> spectacular <u>tenor voice</u> <u>to the role</u> of
                              A                         B                 C
               Danny. <u>An amazing voice!</u>   <u>No error</u>
                         D                 E

Ⓐ Ⓑ ● Ⓓ Ⓔ  **7.** The score <u>included songs</u> from <u>the original</u> Broadway
                            A                       B
             <u>production, some</u> songs <u>from the movie</u> were added.
                    C              D
      <u>No error</u>
          E

Ⓐ Ⓑ ● Ⓓ Ⓔ  **8.** Many <u>young people</u> have <u>only seen</u> the film <u>version it</u> was
                       A              B             C
             exciting for them to see the <u>live show</u>.   <u>No error</u>
                                   D            E

Ⓐ ● Ⓒ Ⓓ Ⓔ  **9.** <u>During the closing</u> number, "We Go <u>Together." The</u>
                    A                         B
             <u>audience gave</u> a <u>standing ovation</u>.   <u>No error</u>
              C             D          E

● Ⓑ Ⓒ Ⓓ Ⓔ  **10.** <u>Congratulations in order</u> for the Springfield <u>Community</u>
                    A                           B
            <u>Theater</u>. They staged <u>the best</u> show <u>our town has seen in a</u>
                           C                        D
            <u>long time</u>.   <u>No error</u>
                    E

## B. Revising Sentences

Revise each sentence below on a separate sheet of paper. Delete any unnecessary words, and add precise details.

Answers will vary. Sample answers are shown.

**1.** We're planning a surprise party.
   My family is planning a surprise birthday party for my sister Janie next Saturday.

**2.** Due to the fact that my sister will be turning the age of sixteen, it will be quite a celebration for the most part and not an average birthday party at all.
   Because Janie is turning sixteen, it will be an elegant and formal celebration.

**3.** A band will play music and songs.
   My best friend's band, The MereCats, will play rock music all evening long.

**4.** We're having the party in the backyard and not inside the house because we expect so many people to come that it will be crowded.
   We're having the party in the backyard because we expect such a large crowd.

**5.** Janie will be surprised.
   Janie will be surprised when she comes home from gymnastics to see fifty people waiting for her!

## C. Choosing the Right Words

Each sentence below contains vague words and informal English. On a separate sheet of paper, rewrite each sentence to include precise words and formal English. Answers will vary. Sample answers are shown.

1. Locks of Love is a very cool organization.
   Locks of Love is a charitable organization.
2. The guys in it collect hair for kids who've lost their own hair from some medical stuff.
   Members collect hair for young people who have lost their own hair from medical treatments.
3. It's one of the easiest ways to give stuff. All you gotta do is get a haircut!
   It is one of the simplest ways to donate to charity. The only requirement is to get a haircut.
4. If you've got short hair, you can grow it out so you have a lot of hair to cut off later.
   If you have short hair, you can let it grow and then have it cut.
5. The program has tons of people in it, and many kids in our school go to it. The program is popular, and thirty students in our school participate in it.

## D. Correcting Sentence Problems

Revise each sentence below. Correct any fragments, run-ons, and uses of passive voice. You can add, delete, and rearrange words as necessary.
Answers will vary. Sample answers are shown.

1. Exercise can benefit you in many ways your body and your mood can both be improved by it.
   Exercise can benefit you in many ways. It can improve both your body and your mood.
2. It is shown by studies that exercise is good for depression. Because your mood is improved by it.
   Studies show that exercise is good for depression because it improves your mood.
3. When you're active, changes are produced by your body that lift your mood. When you're active, your body produces changes that lift your mood.
4. These changes are powerful they have a dramatic effect on the brain. These changes are powerful, and they have a dramatic effect on the brain.
5. Mood changes are also triggered by eating chocolate, exercising is much better for you!
   Eating chocolate also triggers mood changes, but exercising is much better for you!

## E. Improving and Evaluating a Speech

Carefully read the speech that follows. On a separate sheet of paper, answer the questions below, and rewrite the speech. You may add, delete, or rearrange sentences and details as needed.

Students' rewrites will vary. See sample answer in Answer Key at www.grammarforwriting.com. Sample answers to the questions are shown.

**Writing Model**

[1]It's possible that Millner Junior High might benefit from an antibullying program. [2]Often we see students being harassed in the halls. [3]That's a crying shame. [4]Teachers and parents should probably be educated. [5]Also the victims and the bullies.

[6]Many schools that have begun antibullying programs they report awesome results. [7]School violence decreased at Wagner School. [8]Students are less unhappy and definitely happier. [9]They feel safer walking in the halls, eating in the cafeteria, and when they go to gym class.

[10]Millner should follow the example set by these schools. [11]It would be as easy as falling off a log to get a program started, it could change the quality of life here.

**1.** How could the writer strengthen the opinion stated in sentence 1?

The speaker needs to take a more definite stand on the issue and eliminate the phrase "It's possible."

**2.** What are two other suggestions you would give to the writer about how to improve the speech?

I would suggest that the writer eliminate fragments, run-ons, clichés, and wordiness to make the sentences more effective. Also, I would suggest that the writer provide more persuasive evidence to back up his or her opinion.

# Sentence Variety and Structure

# Kinds of Sentences

Using different kinds of sentences helps make your writing more interesting.

▌➡ Sentences may be classified according to their purpose. There are four kinds of sentences: **declarative, imperative, interrogative,** and **exclamatory.** Be sure to use the correct end punctuation mark for each kind of sentence.

**Remember**

*You* is the subject of a request or command, even if the word *you* never appears in the sentence. *You* is called the **understood subject.**

[You] Imagine the deepest part of the ocean.

| Kind of Sentence | Purpose | Example |
|---|---|---|
| Declarative | to make a statement | Winds cause ocean currents**.** |
| Imperative | to make a request or give a command | Please point to the Pacific Ocean**.** |
| Interrogative | to ask a question | Why is the sea salty**?** |
| Exclamatory | to express strong feelings | What an amazing photograph of the ocean that is**!** |

## EXERCISE 1 Writing Sentences

Read the sentences below. On a separate sheet of paper, change each item to the kind of sentence identified in parentheses. You may add, drop, or rearrange words as necessary. Remember to use the correct end punctuation for that type of sentence.
Answers will vary. Sample answers are shown.

For more information about end punctuation marks, see **Lesson 11.1.**

**EXAMPLE**    I enjoyed the view from the Willis Tower. (exclamatory)

The view from the Willis Tower was fantastic!

1. The elevator goes to the very top floor. (interrogative)
Does the elevator go to the very top floor?
2. Is the Willis Tower in Chicago? (declarative)
The Willis Tower is in Chicago.
3. How old is the Taj Mahal? (imperative)
Tell me when the Taj Mahal was built.
4. Did your teacher tell you that it is built entirely of white marble? (declarative)
The temple is built entirely of white marble.
5. Shah Jahan built it in memory of his wife. (interrogative)
Did Shah Jahan build it in memory of his wife?
6. Did the temple cost 35 million rupees to build? (declarative)
The temple cost 35 million rupees to build.

**7.** The Taipei 101 building is 1,667 feet tall. (interrogative)
Is the Taipei 101 building 1,667 feet tall?

**8.** I think it is located in Taiwan. (interrogative)
Is it located in Taiwan?

**9.** Can you describe the even taller building that is under construction? (imperative)
Describe the even taller building that is under construction.

**10.** Amazingly, the new building may be over 2,100 feet tall! (declarative) The new building may be over 2,100 feet tall.

## EXERCISE 2 Proofreading an Ad

Proofread the ad below, correcting errors in end punctuation. Use the proofreading symbols to mark your corrections.

**Proofreading Symbols**

| | |
|---|---|
| ℣ | Delete. |
| ∧ | Add. |
| ⊙ | Add a period. |

¹Do you and your parents disagree about the ideal vacation spot?²Do you want to visit a place that is exciting, but your parents want a place that is relaxing? ³If so, Spring Waters Resort is the perfect compromise. ⁴This 10,000-acre resort offers a variety of enjoyable and exciting amusement parks for young people as well as relaxing spas and quiet adult swimming pools for parents. ⁵Start out your vacation the right way with this fun and relaxing resort. ⁶Have a spectacular vacation at Spring Waters Resort!

## EXERCISE 3 Writing an Ad

On a separate sheet of paper, write an ad about an interesting place you have visited. Make sure you use all four kinds of sentences. Then proofread your draft, paying close attention to end punctuation. Answers will vary. See sample answers in Answer Key at www.grammarforwriting.com.

# Varying Sentence Length

Try to avoid a string of short or long sentences in a row. Vary the length of your sentences to create a lively writing style with **sentence variety.**

➤ Too many short sentences in a row make a passage sound choppy. Look for ways to combine or reword sentences.

ORIGINAL    Michelle lived on a quiet street. Her house was quiet. She lived a peaceful life. Her life was ordinary. Michelle came home from work each night at 5:30. She followed a routine. It was predictable.

REVISED    Michelle lived on a quiet street in a quiet house. She lived a peaceful, ordinary life. When she came home from work each night at 5:30, she followed a predictable routine.

➤ Too many long, rambling sentences can also sound monotonous. Cut out unnecessary words to create shorter sentences that will flow smoothly together. A short sentence in the middle of longer ones will catch the reader's attention.

ORIGINAL    The moonlight cast an eerie shadow across the floor, and the curtains fluttered in the breeze, and the chilly air made Michelle shake and shiver. She collapsed on the sofa because she was exhausted, and she wanted to sleep, so she closed her eyes, and she pulled the blanket up and over her legs, and then she drifted off to sleep, but that was when she smelled the smoke.

REVISED    The moonlight cast an eerie shadow across the floor, and the curtains fluttered in the breeze. The chilly air made Michelle shiver as she collapsed on the sofa. Exhausted, she closed her eyes and pulled the blanket over her legs. That's when she smelled the smoke.

1. Sentence 3 is the shortest. It slows the reader down and makes the reader think about what the author is trying to say.

# EXERCISE 1 Analyzing Sentence Variety

Read the literary model on the next page aloud with a partner. Discuss the answers to the following questions.
Answers may vary. Sample answers are shown.

1. Which sentence is the shortest? What is its effect?

2. Identify the longest sentence in the literary model. How well has the author varied the sentences in his writing?

2. Sentence 4 is the longest sentence. The writer varies his sentences very well. The paragraph sounds good when you read it aloud. One sentence is seven words, and the longest is twenty-three words.

**Literary Model**

[1]When trouble came to me, it didn't involve anybody I thought it would. [2]It involved the nice, normal, smart boy by the name of John Quinn. [3]Life does that to us a lot. [4]Just when we think something awful's going to happen one way, it throws you a curve and the something awful happens another way.

—Excerpt from *The Pigman & Me* by Paul Zindel

# EXERCISE 2 Varying Sentence Length

Read the sets of sentences below.
Answers will vary. Sample answers are shown.

1. On a separate sheet of paper, identify the problem in sentence length or variety.

2. Then rewrite each item to include both long and short sentences.

**EXAMPLE**    Everybody has a talent. Lots of people have many talents. Sometimes talents are passions. Sometimes they are not. [There are too many short sentences.]

Everybody has a talent. Some people even have many talents. Talent can come in the form of passion, and other times people are talented in areas in which they are not particularly interested.

1. Jordan started playing the piano when he was fifteen, and he was fascinated by the various feelings and sounds that come from piano music, so he wanted to explore the ways in which he could express himself through music.

2. Shelby never took a dance class. She has really good rhythm. She likes to listen to hip-hop music.

3. Jessie likes communication. She likes to help people. She can always make me feel better. She asks all the right questions. When she grows up, she wants a job to help others talk about and understand their feelings.

**HINT**

You may add details or other kinds of information.

1. (This sentence is too long.) Jordan started playing the piano when he was fifteen. He was fascinated by the various feelings and sounds that come from piano music. His interest grew as he explored the ways in which he could express himself through music.

2. (There are too many short sentences.) When she was growing up, Shelby never took a dance class. However, she has developed a natural rhythm and likes to listen to hip-hop.

3. (There are too many short sentences.) Jessie likes communication. She can always make me feel better simply by asking all the right questions. When she grows up, she wants to work at a job where she can help others talk about and understand their feelings.

4. If we get lost, Zoe has a good sense of direction and can lead us in the right direction, but I don't know if reading maps and following directions are what she likes. Yet Zoe is a great resource to have when traveling to unfamiliar places because she can always figure out where we are.

5. Faye writes wonderful poetry by capturing images with words and presenting them in a fresh and original way, and she takes simple words and strings them together in a way that is surprising and interesting, creating a unique poem that keeps the reader's attention through the entire poem.

4. (Both sentences are long.) If we get lost, we always rely on Zoe. She has a good sense of direction and can lead us in the right direction. I don't know if reading maps and following directions are what she likes. However, Zoe is a great resource to have when traveling to unfamiliar places because she can always figure out where we are.

5. (The sentence is too long.) Faye writes wonderful poetry by capturing images with words and presenting them in a fresh and original way. She takes simple words and strings them together in a surprising and interesting way. Her unique poems keep the reader's attention.

## Exercise 3 Writing About a Graph

Study the graph below. Write a five-sentence paragraph about the graph on a separate sheet of paper. Make sure to use sentences of different lengths.

Answers will vary. Sample answers are shown.

**EXAMPLE**   The chart lists four occupations.

**EXAMPLE**   The results show that more girls in the class dream of being doctors, which I think is the result of the media's emphasis on an increasing number of women in high-powered medical jobs.

According to the graph, most girls in Mr. Zach's class want to become doctors when they grow up. Being a teacher is the second highest-ranking job for girls. Being a coach ranks last. For boys, the top three dream jobs are being an astronaut, a teacher, or a coach. Fewer boys than girls are interested in becoming doctors.

# Varying Sentence Beginnings

Good writing includes sentences that begin in different ways.

▐▶ Use a **variety of sentence beginnings** to make your writing sound natural and interesting. Try the ways below.

**1.** Start with the subject.

> **Beavers,** the largest rodents in North America, can weigh up to sixty-six pounds.

**2.** Begin with a subordinate clause. (See Lesson 3.4 for more about subordinate clauses.)

> **Because beaver lodges are large,** they can be home to up to eight beavers.

**3.** Add a transition word or phrase before the subject. (See Lesson 4.4 for more about transitions.)

> **In addition,** beavers huddle and rest during the winter.

**4.** Lead off with a phrase. (See Lesson 9.6 for more about a common kind of phrase, the prepositional phrase.)

> **At about seven feet long,** prehistoric beavers were the size of black bears.

Notice the different sentence beginnings in the passage below.

## Some Words That Begin Subordinate Clauses

| | |
|---|---|
| after | since |
| although | until |
| because | when |
| before | while |
| if | |

## Common Transitions

| | |
|---|---|
| also | for instance |
| as a result | in addition |
| before | later |
| finally | second |
| first | then |

### Literary Model

Subordinate clause

Subject

Transition word

[1]<u>When the train arrived,</u> all sputtering and blustery, porters had hurried to escort them, showing them the way to their car. [2]<u>Papa</u> took her hand and Miguel's and they boarded, waving good-bye to Alfonso and Hortensia. [3]The compartment had seats of soft leather, and she and Miguel had bounced happily upon them. [4]<u>Later,</u> they ate in the dining car at little tables covered in white linens and set with silver and crystal.

—Excerpt from *Esperanza Rising* by Pam Muñoz Ryan

### Reading as a Writer
Answers will vary. Sample answers are shown.

**1.** How well has the author varied sentence beginnings?
The variety is good. Three of the four sentences begin in different ways.
**2.** How could you revise the third sentence so that it begins with a phrase?
In the compartment, she and Miguel bounced happily on the soft leather seats.

## EXERCISE 1  Revising Sentences

Read the sentences below. Rewrite the sentence beginnings according to the directions given in the parentheses. You can add, delete, or rearrange words as necessary.
Answers will vary. Sample answers are shown.

**CONNECTING**
*Writing & Grammar*

Remember to add a comma after a beginning subordinate clause or phrase. See **Lesson 11.4.**

**When I see a commercial,** I change the channel.

**EXAMPLE**  Many TV commercials are less than thirty seconds. (phrase)

On many TV shows, commercials are less than thirty seconds.

**1.** I have watched many commercials in the last year. (phrase)
In the last year, I have watched many commercials.
**2.** Companies try to convince you to choose their products in a commercial. (phrase)
In a commercial, companies try to convince you to choose their products.
**3.** Commercials, flyers, and pop-up ads are common forms of advertising. (transition)
For example, commercials, flyers, and pop-up ads are common forms of advertising.
**4.** My sister works at an advertising agency and has to write catchy ads about cheese. (subordinate clause)
Because my sister works at an advertising agency, she has to write catchy ads about cheese.
**5.** Some ads are really annoying and make consumers dislike the product. (transition)
In fact, some ads are really annoying and make consumers dislike the product.
**6.** Advertising often costs a lot in movies. (phrase)
In movies, advertising often costs a lot.
**7.** It's a form of advertising when you see a toothpaste or clothing brand on a TV show. (subordinate clause)
When you see a toothpaste or clothing brand on a TV show, it's a form of advertising.
**8.** Companies pay millions of dollars to show their commercials during the Super Bowl. (phrase)
During the Super Bowl, companies pay millions of dollars to show their commercials.
**9.** Study communications or English if you're interested in pursuing advertising. (subordinate clause)
If you're interested in pursuing advertising, study communications or English.
**10.** Think about how advertising affects how or why you buy products. (transition)
Finally, think about how advertising affects how or why you buy products.

**Working Together**

# EXERCISE 2 Revising a Draft

With a partner, revise this draft on a separate sheet of paper.
Try to improve the sentence beginnings by using at least one of
each of the four methods introduced in the lesson. You may add,
delete, or rearrange words as necessary.
Answers will vary. See sample answer in Answer Key at www.grammarforwriting.com.

[1]NPR stands for National Public Radio. [2]It is a
nonprofit organization that provides news and
entertainment for listeners. [3]NPR averages about 26
million American listeners a week. [4]It was founded
in 1970 and immediately became important. [5]NPR is
a national organization, but many cities across the
country have their own shows. [6]This is convenient.
[7]People in New York don't hear the Chicago weather
and vice versa. [8]The name is misleading because NPR is
actually not a radio station. [9]It is an organization that is
made up of more than 860 public radio stations.

## Write What You Think

Respond to the question below in a paragraph of at least five
sentences. Use a variety of sentence beginnings.
Answers will vary. See sample answer in Answer Key at www.grammarforwriting.com.
What type of news do you enjoy reading or hearing about most?
For example, do you like news about sports, current events, people,
or new products?

# Independent and Subordinate Clauses

A **clause** is a group of words with a subject **(s)** and verb **(v).** There are two kinds of clauses: independent and subordinate.

▸ An **independent** (or **main**) **clause** expresses a complete thought. Since it can stand alone as a sentence, it is called *independent*. Every complete sentence contains at least one independent clause.

> s         v
> **I recently visited Boston, Massachusetts.**
> [one independent clause]
>
> s    v                    s    v
> **Our family flew there last month,** and **we stayed for six days.** [two independent clauses]

▸ A **subordinate** (or **dependent**) **clause** cannot stand by itself as a complete sentence. A subordinate clause must be attached to an independent clause in order for its meaning to be complete. By itself, it is a **sentence fragment.** (See Lesson 2.1 for more about fragments.)

> s    v
> **While we were there**, we went to a Boston Red Sox game.
> [one subordinate clause, followed by an independent clause]
>
> s    v
> I ate a lot of clam chowder, **which is a Boston specialty**.
> [one independent clause, followed by a subordinate clause]
>
> s    v
> Many buildings **that we saw on the bus tour** were built before the Revolutionary War.
> [one subordinate clause in the middle of an independent clause]
>
> s    v
> **After we walked around the Boston Common,** we visited the
> s    v
> New England Aquarium, **which first opened in 1969.**
> [two subordinate clauses, before and after an independent clause]

▸ Words that introduce a subordinate clause are called **subordinating conjunctions.** Not every subordinate clause starts with one, but most do.

**R**emember

A subordinate clause is not the same as a phrase. Phrases do not have subjects and verbs, while clauses do.

sleeping on the floor [phrase]

although <u>we</u> <u>were</u> <u>sleeping</u> on the floor [subordinate clause]

## Common Subordinating Conjunctions

| | | | |
|---|---|---|---|
| after | before | than | when |
| although | if | though | where |
| as | since | unless | which |
| because | so that | until | while |

# EXERCISE 1 Writing Sentences with Clauses

Remember to set off an introductory subordinate clause with a comma.

If you want to take a close-up picture**,** push the zoom button.

Read the subordinate clauses below.
Answers will vary. Sample answers are shown.

**1.** Add an independent clause to each one to create a sentence.

**2.** Underline the subject of both clauses once and the verbs of both clauses twice.

**3.** Add capital letters and punctuation marks as necessary.

**EXAMPLE**  since I detest spiders

Will you clean the basement since I detest spiders?

**1.** because the photographs are old
Because the photographs are old, the colors are faded.

**2.** if you want a picture
If you want a picture, I will take it.

**3.** since it is dark outside
We used the flash since it is dark outside.

**4.** while we took a family portrait
While we took a family portrait, the sun went down.

**5.** although the baby cried
The pictures look great, although the baby cried.

**6.** before it got windy
We took the pictures quickly before it got windy.

**7.** unless it rains
Unless it rains, we will take more pictures tomorrow.

**8.** so that we all smile
The photographer makes jokes so that we all smile.

**9.** when you buy a photo album
When you buy a photo album, you can select the best pictures.

**10.** after the photographer gave us the signal
After the photographer gave us the signal, we smiled.

In your sentences, also underline helping verbs, such as *will* and *should*. See **Lesson 8.1.**

If you smile, the picture **will** look great.

# EXERCISE 2 Identifying Clauses

Read the book review below. Identify the bold portion of each sentence as either an *independent* or a *subordinate clause*. Answers are shown.

> [1]**The BFG, by Roald Dahl, is a perfect combination of fantasy and reality.** [2]The BFG, **which stands for "Big Friendly Giant,"** is a gigantic creature that doesn't exist in real life. [3]**Even though the BFG is a monster,** he becomes friends with an orphan child named Sophie. [4]**The BFG collects dreams in the night,** which he distributes to children through a trumpet. [5]**When the other giants, such as the Fleshlumpeater or the Bonecruncher, go out in the night,** they are a danger to children. [6]**Sophie and the BFG approach the Queen of England and ask for her help** since the children must be saved from these monsters. [7]**The queen has the giants tied up and sent to a large pit in London.** [8]**Because of its great characters and action,** I very much enjoyed reading this book.

1. independent clause
2. subordinate clause
3. subordinate clause
4. independent clause
5. subordinate clause
6. independent clause
7. independent clause
8. subordinate clause

# EXERCISE 3 Writing a Summary

Summarize one of your favorite books or movies in a single paragraph of at least five sentences.
Answers will vary. See sample answer in Answer Key at www.grammarforwriting.com.

1. Use a subordinate clause in at least three sentences. (If you need help beginning your subordinate clauses, refer to the list of common subordinating conjunctions on the previous page.)

2. Underline each subordinate clause.

Remember to italicize or underline the title of a book or movie.

My favorite book is *Brian's Winter*.

For more information about titles, see **Lesson 12.2.**

# Varying Sentence Structure

Keep your readers interested by varying the **structure** of your sentences. Structure refers to the number and kinds of clauses a sentence contains. In this lesson, you will learn about four basic types of sentences.

⟩ All **simple sentences** have only one independent clause and no subordinate clauses. However, simple sentences are not all short. If they have compound subjects and verbs or several prepositional phrases, they may be long and complicated.

| | |
|---|---|
| ONE SUBJECT AND ONE VERB | **Water is** important. |
| COMPOUND SUBJECT AND COMPOUND VERB | All **plants** and **animals need** a surprising amount of water and **depend** on it to stay healthy. |

⟩ **Compound sentences** have two or more independent clauses and no subordinate clauses. In most compound sentences, the independent clauses are joined by a comma and a coordinating conjunction, such as *and*, *or*, *but*, or *so*. You may also join the independent clauses with a semicolon (**;**) if they are closely related.

| | |
|---|---|
| TWO INDEPENDENT CLAUSES | Last year we learned a lot about air pollution**,** **but** we hardly studied water pollution. |
| TWO INDEPENDENT CLAUSES | Baths usually require a lot of water**;** you may need more than forty gallons to fill a tub. |

⟩ **Complex sentences** contain one independent clause and at least one subordinate clause. The subordinate clause may go before, after, or in the middle of the independent clause.

| | |
|---|---|
| ONE BEGINNING SUBORDINATE CLAUSE | **If people make an effort,** they can find ways to conserve water. |
| TWO SUBORDINATE CLAUSES AT THE END | Polluted water may kill fish and other animals **unless we can clean up lakes, rivers, and oceans where pollution occurs.** |

---

**WRITING HINT**

Not all pairs of sentences make good compound sentences.

We should conserve water. My father is a plumber.

The sentences above are about two different ideas. Join two independent clauses in a compound sentence only if the two ideas are closely related.

---

▮▶ **Compound-complex sentences** have two or more independent clauses and at least one dependent clause. The subordinate clause may go before, after, or in the middle of one of the independent clauses.

| | |
|---|---|
| ONE BEGINNING SUBORDINATE CLAUSE | **Because conservation is an important issue,** I think many students are interested in it, and I believe a conservation club would be popular. |
| SUBORDINATE CLAUSE IN THE MIDDLE | The high school already has a conservation club, but middle school students **who are interested in the environment** might want to create their own club. |

# Exercise 1  Identifying Sentence Types

Read each sentence below, and identify whether it is *simple, compound, complex,* or *compound-complex.* Answers are shown.

1. S.E. Hinton is the author of *Rumble Fish* and *The Outsiders.* simple

2. S.E. Hinton wrote her first novel when she was only sixteen years old. complex

3. The main character of *Rumble Fish* is Rusty-James, who is a tough kid who always gets into trouble. complex

4. Rusty-James is one interesting character, and Motorcycle Boy is another. compound

5. Finally, Rusty-James lands in so much trouble that even his friend Motorcycle Boy cannot get him out of it. complex

6. Hinton wrote *The Outsiders* in 1976. simple

7. The main character is Ponyboy Curtis; he belongs to a gang. compound

8. I can relate to many of the characters, but I can especially relate to Ponyboy when he imagines how his life would be different. compound-complex

9. Since the book explored the lives of teens from low-income backgrounds, it was groundbreaking. complex

10. If you enjoyed the book, you should watch the movie, which was made in 1983. complex

## Exercise 2 Writing Sentences with Varied Structure

Read the topics below. Write a sentence about each topic, using the sentence structure indicated in parentheses. Make sure to check for punctuation and grammar errors. Remember to italicize or underline the titles of books and movies.

Answers will vary. See sample answers in Answer Key at www.grammarforwriting.com.

**EXAMPLE**   favorite book (complex sentence)

Although <u>The Chocolate War</u> is my favorite book, I also really like <u>Hatchet.</u>

**1.** favorite author
(compound sentence)

**2.** funny characters
(simple sentence)

**3.** TV show
(complex sentence)

**4.** well-known actor
(compound-complex sentence)

**5.** action movie
(complex sentence)

## Exercise 3 Varying Sentence Structure

Read the text of a brochure below. Work with a partner to revise it on a separate sheet of paper. Use a variety of sentence structures. Then read your revision aloud to the class.

Answers will vary. See sample answer in Answer Key at www.grammarforwriting.com.

¹Have you ever wanted to be in a movie? ²Do you think you can act? ³This Saturday we are holding auditions for extras. ⁴The film is *Shake It Up*. ⁵It stars teen idol Sarah Dominick. ⁶We need people to dance. ⁷The people need to dance in a prom scene. ⁸We need people to sing. ⁹They need to sing in the choir. ¹⁰We even need track runners. ¹¹So come on down. ¹²Go to the Center Arena at 10 A.M. ¹³Prove your talent to the world!

# Combining Sentences: Compound Parts

▪️➡️ You can smooth out your sentences and avoid repetition by using **compound subjects** and **compound verbs.** To do that, you can combine two or more related sentences.

| | |
|---|---|
| ORIGINAL | Finland joined the United Nations (UN) in 1955. Albania joined the United Nations in 1955. Portugal joined the United Nations in 1955, too. |
| COMPOUND SUBJECT | **Finland, Albania,** and **Portugal** joined the United Nations in 1955. |
| ORIGINAL | The United Nations promotes peace throughout the world. The United Nations develops cooperation among countries. |
| COMPOUND VERB | The United Nations **promotes** peace throughout the world and **develops** cooperation among countries. |

▪️➡️ When two short sentences are related, consider combining them to create a **compound sentence.** Use the **coordinating conjunctions** *and* (to show similarity), *but* (to show contrast), and *nor* or *or* (to show choice). Remember to use a comma before the coordinating conjunction that joins the two sentences.

| | |
|---|---|
| ORIGINAL | The headquarters of the United Nations is in New York City. The building and grounds are not part of the United States. |
| COMPOUND SENTENCE | The headquarters of the United Nations is in New York City, **but** the building and grounds are not part of the United States. |

▪️➡️ If two sentences are closely related, you may also use a **semicolon (;)** to join them.

| | |
|---|---|
| COMPOUND SENTENCE | The United Nations is an international zone; it has its own flag and security. |

**CONNECTING**
*Writing & Grammar*

Avoid using a comma between two parts of a compound subject or a compound verb.

INCORRECT My history teacher, and his wife visited New York City, and toured the UN.

CORRECT My history teacher and his wife visited New York City and toured the UN.

# EXERCISE 1  Combining Sentences

Read the groups of sentences below, and combine the sentences in each group. Then tell how you combined each group: with a compound subject, compound verb, or compound sentence.
Answers will vary. Sample answers are shown.

**EXAMPLE**    The East Coast is famous for its fall foliage. The trees are full of orange, red, and yellow leaves.

*The East Coast is famous for its fall foliage; the trees are full of orange, red, and yellow leaves. (compound sentence)*

1. I took lots of pictures of leaves. I also raked a lot of leaves.
I took lots of pictures of leaves and also raked a lot of them. (compound verb)
2. Maine is full of oak trees. New Hampshire has oak trees, too. Oak trees are also in Vermont.
Maine, New Hampshire, and Vermont have oak trees. (compound subject)
3. My friend Jamie likes to look at the foliage from inside. Jamie has seasonal allergies.  My friend Jamie has seasonal allergies, but she likes to look at the foliage from inside. (compound sentence)
4. Growing up, my dad made fifty cents an hour raking leaves for his neighbors. He grew up in Connecticut.  My dad grew up in Connecticut and made fifty cents an hour raking leaves for his neighbors. (compound verb)
5. People on the West Coast and in the South don't see a big change between the seasons. They stay warm year-round.  People on the West Coast and in the South don't see a big change between the seasons; they stay warm year-round. (compound sentence)
6. It rarely snows in California. It rains in California.
It rarely snows in California, but it does rain. (compound sentence)
7. Chicago is freezing in the winter. It is very hot during the summer.  Chicago is freezing in the winter, but it is very hot during the summer. (compound sentence)
8. Portland has a lot of rainfall. It rains a lot in Seattle.
Portland and Seattle have a lot of rainfall. (compound subject)
9. Some people like the cold. Winter is my least favorite season.
Some people like the cold, but winter is my least favorite season. (compound sentence)
10. My uncle lives in Florida. He likes hot weather.
My uncle lives in Florida and likes hot weather. (compound verb)

# EXERCISE 2  Improving Your Writing

Reread an essay or piece of work that you have recently written.
Answers will vary.

1. Find two examples of sentences that you could have combined.

2. Write the original sentences and your revisions on a separate sheet of paper.

# Combining Sentences: Key Words and Phrases

 One way of combining two or more short sentences is to take a key word from one sentence and add it to another. You can often cut out the other words.

> ORIGINAL   Sasha ran quickly to the dog. The dog was whimpering.
>
> COMBINED   Sasha ran quickly to the **whimpering** dog.

 Sometimes you may need to change the form of the word before you can insert it. For instance, you might have to add an *-ly* or use the *-ed* or *-ing* form of the word.

> ORIGINAL   She stroked the animal. She was gentle. It had begun to tremble.
>
> COMBINED   She **gently** stroked the **trembling** animal.

You can also combine two or more related sentences by taking a phrase from one sentence and adding it to another. Experiment with different ways to combine and emphasize your ideas. You may need to add one or more commas to your new sentence.

> ORIGINAL   The dog was curled up. It was on the wet grass. It was a small black terrier.
>
> COMBINED   The dog**, a small black terrier,** was curled up **on the wet grass.**
>
> COMBINED   **Curled up on the wet grass** was a small black terrier.

## EXERCISE 1   Inserting Key Words

Read the following groups of sentences. On a separate sheet of paper, combine the sentences by inserting a key word from the second sentence into the first sentence. You may need to change the form of the word.

> **EXAMPLE**   Pam writes stories. Her stories are brilliant.
>
> *Pam writes brilliant stories.*

---

**CONNECTING**
Writing & Grammar

You may decide to use an **appositive phrase** to combine two sentences. It renames or identifies a noun or pronoun in the sentence. Use commas to set off the appositive phrase from the rest of the sentence.

ORIGINAL Sasha has two dogs. She is my oldest cousin.

COMBINED Sasha**, my oldest cousin,** has two dogs.

---

1. Pam lives in an apartment building. The building is huge.
   Pam lives in a huge apartment building.
2. Pam is an athlete. She is talented.
   Pam is a talented athlete.
3. For homework, she was assigned a paper about a sport. It has to be a research paper.
   For homework, she was assigned a research paper about a sport.
4. Her school library opens on Friday. The library is new.
   Her new school library opens on Friday.
5. Pam will go to the library on Monday. She will go early.
   Pam will go to the library early on Monday.

## EXERCISE 2  Inserting Phrases

Read the pairs of sentences below. Take a phrase from the second sentence, and insert it into the first. Write your combined sentences on a separate sheet of paper.

**Remember**

Remember to add a comma after an introductory phrase.

After the long movie, we had a discussion.

See **Lesson 11.4** for more about using commas with phrases.

1. We watched a movie. We saw it with Mrs. Kelso's class.
   We watched a movie with Mrs. Kelso's class.
2. Mrs. Kelso just returned from teaching abroad. She is a science teacher.
   Mrs. Kelso, a science teacher, just returned from teaching abroad.
3. We have been studying healthy eating. We have studied it for the last three weeks.
   We have been studying healthy eating for the last three weeks.
4. After the movie, Mrs. Kelso led a discussion. It was about nutrition.
   After the movie, Mrs. Kelso led a discussion about nutrition.
5. When the bell rang, everyone left class. The bell rang at 3 P.M.
   When the bell rang at 3 P.M., everyone left class.

## EXERCISE 3  Combining Sentences

Read the groups of sentences below, and combine each group into one sentence. Combine them using key words and phrases.
Answers will vary. See sample answers in Answer Key at www.grammarforwriting.com.

1. My grandmother does crossword puzzles to help slow down the effects of aging. She is sharp.

2. These crossword puzzles are hard. They are printed in our local paper. The local paper is the *Longwood News*.

3. Crossword puzzles are challenging word games. Like other challenging word games, they help improve your vocabulary.

# Story

Stories have always been a part of your life. You have seen stories on the screen, on the stage, and in books and magazines. You have heard stories told by friends and family.

When you write a **story,** you are writing a narrative, or telling about a series of related events. Most stories have characters, a setting, a plot, and a theme. Here is a diagram that shows the plot of the folktale "John Henry."

**Climax**
John Henry challenges a machine to a steel-driving race.

**Rising Action**
John Henry drives steel for the railroad.

**Resolution**
Though John Henry dies, his legend lives on.

**Exposition**
John Henry is born stronger than others.

**Falling Action**
John Henry defeats the machine but dies in the process.

Now focus on these key features for writing a story.

## Key Features

- characters, setting, point of view, and series of events
- dialogue and description
- transition words to signal shifts in time and events
- descriptive details and sensory language
- ending that concludes and reflects on the narrative's events

## ASSIGNMENT

**TASK:** Write a three- to four-page **story** about a problem between two characters. Your story can be entirely imagined or based on an experience.

**AUDIENCE:** your classmates

**PURPOSE:** to entertain

## Prewriting

**Set the Scene** First, choose the **setting,** or the time and place described in your story. Your setting can be realistic or imaginary.

- A realistic setting might take place in the present or during a particular historical period.
- An imaginary setting can be set in any time or in any place and should include colorful, fantastic details.

The setting you choose will affect the **mood** of your story. Mood is the feeling your story creates for readers.

| Setting | Mood |
|---|---|
| outer space | exciting, curious |
| haunted castle | spooky, mysterious |
| playground | fun, full of energy |
| apple orchard | peaceful, relaxing |

**Create Your Characters** Stories have different kinds of characters. If a character changes during a story, he or she is called a **dynamic character.** If a character stays the same, the character is called a **static character.**

Create a chart to plan characters in your story.

| | Physical Description | Personality |
|---|---|---|
| Character 1 (Rick) | curly red hair, short | serious and nervous |
| Character 2 (Karyn) | wears stylish clothes, brown hair | impatient and hardworking |

# Prewriting

**Brainstorm a Conflict and Theme** Next, figure out the **conflict,** or the central problem around which your story will revolve. The conflict is usually introduced or hinted at near the beginning of the story. There are different types of conflict.

|  | Definition | Example |
|---|---|---|
| **Internal** | a struggle in the mind of the main character, such as making a tough decision or overcoming a fear | Rick has not studied for a test and spends all day worrying about it. |
| **External** | a struggle between the main character and another character, society, or nature | Rick wants to write for the student newspaper. The student editor, Karyn, questions his writing skills. |

The conflict often reinforces the story's **theme,** or the general message that the author wants the reader to take away from the story. As you plan a story's conflict, ask yourself, "What message will my conflict suggest to readers?"

**Put the Details in Order** Your story also needs a **plot.** A plot is a series of events often made up of five different parts.

- The **exposition** introduces the setting, the main characters, and the conflict.
- During the **rising action,** the conflict becomes worse.
- The **climax** is the moment of highest tension and the story's turning point.
- During the **falling action,** the tension winds down.
- At the **resolution,** the conflict is resolved.

The resolution acts as the conclusion in a story and often reflects on the story's experiences and events. Usually the theme becomes clear during the resolution.

**WRITING HINT**

Avoid confusing a story's theme, or overall message, with a story's topic, or subject.

TOPIC  baseball

THEME  Teamwork is important.

**WRITING HINT**

Arrange the events in your story chronologically. **Chronological order** means that events are described in the order they occur, from first to last. Use transition words to call attention to time.

**After** his argument with Karyn, Rick felt disappointed.

## CONNECTING
### Writing & Grammar

When you write dialogue, remember to enclose it in quotation marks and create a new paragraph each time the speaker changes.

For rules about using quotation marks, see **Lesson 11.6.**

## Drafting

**Fill In the Details** Include dialogue and sensory details.

1. **Dialogue** is language written as if it were spoken by the characters themselves.

2. Use **sensory details** to describe the setting and your characters' appearance and actions. Be specific.

ORIGINAL    The lunchroom was very loud.

REVISED    The lunchroom buzzed like a beehive.

### Writing Model

Clear setting and sensory details

¹Rick walked into the student newspaper office. ²His brow was damp with perspiration. ³"Is this where I sign up to write for *The Herald*?" he mumbled. ⁴Karyn, the paper's editor, spun around like a crazed top. ⁵"Who wants to know?" she growled.

Dialogue

⁶"I do," said Rick, staring at Karyn. ⁷"I thought you could use another good writer on staff."

⁸"Okay. Go interview some of the new students and see what story you can get from them," Karyn barked.

**Get Perspective** Use only one **point of view.**

- **First-person point of view** is told from the perspective of someone inside the story.

- **Third-person limited point of view** is told from the perspective of someone outside the events of the story who knows only the thoughts of some of the characters.

- **Third-person omniscient point of view** is told from the perspective of a narrator who knows the thoughts of everyone.

# Revising

Use the Revising Questions below to improve your draft.

## Revising Questions

❏ Where can I add sensory details or dialogue?

❏ How clear is the chronological order?

❏ How vivid are the characters, setting, and mood?

❏ How clearly have I hinted at or stated the theme?

❏ How interesting are my introduction, plot, and conflict?

❏ Is the point of view consistent?

### WRITING HINT

Consider some of these ways to create a strong beginning:

● Begin with dialogue.

● Start in the middle of the action.

● Begin with a vivid description.

● Open with a question.

● Foreshadow, or suggest, the conflict that is coming.

Read the opening below from a classic novel.

As you revise, keep in mind the traits of good writing. See **Lesson 1.3.**

### Literary Model

Alice was beginning to get very tired of sitting by her sister on the bank, and of having nothing to do: once or twice she had peeped into the book her sister was reading, but it had no pictures or conversations in it, "and what is the use of a book," thought Alice, "without pictures or conversations?"

—Excerpt from *Alice's Adventures in Wonderland* by Lewis Carroll

1. The author uses vivid description and a question to open the story. He also hints at a conflict (that Alice is bored).

2. The beginning suggests that Alice may try to find a way to rid herself of her boredom. Alice seems like a girl who is curious and thoughtful.

### Reading as a Writer

Answers will vary. Sample answers are shown.

1. What techniques does the author use to strengthen the opening of this story?

2. What does this beginning suggest about Alice?

## Revising

**Vary Your Sentences** To keep your writing interesting, vary your sentences.

For more help with sentence variety, see **Lessons 3.1, 3.2, 3.3,** and **3.5.**

- Add a question or exclamatory sentence, and include a variety of short and long sentences.

- Use a variety of simple, compound, and complex sentences. Combine short sentences with compound subjects or verbs.

- Avoid starting every sentence with the subject. Begin some sentences with a subordinate clause or a phrase.

**Writing Model**

Combine sentences to vary sentence structure.

¹Rick was confused by Karyn's response. ²Rick ~~and he~~ ~~was also unsure of how to fix the problem.~~ ³He wondered what to do. ⁴*Could he do anything at all?* "Maybe I could talk to Mrs. Hill," he thought. ⁵Rick grabbed his backpack and headed to her office.

Vary sentences by adding a question.

⁶"Where are you going?" Karyn asked.

⁷"I'm going to see Mrs. Hill," Rick said quickly before walking away. ⁸Then, he heard footsteps following him. ⁹He turned around. ¹⁰~~He~~ *and* saw a very upset Karyn.

Combine sentences using compound verbs.

¹¹"Rick, I'm sorry I've been so tough on you," Karyn whispered. ¹²"I think you're a great writer. ¹³The first draft of that article was really good."

# Editing and Proofreading

Use the checklist below to edit and proofread your draft.

## Editing and Proofreading Checklist

❏ Are all words spelled and used correctly?
❏ Did I leave out or run together any words?
❏ Have I indented dialogue and paragraphs?
❏ Have I added a comma before a conjunction in a compound sentence?

**Writing Model**

¹Karyn and Rick ended their fight over who was going
to write the article about eliminating gym class, the
hottest topic at there school. ²They decided to dedicate
the entire next issue to the topic. ³The first would present
one side of the argument and the second half would
present the other side. ⁴Finally, they worked as a team

*(Editing marks: "#" over "overwho"; "their" added above "there"; "half" added above "first"; comma mark in "argument and"; delete mark on "as"; period mark after "team".)*

**Proofreading Symbols**

∧  Add.
⅄  Delete.
#  Add a space.
⊙  Add a period.
⋏  Add a comma.

## Publishing and Presenting

Use one of these ways to share your story.

- **Post your work on a blog.** Add pictures or drawings. Invite friends and family to read and comment on your story.

- **Give a dramatic reading of your story to the class.** Before you give the reading, practice reading it aloud.

**Reflect On Your Writing**

- Which character did you develop most successfully?
- What description or dialogue was most effective? Why?

## A. Practice Test

Read each sentence below carefully. Decide which answer choice best replaces the underlined part, and fill in the circle of the corresponding letter. If you think the underlined part is correct as is, fill in the circle for choice *A*.

**EXAMPLE**

Ⓐ Ⓑ Ⓒ Ⓓ Ⓔ Protect yourself online. Choose a safe <u>password. It should be hard to guess</u>.
(A) password. It should be hard to guess.
(B) password that is hard to guess.
(C) password. That is hard to guess.
(D) password, it should be hard to guess!
(E) password. That is hard to guess?

Ⓐ Ⓑ Ⓒ ● Ⓔ **1.** Don't use <u>your name. Don't use your pet's name. Don't use your birthday. Don't use</u> your phone number.
(A) your name. Don't use your pet's name. Don't use your birthday. Don't use
(B) the name of you or your pet, your birthday, or
(C) your name, your pet's name, your birthday. Don't use
(D) your name, your pet's name, your birthday, or
(E) your or your pet's name, don't use your birthday or

Ⓐ Ⓑ ● Ⓓ Ⓔ **2.** One <u>solution is to combine upper- and lowercase letters with numbers. This is easy. It is practical</u>.
(A) solution is to combine upper- and lowercase letters with numbers. This is easy. It is practical.
(B) practical solution is to combine upper- and lowercase letters with numbers and this is easy.
(C) easy and practical solution is to combine upper- and lowercase letters with numbers.

**TEST-TAKING TIP**

When answering questions that ask you to improve sentences, remember that your answer choice must be correct in the context of the rest of the sentence. Don't read the answer choices by themselves. Instead, read each one in place of the underlined part of the sentence.

(D) solution is to combine upper- and lowercase letters with numbers. Easy and practical.

(E) solution is to combine letters with numbers.

ⒶⒷⒸⒹ⬤ **3.** Make sure your password does not take too long to <u>type. Because you never know who's looking over your shoulder?</u>

(A) type. Because you never know who's looking over your shoulder?

(B) type. Because you never know. Who's looking over your shoulder?

(C) type, because you never know, who's looking over your shoulder?

(D) type. Because you never know who's looking over your shoulder!

(E) type. You never know who's looking over your shoulder.

Ⓐ⬤ⒸⒹⒺ **4.** If a hacker obtains your password, <u>it can be dangerous. It can lead to identity theft. This is a crime.</u>

(A) it can be dangerous. It can lead to identity theft. This is a crime.

(B) it can lead to the dangerous crime of identity theft.

(C) it can be dangerous and lead to identity theft. This is a crime.

(D) it can be a crime and it can lead to dangerous identity theft.

(E) it can be dangerous, a crime, and identity theft.

ⒶⒷⒸⒹ⬤ **5.** <u>Never write your password down. Don't share it with anyone else. This is the most important thing.</u>

(A) Never write your password down. Don't share it with anyone else. This is the most important thing.

(B) Never write your password down or share it with anyone else. Is this the most important thing?

(C) This is the most important thing! Never write your password down, never share it with anyone else.

(D) Most importantly, never write your password down, don't share it with anyone else!

(E) Most important, you should never write your password down or share it with anyone else.

## B. Writing Sentences

On a separate sheet of paper, use each clause below to write the type of sentence described in parentheses.
Answers will vary. Sample answers are shown.

- Add words and clauses as needed.
- Then, underline each independent clause once and each subordinate clause twice.

1. although it rained on Monday (complex sentence with one subordinate clause at the beginning)
Although it rained on Monday, the football game went on as planned.

2. Jeremy took his dog for a walk. (compound sentence with two independent clauses joined by a coordinating conjunction)
Jeremy took his dog for a walk, and then he did his homework.

3. when he went to the mall (complex sentence with one subordinate clause at the end)
Jeremy bought lots of clothes when he went to the mall.

4. His family goes shopping together. (simple sentence with a compound verb)
His family goes shopping and eats dinner together.

5. because Jeremy is trying to save money (complex sentence with a compound subject)
Because Jeremy is trying to save money, he and his friends wait for sales.

## C. Revising and Analyzing a Story

Revise the story on the right on a separate sheet of paper. Then answer the questions below. Students' revisions will vary but should meet the criteria indicated in the directions. See sample answer in Answer Key at www.grammarforwriting.com. Sample answers to questions are shown.

- Use at least one sentence of each type: declarative, imperative, interrogative, and exclamatory.
- Vary sentence lengths by combining some sentences. Use compound parts, and insert key words and phrases.
- Vary sentence beginnings by including sentences that begin with a subject, subordinate clause, transition, and phrase.

1. What is the setting?
The setting is a school. It changes from a classroom to a cafeteria.

2. Who are the characters?
The characters are Carly, Elliot, and Ms. Barnes.

3. What is the point of view?
The point of view is third-person limited.

4. What is the conflict?
Carly doesn't want to be friends with Elliot. She's afraid her reputation will become worse than it already is.

¹Carly was sitting. ²She was in the back row of the classroom. ³Then the new kid walked in. ⁴He was tall. ⁵He was skinny. ⁶He had freckles. ⁷Ms. Barnes asked him to introduce himself. ⁸His name was Elliot. ⁹"I hope he doesn't sit next to me," thought Carly. ¹⁰He did.

¹¹Elliot tried to be friendly to Carly. ¹²He tried every day. ¹³Carly just ignored him. ¹⁴Carly was a bit of a loner. ¹⁵She had a reputation. ¹⁶It was for being "weird." ¹⁷She felt like a green, one-eyed alien already. ¹⁸This was when she walked down the hall. ¹⁹She couldn't be seen talking to Elliot. ²⁰She would look even weirder.

²¹Carly was in the cafeteria. ²²It was Tuesday. ²³She was alone. ²⁴She was eating. ²⁵It was a sandwich. ²⁶It was her favorite. ²⁷It had peanut butter. ²⁸It had potato chips. ²⁹People thought it was gross. ³⁰Carly didn't care. ³¹Elliot walked over. ³²He asked to sit down. ³³Carly wanted to say no. ³⁴She didn't have the nerve. ³⁵Elliot sat down. ³⁶He unwrapped his lunch. ³⁷It was a sandwich. ³⁸It had peanut butter. ³⁹It had potato chips. ⁴⁰Carly smiled. ⁴¹Maybe she wasn't so weird after all.

# Effective Paragraphs

# Supporting the Main Idea

In effective **paragraphs,** sentences work together to develop a **main idea,** or point.

▸ Some paragraphs (especially ones that inform or persuade) state the main idea in a **topic sentence.** Topic sentences often begin paragraphs, but they may appear in the middle or the end.

> [1]During the Middle Ages, both nobles and peasants enjoyed a surprising variety of entertainment. [2]In castles and nearby villages, traveling singers, acrobats, and musicians performed at gatherings and special feasts. [3]Jousting tournaments, held on the castle grounds, included exciting mock battles, and crowds gathered to watch actors perform short plays. [4]Evening life inside the castle often included mimes, storytellers, and jesters.

The topic sentence tells the main idea.

**WRITING HiNT**

Besides making your main idea clear, a good topic sentence captures readers' attention and makes them want to read on.

▸ You may want to **imply,** or suggest, your main idea rather than announce it directly. In a paragraph with an **implied main idea,** include details so that your overall point is clear.

> [1]Castle walls, often made of stone, were very thick so they could withstand bombardment or battering. [2]Windows were narrow slits through which soldiers shot arrows, and gatehouses featured heavy iron grates and massive doors that could be barred shut. [3]Many castles were built atop steep hills and surrounded by deep, hard-to-cross ditches or water-filled moats. [4]Drawbridges could be pulled up quickly to keep enemy invaders out.

The implied main idea is that castles were built to be strong and safe during battle.

�➡ To build an effective paragraph, you need to include enough **supporting details** to **elaborate,** or explain, the main idea fully. Some details will come from your memory or experiences, and others will come from research.

| Kinds of Supporting Details | |
|---|---|
| Facts | statements that can be proved true |
| Examples | specific cases or instances |
| Sensory Details | details about how something looks, sounds, smells, feels, or tastes |
| Anecdotes | brief stories or incidents |
| Quotations | spoken or written words from an expert |

As you read the paragraph below, pay attention to how the main idea is supported.

**Literary Model**

The topic is life inside a typical French castle in the Middle Ages.

[1]The Norman castle was built for security, not for comfort. [2]The lord and lady of the castle usually slept behind a curtain in the main dining hall. [3]Also sleeping in the hall might be a small mob of knights, guests, servants, and dogs. [4]The floor was covered with herbs to keep down the smell of bones and other refuse. [5]On a winter morning, inhabitants would wash by plunging their arms through ice-crusted water in a bucket.

—Excerpt from *Across the Centuries*

**Reading as a Writer**    Answers will vary. Sample answers are shown.

1. The main idea is that life in the Norman castle was not very comfortable.

2. The author mentions that the castle lacked many basic necessities, such as bedrooms, trash areas, and showers. The facts, examples, and sensory details are very effective.

3. The author could have added anecdotes from an inhabitant's journal or a quotation from a historian.

**1.** What, in your own words, is the main idea of this paragraph?

**2.** What kinds of supporting details are included? How effective are they?

**3.** What other kinds of details might the author add to elaborate the main idea? Think of one or two specific suggestions.

# EXERCISE 1 Identifying Main Ideas

In each paragraph that follows, underline the topic sentence. If there isn't a topic sentence, write a one-sentence statement of the main idea in your own words. Students' responses for paragraph 2 may vary slightly. Sample answer is shown.

[1]One of the largest plant-eating dinosaur skeletons ever found is more than 105 feet long. [2]Discovered in Patagonia, the dinosaur is estimated to be 88 million years old. [3]<u>Patagonia continues to be the site where the largest plant-eating dinosaur skeletons have been discovered.</u> [4]The other two skeletons discovered in Patagonia measure between 115 and 131 feet long.

[1]Archaeologists in Peru have discovered what might be the oldest mural in the Americas. [2]Carbon dating shows the mural and the temple in which it was found are about 4,000 years old. [3]The mural and temple surprised archaeologists. [4]They had previously believed that such complex art and architecture developed later in Peru.

Paragraph 2: Archaeologists were surprised by the age of a certain mural and temple in Peru.

# EXERCISE 2 Supporting a Main Idea

Read each main idea below, and choose one.
Answers will vary. See sample answer in Answer Key at www.grammarforwriting.com.

- Styles of fashion and music often make a comeback.
- Text messaging is better than making a phone call.
- Exotic animals, such as reptiles or ferrets, make good pets.

**1.** For the main idea you chose, write a paragraph that elaborates on it. Write your paragraph on a separate sheet of paper.

**2.** Include at least two different types of details in your paragraph. Write at least six sentences.

# Paragraph Unity

▶ A paragraph has **unity** if all of its sentences stay on one topic and work together to support the main idea. As you read the model below, notice how each sentence relates directly to the author's point about cowboy boots.

### Literary Model

The paragraph explains how the boots were practical.

[1]The earliest cowboy boots, influenced by the riding gear of the Mexican *vaquero*, were created by bootmakers in Kansas. [2]<u>These plain black or dark brown cowhide boots weren't fancy, but they were practical.</u> [3]Their narrow toes slipped easily into stirrups. [4]When the cowboy stood up in the saddle to rope a steer, the reinforced steel arches helped brace his feet. [5]If the cowboy's horse stopped or turned unexpectedly, high, underslung heels helped his feet stay in place in the stirrups.

—Excerpt from *Where Will This Shoe Take You? A Walk Through the History of Footwear* by Laurie Lawlor

▶ Including a **topic sentence** that directly states your main idea can help you stay focused. As you revise, delete any details that do not relate to the topic sentence.

Topic sentence focuses on one main idea.

[1]<u>The cowboys, or "cowpunchers," who worked on cattle drives in the Old West had to work under hard and dangerous conditions.</u> [2]They had to endure scorching heat, soaking rains, dust storms, and lack of sleep for weeks at a time. [3]Hunger, thirst, and lack of medical supplies were constant problems. [4]Some cowboys were injured or killed in stampedes or encounters with cattle thieves. [5]~~Some cowboys today enjoy participating in rodeos.~~

Irrelevant information disrupts paragraph unity.

# EXERCISE 1 Identifying Unity Problems

Decide which paragraph has a problem with unity, and explain why. Then revise it by deleting detail(s) that are unrelated.

> [1]Data from the U.S. Census Bureau reveal interesting comparisons between men and women. [2]For example, a total of 154 million females live in the United States, 5 million more than males. [3]Also, 32 percent of women age 25 to 29 earned a bachelor's degree or higher in 2006, compared to 25 percent of men. [4]However, men continue to earn more money than women, with women earning 77 cents for every dollar a man earns.

> [1]The busy holiday shopping rush forces stores to hire temporary workers. [2]The U.S. Census Bureau notes that in December 2006, retail sales totaled $31.4 billion. [3]That was a 44 percent increase from November. [4]~~The only people probably busier are postal carriers.~~ [5]To handle the shopping rush, 1.7 million people were employed by department stores.

# EXERCISE 2 Writing a Paragraph

Write a unified paragraph of at least four sentences based on the graphic below. Begin with a clear topic sentence.

Answers will vary. See sample answer in Answer Key at www.grammarforwriting.com.

**Favorite Sports of Students in Ms. Hirst's Classes**

# Patterns of Organization

A paragraph has **coherence** when all of the sentences fit logically together.

▐▶ Arranging details in an order that makes sense is one way to make sure your paragraphs are clear and coherent. Your organization of a paragraph depends on your topic and purpose.

▐▶ Below are four common patterns of organization for paragraphs.

1. **Chronological Order** When you organize ideas in chronological (time) order, you present them in the order in which they occur. Use chronological order to tell a story, describe a historical event, or explain the steps in a process.

### Writing Model

[1]At first we couldn't decide if the low rumbling we heard was from a train or thunder. [2]But, within five minutes, the blackening sky gave us the answer. [3]While I grabbed the picnic basket, my dad yelled to everyone to head to the cabin. [4]Before we had gone twenty yards, we were completely drenched.

2. **Spatial Order** Use spatial order to help your readers visualize a person, place, or object. Describe details according to their location, such as front to back, top to bottom, left to right, near to far, or inside to outside.

### Writing Model

[1]The sky to the left was a bright blue, with sunlight streaming between an occasional fluffy white cloud. [2]Straight above us, the sky was almost gray, and the clouds hung lower to the ground. [3]However, to our right was an even scarier scene. [4]Jagged bolts of lightning were exploding in the air.

3. **Order of Importance** Use order of importance when you want to show readers the significance of different facts, reasons, or examples. Start with the least important detail and end with the most important one, or start with the most important detail and end with the least important.

**Writing Model**

¹What is the air you breathe made of? ²The answer is that the atmosphere is a mixture of gases, including tiny amounts of such gases as neon and helium. ³Then come carbon dioxide, which helps plants make food, and water vapor. ⁴The most abundant and important gases are nitrogen and oxygen. ⁵Without nitrogen, living things could not make the proteins necessary to grow. ⁶Without oxygen, humans could not breathe.

Ends with the most important detail

4. **Logical Order** When you organize details in logical order, you group together related information in a way that helps readers follow your key points. For example, to compare and contrast two things, you might discuss all the similarities first and then all the differences.

**Writing Model**

¹Hurricanes that occur in the Northern and Southern Hemispheres share many similarities. ²In both areas, they develop over warm water, have winds in excess of 74 miles per hour, and lose power as they move over land. ³However, in the Northern Hemisphere, hurricane winds rotate counterclockwise. ⁴In the Southern Hemisphere, they rotate clockwise. ⁵In addition, most hurricanes in the Northern Hemisphere occur between July and October, but in the Southern Hemisphere a shorter hurricane season lasts only from January to March.

Starts with similarities

Ends with differences

## Exercise 1 Organizing Your Ideas

For each subject below, list at least three details. Arrange your details, using one of the four patterns of organization. Label the pattern you used.

Answers will vary. See sample answers in Answer Key at www.grammarforwriting.com.

**1.** choosing a cell phone

**2.** an interesting building

**3.** your ideal weekend

**4.** buying clothes

**5.** baseball and basketball

## Exercise 2 Improving Paragraph Organization

Read the draft below.

Answers will vary. See sample answer in Answer Key at www.grammarforwriting.com.

**1.** Identify the pattern of organization you would suggest for revising the draft.

**2.** Then rewrite the draft based on your suggestion. You may add, delete, combine, or move words and sentences.

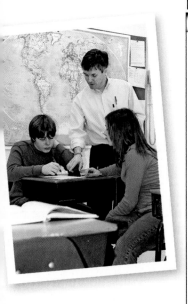

[1]For several reasons, some schools are extending the school day by an hour or two. [2]For example, students have time to learn science through real-life activities, such as cooking and gardening. [3]Extra time in school also allows for fun subjects like art, gym, and theater. [4]The most important reason schools are doing this is to give students more help in math, science, and reading. [5]With more time, schools can give students hands-on experience with these subjects. [6]The least important reason to extend the school day is that students will have additional time for tutoring and study halls.

# Transitional Words and Phrases

▣▶ Using **transitional words and phrases** helps make writing easy to follow. Transitions show readers how ideas are logically related. The chart below lists some commonly used transitions.

| To show **time** | after, at last, before, during, finally, later, meanwhile, soon, then, when |
|---|---|
| To show **location** | above, across, below, in front of, on top of, to the left/right of, under |
| To show **order of importance** | first, last, less/more important, mainly, of least/most significance |
| To show **cause and effect** | as a result, because, consequently, since, so, therefore |
| To show **examples** | for example, for instance, in addition, namely |
| To show **similarities and differences** | also, but, however, in contrast, likewise, on the other hand |

**CONNECTING**
Writing & Grammar

When you begin a sentence with some transitions, such as *for example*, *therefore*, and *however*, use a comma after the transition. See **Lesson 11.4.**

However, Javi thought it was a good idea.

▣▶ You can use transitions to connect one sentence to another or one paragraph to the next, as the passage below illustrates.

### Literary Model

¹At that moment the lights flickered several times and went out. ²The entire library plunged into darkness. ³In the next few seconds, Amy and Kimberly shrieked, Robert and Max hooted, and Ms. Watkins screeched, "Quiet, children, quiet!"

⁴Then the lights flashed back on, followed by the loud *whoosh* of the air conditioner.

—Excerpt from *Something Wicked's in Those Woods* by Marisa Montes

Transitions show clear time order.

## Exercise 1  Adding Transitions

The paragraphs below lack transitions. On a separate sheet of paper, rewrite the paragraphs. Add transitions between sentences and between the paragraphs to show how ideas are related. You may combine sentences as needed.
Answers will vary. See sample answer in Answer Key at www.grammarforwriting.com.

[1]Twelve o'clock smacked me in the head like a thick rubber band. [2]Jackie sent me a text message asking me where I was. [3]I forgot that we were supposed to audition for the school talent show. [4]I woke up late. [5]I had to go grocery shopping with my parents. [6]My brother needed help with his homework. [7]Today everything was going wrong. [8]That's why I forgot about our audition.

[9]I slung my guitar around my shoulder and asked my mom to drive me to school. [10]We performed our song. [11]The judges nodded their heads and whispered to each other. [12]They told us that we had made the cut.

Working Together

## Exercise 2  Writing About a Photo

Write a paragraph about the photo to the right. You may describe the photo, use it to explain a topic, or use it to inspire a short story. Include at least three transitional words and phrases in your paragraph. Then exchange your writing with a partner, and talk about how effective the transitions are.

Answers will vary. See sample answer in Answer Key at www.grammarforwriting.com.

# Types of Paragraphs

The four main types of paragraphs are narrative, descriptive, expository, and persuasive. The type of paragraph you write depends on your purpose.

▐▌▶ Use a **narrative paragraph** to tell a story or relate a series of events. The details in narrative paragraphs are usually arranged in **chronological order,** in the order the events happened.

### Writing Model

¹With a bowl of popcorn in one hand, <u>Max grabbed the remote control with the other and plopped down on the floor</u> in front of the television. ²Within a couple of minutes, <u>he fell asleep.</u> ³<u>When Max opened his eyes next,</u> the television was off, and the room was filled with an eerie silence.

Three events

▐▌▶ Use a **descriptive paragraph** to create a picture of a person, place, animal, or object. Effective descriptions often contain **sensory details** that show how something looks, sounds, smells, feels, or tastes.

### Writing Model

¹<u>Two bright, rectangular lights hang from the ceiling</u> and make the small television studio <u>uncomfortably hot.</u> ²The <u>smell of stale coffee</u> lingers in the <u>humid air.</u> ³A few <u>beads of perspiration</u> appear on the forehead of the young news announcer. ⁴<u>Sitting stiffly</u> behind the huge anchor desk, she <u>taps her fake fingernails nervously on the dark wood.</u> ⁵Only the <u>low whirring noise of a rusty fan</u> in the back of the studio breaks the <u>silence.</u>

Sight, smell, touch, and sound details

▐▌▶ **Expository,** or informative, **paragraphs** give information. They may compare and contrast two things, explain a process, define a term, present facts, or discuss causes and effects.

**Writing Model**

Main idea followed by supporting facts

¹A television set changes electronic signals into sound and pictures, but do you know how the signals get to your TV? ²<u>There are several different ways.</u> ³First, the signals may be sent from the TV station to your home by a satellite. ⁴Second, the signals may be picked up by an antenna on your TV. ⁵In other places, the signals are sent out along underground fiber-optic cables.

■➡ **Persuasive paragraphs** state an opinion or present an argument. To be effective, a writer needs to present sound reasons and evidence that will convince readers to agree with his or her opinion. Some persuasive paragraphs also try to persuade readers to take action.

**Writing Model**

Clear opinion

¹<u>Parents who allow their young children to have TVs in their bedrooms are making a huge mistake.</u> ²Not only are they not sure *what* their kids are watching, but they don't know *when* the TV is on. ³Children may stay up too late, watch programs with adult content, or be by themselves too much.

Call to action

⁴<u>Parents should keep television sets in rooms where they can easily monitor—and limit—their children's TV viewing.</u>

**Working Together**

## Exercise Identifying Paragraphs

With a partner, read the paragraphs that follow. Identify which type each paragraph is. In one or two sentences, explain each choice, and identify the author's purpose.

¹Cradled in the heart of Memphis and surrounded by trees, the National Civil Rights Museum is a large, tan building. ²In one exhibit hall, oversized illuminated photographs hang on the walls. ³The black-and-white photos show the funeral procession of Dr. Martin Luther King, Jr. ⁴One photo shows a man with his head lowered and his face wet with tears.

This is a descriptive paragraph. The author's purpose is to describe the museum.

¹Cesar Chavez had firsthand experience with the poor working conditions that farmworkers faced. ²His experience inspired him to organize farmworkers to fight for their rights. ³In September 1965, he led a successful nationwide boycott of California grapes. ⁴The purpose was to protest the working conditions. ⁵In 1972, along with Dolores Huerta, Chavez created the United Farm Workers of America (UFW), the first union of its kind. ⁶Through continued peaceful actions, Chavez managed to win significant rights for farmworkers.

**Cesar Chavez**

This is an expository paragraph. The author's purpose is to give information about Cesar Chavez's work for farmworkers' rights.

## Write What You Think

Answers will vary. See sample answer in Answer Key at www.grammarforwriting.com.

Read the statements below.

- More change has been made through peace than through war.
- Many teens today think too much about possessions and money.
- A sense of humor can get you through the toughest situations.

1. Pick one, and state whether you agree or disagree with it.
2. Turn your opinion into a topic sentence for a persuasive paragraph.
3. In your paragraph, include the reason you hold that opinion and at least two strong supporting details to persuade readers to agree with you.

# Descriptive Paragraph

When you see something beautiful, experience something unusual or exciting, or meet an amazing person, you probably want to share your experience with others. Sharing your experiences often involves the use of description. When you write a **descriptive paragraph,** you use words to create a picture of a person, place, event, or object.

When you write a descriptive paragraph, remember to include the features below.

## Key Features

- clear order and transitions
- precise word choice
- sensory details and imagery
- your feelings about the topic

## ASSIGNMENT

**TASK:** Write a **descriptive paragraph** about an interesting person you know who has a characteristic that makes him or her stand out. Describe this person, and focus mostly on the characteristic.

**PURPOSE:** to describe

**AUDIENCE:** your teacher, parents, and classmates

**KEY INSTRUCTIONS:** Write at least eight sentences.

**Choose a Topic** First, make a list of people you find interesting. Next to each person's name, jot down characteristics that make that person unique.

Grace—incredibly funny, great impersonator

Jesse—coolest kid at school, fearless

Ms. Gunther—excellent math teacher, curious

See **Lesson 1.1** for more ideas about choosing a topic.

Then, choose a person you can describe in detail and you think your audience will enjoy reading about. Write as many details as you can, such as how the person looks and acts. Add details about the characteristic you will focus on.

**Be Clear** As you write your description, organize your paragraph in a logical way. Use **transitional words and phrases,** such as *first, in addition*, and *also*, to connect one sentence to the next. Also, make sure that all the details relate to your purpose so that your paragraph has **unity.** (See Lesson 4.2.)

Look at the draft below. What other unrelated sentence might be deleted to improve paragraph unity?

¹No one gets your attention better than Jesse. ²Maybe Kristen does, too. ³Jesse is the "cool kid" at school. ⁴He is very friendly. ⁵Also, Jesse is fearless, and he's always the first to jump at a silly dare. ⁶My cousin once dared my brother to skateboard down a ramp at a skateboard park. ⁷My brother was scared.

**CONNECTING**
**Writing & Grammar**

When you begin a sentence with a transitional phrase, add a comma after the phrase. See **Lesson 11.4.**

In addition**,** people always stare at Jesse when he walks by.

**Be Specific** As you draft your paragraph, make your details specific and your word choice precise. Avoid overly general or vague words.

| | |
|---|---|
| GENERAL | Jesse isn't scared of stuff. |
| SPECIFIC | Jesse is fearless, and he's usually the first to jump at a silly dare. |
| GENERAL | I would be nervous. |
| SPECIFIC | My stomach would be knotted like a pretzel. |

Remember that your readers were not there, so you have to paint a picture with your words. The more precise you are, the better your descriptive paragraph will be.

**Add Life to Your Description** Add details to help your readers picture the person you are describing. Help readers feel as though they can see and hear this person. To make your description come alive, use sensory details and imagery.

| Types | Definition | Examples |
|---|---|---|
| **Sensory Details** | details that appeal to the five senses (touch, smell, taste, sight, and sound) | Jesse's voice is soft like a gentle ocean wave. Long blond bangs cover the side of his face. |
| **Imagery** | details that create a picture in the mind of the reader | Before a dare, Jesse's eyebrows curl into lightning bolts. He sways back and forth like a tree branch in the wind. |

**Remember**

In your paragraph, make sure to express at least one feeling you have about your topic.

~~Jesse is brave.~~

I admire Jesse's bravery.

**Real-World Writing**

Good writers know the importance of imagery.

"Imagery is powerful shorthand. It says in four or five words what might otherwise take you sentences to describe—and not as vividly."

—Sid Fleischman

**Revise Your Paragraph** Use this checklist to help you review and revise your paragraph. The model below shows one writer's descriptive paragraph.

## WRITING CHECKLIST
### Did you...

✔ use a clear order and precise words?

✔ include sensory details and imagery?

✔ include your feelings about your topic?

✔ write at least eight sentences and check for spelling, usage, punctuation, and grammar mistakes?

**Writing Model**

¹No one gets your attention better than Jesse. ²Jesse is the "cool kid" at school, the confident kid with faded jeans and colorful T-shirts from bands no one else has heard of. ³Jesse is so friendly that everyone likes to be around him. ⁴His soft voice and big grin put everybody at ease. ⁵Jesse is also fearless, and he's usually the first to jump at a silly dare, like wading in the icy waters of the lake on a chilly morning. ⁶While other people, like me, would hesitate and have their stomachs knotted like pretzels, Jesse is calm and relaxed. ⁷Before a dare, he always crunches up his eyebrows like lightning bolts. ⁸Then, with a grin, he takes action. ⁹Jesse is the person my friends and I want to be like.

Precise words

Characteristic that makes Jesse unique

Imagery

Writer's feelings

## A. Practice Test

Read the draft and questions below carefully. The questions ask you to choose the best revision for sentences or parts of the draft. Fill in the corresponding circle for your answer choice.

**(1)** Harper Lee grew up in the 1930s in a rural part of southern Alabama. **(2)** In *To Kill a Mockingbird*, her only novel, Lee writes about a young girl named Scout Finch, who also grows up in the 1930s in southern Alabama. **(3)** Alabama's state capital is Montgomery, although its largest city is Birmingham.

**(4)** When Harper Lee was six years old, a famous trial took place in Alabama in which several African-American men were falsely accused of a crime. **(5)** *To Kill a Mockingbird* features the court case of Tom Robinson, an African-American being tried for a crime he did not commit. **(6)** Lee was only six years old when the real-life Scottsboro trial took place, but she was likely familiar with the details because it was covered in all the papers, and Lee began reading at a very young age. **(7)** Scout Finch is able to read her local newspaper by the time she enters first grade. **(8)** By drawing from her own experiences, Harper Lee was able to make her novel come to life.

Ⓐ Ⓑ Ⓒ ● Ⓔ  **1.** Which of the following makes the best topic sentence for the paragraph (inserted before sentence 1)?
(A) Harper Lee's only novel was at first rejected by publishers.
(B) Harper Lee's only novel was a great success.
(C) Harper Lee's only novel was turned into a film in 1962.
(D) Harper Lee's only novel contains many details from her own life.
(E) Harper Lee wrote a book.

Ⓐ Ⓑ Ⓒ Ⓓ ●  **2.** Which is the best transition to use at the beginning of sentence 4?
(A) For example,
(B) In the meantime,
(C) However,
(D) Later on,
(E) It is correct as is.

Ⓐ Ⓑ ● Ⓓ Ⓔ  **3.** Which of the following sentences should be removed to improve paragraph unity?
(A) sentence 1
(B) sentence 2
(C) sentence 3
(D) sentence 4
(E) sentence 5

Ⓐ Ⓑ Ⓒ Ⓓ ●  **4.** Which of the following sentences could be added to the second paragraph without disrupting its unity?
(A) Truman Capote, a famous writer, was Lee's neighbor.
(B) In 1949, Lee moved to New York City.
(C) After graduating from the University of Alabama, Lee went to study at Oxford University in England.
(D) A year after it was published, *To Kill a Mockingbird* had already been translated into ten languages.
(E) In addition, Lee's father was an attorney, as is Scout's father in the novel.

● Ⓑ Ⓒ Ⓓ Ⓔ  **5.** Which is the best transition to begin sentence 7?
(A) Similarly,
(B) Meanwhile,
(C) As a result,
(D) In contrast,
(E) Most important,

## B. Matching Purpose to Organization

Read each writing purpose in the first column.

1. Decide which type of paragraph and organization best fits with each one.

2. Write the letter of the correct choice in the space provided.

<u>c</u> **1.** to retell the plot of a recent episode of a favorite TV show

    **a.** persuasive paragraph, order of importance

<u>e</u> **2.** to explain the process of how forest fires spread

    **b.** descriptive paragraph, spatial order

<u>d</u> **3.** to clarify differences between rats and mice

    **c.** narrative paragraph, chronological order

<u>a</u> **4.** to explain reasons that your highway needs a car-pool lane

    **d.** expository paragraph, logical order

<u>b</u> **5.** to tell tourists what a historic site looks like

    **e.** expository paragraph, chronological order

## C. Writing Supporting Details

On a separate sheet of paper, write at least three supporting sentences for each topic sentence below. The type of paragraph and type of detail are indicated in parentheses. Answers will vary. Sample answers are shown.

1. **The kitchen is my favorite room. (descriptive, sensory details)**
It is full of the great smell of home-cooked meals. The warmth of the oven makes it cozy. My family's laughter echoes off the walls.

2. **Teens benefit from reading. (expository, examples or anecdotes)**
My cousin is a bookworm and is curious about everything. Reading more this year has helped my vocabulary. My best friend, who reads a book a week, is an A student.

3. **Many Americans should exercise more. (persuasive, facts)**
Studies show that many Americans are dangerously overweight. Regular exercise can improve physical and emotional health. According to Dr. Smith, "Regular exercise adds years to a person's life."

4. **The first meal I cooked was a disaster. (narrative, sensory details)**
The fruit salad was a sticky, watery mess. The chicken and vegetables had blackened edges and tasted burned. The pumpkin muffins looked gray and were as hard as baseballs.

5. **With practice and time, you can enjoy a hobby. (expository, anecdotes)**
When my mom took up knitting, she was awful at first, but soon she knitted a beautiful sweater for me. My brother collects anything having to do with baseball, and his collection was featured in a magazine. I signed up for a tennis class last year, and now I play tennis well.

## D. Revising a Description

Read the draft below.
Answers will vary but should eliminate sentences 7 and 11.

1. Cross out any sentences that disrupt paragraph unity.

2. Insert transitions where needed.

**Proofreading Symbols**

∧ Add.

/ Make lowercase.

⋎ Delete.

¹My dog Bailey is quite a character. ²On the outside, he looks like an average dog. ³For instance, He is scruffy and cute, with big brown eyes. ⁴However, On the inside, he has some very unusual personality traits. ⁵For example, He loves music. ⁶His favorite vocalist seems to be Adele, because whenever I play her albums, he howls along like the worst karaoke performer in history. ⁷~~Adele is known for her soulful lyrics and deep voice.~~ ⁸In addition, He is the only dog I know who actively watches TV. ⁹Whenever a dog comes on-screen, Bailey begins growling. ¹⁰Then He leaps off the couch and storms the television set, pawing the screen as if he is trying to reach the dog inside. ¹¹~~Our TV is on a wood table.~~ ¹²When the dog leaves the screen, Bailey looks as puzzled as a rat in a maze as he walks around the TV in circles, trying to see where the dog went! ¹³Bailey is a better pet than a fish or a bird could ever be.

# Writing an Essay

# Parts of an Essay

Knowing how to write a short **essay** is useful anytime you want to express your thoughts. In fact, writing is an excellent way to form your own opinion about an issue.

In addition, knowing how to write an effective essay is useful because you will be assigned essays to write and you will take essay tests throughout your school years.

➡ You already know about paragraphs. The form of an essay is similar to that of a paragraph.

| Paragraph | Function | Essay |
|---|---|---|
| Topic Sentence | states main idea | Introductory Paragraph |
| Supporting Sentences | develop main idea | Body Paragraphs |
| Concluding Sentence | restates main idea | Concluding Paragraph |

> Review **Lesson 4.1** for more about main ideas and topic sentences.

### Organization of an Essay

| Introduction | Body | Conclusion |
|---|---|---|
| The introduction of an essay includes a clear statement of the main idea. Start with an attention-getting sentence to keep your readers interested. | Body paragraphs include facts, details, examples, sensory details, and quotations to support the main idea. | The last paragraph sums up the points made in the essay. It restates the main idea and draws the essay to a close. |

> **R**emember
>
> The three parts of an essay mostly appear in expository and persuasive essays. Many descriptive and narrative essays do not have these features.

➡ The introduction and conclusion are usually only one paragraph long, while the body of an essay includes three or more paragraphs.

## EXERCISE   Identifying Parts of an Essay

The essay on the next page needs to be rewritten. Read it once through.

1. Use the proofreading symbol ¶ to start a new paragraph where you think each new one should begin.

2. Label the introductory paragraph and concluding paragraph, and underline the main idea in each.

introductory paragraph

Look for the three topic sentences. They will help you find the individual body paragraphs.

¹Today, women take their independence for granted. ²Their grandmothers and great-grandmothers, however, laid the groundwork. ³At the turn of the twentieth century, women often had long hair and wore ankle-length skirts. ⁴In the next decades, women began working outside the home. ⁵They even did work that had been considered "men's work." ⁶The women living from the 1920s through the 1970s made possible the independence women know and expect today.¶⁷In the 1920s, flappers insisted on freedom in their clothing and way of life. ⁸They chose short skirts that allowed them to move freely, and they cut their hair in short, easy-to-care-for styles. ⁹They danced the Charleston in clubs and wore fringed skirts. ¹⁰They even began driving cars!¶¹¹During World War II, women were needed in factories because the men were off fighting, and these "Rosie the Riveters," as they were called in the 1940s, went to work wearing pants. ¹²Their attitude was, "If it needs to be done, I can do it." ¹³They were the first middle-class women to go off to work and raise families at the same time.¶¹⁴By the 1960s, more women were working outside the home than ever before. ¹⁵The numbers grew through the decade. ¹⁶According to the U.S. Department of Labor, 40.8 percent of women were in the labor force in 1970.¶¹⁷In the twenty-first century, women can choose any career, can marry or remain single, and can own their own homes. ¹⁸Rules of correctness do not tell them how to dress, where to work, or how to act. ¹⁹Today, women owe their current variety of choices to women of the past, who fought for and won the independence women cherish today.

concluding paragraph

# Thesis Statements

A **thesis statement** is a sentence or two that states your main idea about your subject. Sometimes it is also called a **claim** or **controlling idea.** It can come anywhere in the introduction, but it often is the last sentence in the first paragraph.

⬛➤ To write an effective thesis statement, start with your subject. Collect your information, and look for connections to explore. Then ask yourself, "What main point do I want to make about this subject?"

⬛➤ Your thesis statement should be specific. If it is too general, it won't grab your readers' interest. On the other hand, if it is too specific or simply a fact, you won't have enough material to develop an essay. Suppose your topic is "paintings."

| Too Broad | Paintings are beautiful. |
|---|---|
| Too Narrow | Claude Monet painted *Water Lilies* in 1906. |
| Lacks a Main Idea | Claude Monet was an impressionist painter. |
| Strong Thesis, or Claim | Claude Monet was an important impressionist painter. |

⬛➤ It is a good idea to use your thesis statement, or claim, to preview the essay's organization. Mention your key ideas in the order in which you will discuss them in your body paragraphs. See Lesson 5.4 for more about thesis statements that give clues about how an essay will be organized.

Claude Monet's **quick brushstrokes** and **use of bright colors** made him an important impressionist painter.

Writing a thesis statement before you begin will give your essay a focus and keep you on track. You may want to revise your thesis statement, or claim, during the process of writing as you discover new information.

Claude Monet

# EXERCISE 1  Identifying a Thesis Statement, or Claim

Underline the thesis, or claim, in the introductory paragraph.

[1]Claude Monet and Pierre-Auguste Renoir both showed unusual artistic talent at a young age. [2]Monet was first recognized for his ability when he was fifteen years old. [3]Renoir's talent was recognized early, too. [4]His family had him work in a factory painting flowers on plates when he was just thirteen.

# EXERCISE 2  Writing a Thesis, or Claim

Below is a Venn diagram that compares plasma and LCD televisions. Use the details in the graphic organizer to write a strong thesis, or claim. Answers will vary. Sample answer is shown.

1. Assume your paper needs to be two or three pages long.

2. Remember to make a point about your subject. You may choose to use some or all of the details to preview your key points.

Through modern technology, we now have two kinds of thin flat-screen televisions. The LCD sets seem to be more popular because they are lighter, use less power, and last longer.

**Plasma**
- may have better viewing angles
- brighter picture
- less popular

**Both**
- flat-screen televisions
- thin profiles

**LCD**
- use less power
- weigh less
- in the largest sizes more costly
- last longer

# Introductions

Consider the **introduction** of your essay an invitation. It should catch your readers' attention and invite them to read more.

▥➤ The first paragraph of many essays introduces the topic and usually includes a **thesis statement,** or **claim,** which states your main idea. One commonly used structure for an introductory paragraph begins with a general sentence and ends with a specific statement. This organization can help focus your essay.

**WRITING HINT**

Although readers read the introduction first, you do not have to write it first. Try starting in the middle of your paper. Then go back to the introduction later.

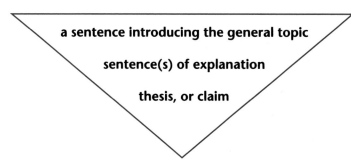

a sentence introducing the general topic

sentence(s) of explanation

thesis, or claim

▥➤ Below are some effective ways to begin an essay.

- an amazing fact
- an unusual comparison
- a question
- a contradiction
- an example
- an anecdote
- a quotation
- brief mention of an opposing view

▥➤ The length of an introductory paragraph depends on the topic of the essay. Your introduction should quickly introduce the main idea that you will develop in the body of the essay. Two to five sentences are usually ideal. Occasionally, your introduction may be more than one paragraph.

▥➤ Avoid starting with phrases such as, "This essay is about…" or "I will write about…" Also try to avoid vague, general statements. They often don't add any content or spark interest in your readers.

CONNECTING
Writing & Grammar

To improve sentence style, combine short, choppy sentences. Use conjunctions, such as *and*, to combine ideas. See **Lesson 3.6.**

ORIGINAL Gabriel paints with oils. He uses bold brushstrokes.

REVISED Gabriel paints with oils **and** uses bold brushstrokes.

| Weak | Mary Cassatt (1844–1926) was a famous artist. She is well known for her paintings and prints. |
|---|---|
| Weak | This paper deals with the life and work of Mary Cassatt, a painter. She was born in America. Then she settled and lived in France. Her Impressionist paintings were about daily life. |
| Revised | Who was the only woman invited to exhibit her paintings in Paris with Pierre-Auguste Renoir, Claude Monet, and Edgar Degas? She was an American named Mary Cassatt, who lived most of her life in Paris. Her works are recognized as significant Impressionist paintings. |

# EXERCISE 1  Revising Introductions

Read the three introductory paragraphs below. Revise them, using the ideas from this lesson to make improvements. Underline the thesis statement, or claim, in each revision.

Answers will vary. Students' paragraphs should include a thesis statement and a method to catch readers' interest. See sample answers in Answer Key at www.grammarforwriting.com.

¹Visiting an art museum is fun. ²It's interesting to rent earphones and learn about the works you are seeing.

¹This paper is about looking at a building as a work of art. ²Designing a building is a form of art. ³The kind of structure doesn't matter. ⁴An architect decides where to place windows and doors and how to connect rooms to each other.

¹There are many forms of art, such as painting and sculpture. ²Cartoons are a form of art, too, and good ones are not easy to create. ³Even if the cartoon is simple, the way the lines are put together is important.

# EXERCISE 2  Evaluating an Introduction

Read the introductory paragraph below. In your own words, describe the strategies the author has used to begin his essay.

Answers will vary. Students may mention the example of the shoes, the attention-grabbing humor in the exaggerated number of pairs of shoes, the quote from a review, and the comparison of shoe technology with space program technology.

**Literary Model**

[1]I have a teenage son who is a runner. [2]He has, at a conservative estimate, sixty-one hundred pairs of running shoes, and every one of them represents a greater investment of cumulative design effort than, say, the Verrazano Narrows Bridge. [3]These shoes are amazing. [4]I was just reading a review in one of his running magazines of the latest in "Sport Utility Sneakers," as they are evidently called, and it was full of passages like this: [5]"A dual density EVA midsole with air units fore and aft provides stability while a gel heel-insert absorbs shock, but the shoe makes a narrow footprint, a characteristic that typically suits only the biomechanically efficient runner." [6]Alan Shepard went into space with less science at his disposal than that.

—Excerpt from "Design Flaws" in *I'm a Stranger Here Myself* by Bill Bryson

# EXERCISE 3  Writing an Introduction

Working Together

Below is a list of topics for two-page expository essays. Work with a partner to discuss the most effective ways to begin introductory paragraphs for them. (See list on page 117.) Write your ideas on a separate sheet of paper. Then, choose one topic, and write an introduction with a thesis statement, or claim.

Answers will vary. Sample answers are shown. For sample introduction, see Answer Key at www.grammarforwriting.com.

1. values of walking versus riding
   a question, an example, an anecdote
2. comparison of two cities
   an unusual comparison, a contradiction, an example, a question
3. balancing extracurricular activities and homework
   an amazing fact, a comparison, a contradiction, an anecdote, a hint of an opposite view
4. my favorite food
   an amazing fact, a question, a contradiction, an example, a quotation
5. a good friend
   a question, an example, an anecdote, a quotation

# Body Paragraphs

**Body paragraphs** come between the introduction and the conclusion. They provide examples and explanations to support the thesis of your essay. By keeping your thesis in mind as you write the body paragraphs, you will give your essay **unity.**

▶ Keep each body paragraph unified by developing a single main idea. Your **thesis statement,** or **claim,** can point to the topics you will develop. (See Lesson 5.2.) For example, the thesis statement below about the painter Camille Pissarro suggests the essay will focus on three points.

To make sure each body paragraph is effective and unified, ask yourself:

1. Is the topic stated clearly? Does it relate to the thesis, or claim?

2. Are there enough examples, facts, or details to develop the topic sentence?

3. Does each sentence relate to the topic?

> Pissarro is noted for his [1] paintings of landscapes, [2] his special brushstrokes, and [3] his ability to create reflections of light and dark.

The body paragraphs will focus on these three points in the same order they are mentioned in the thesis statement.

▶ Writing a **topic sentence** for each body paragraph will help focus your writing. Then you can develop the main idea with details, examples, anecdotes, quotations, and facts.

Notice, for example, how the paragraph below about Pissarro's landscapes explains the first idea in the thesis statement.

Topic sentence

Two examples of rural landscapes

One example of city landscapes

> [1] Pissarro's paintings of landscapes are among his most well-known works. [2] He first painted rural landscapes, such as scenes of the West Indies of his childhood. [3] His next paintings were rural landscapes done directly from nature. [4] Later, he turned to city landscapes, such as scenes in London.

⏭ Use a **pattern of organization** to help your reader follow your ideas. Arrange your body paragraphs—and the sentences in each one—logically, depending on your purpose. (Chronological order is used in the paragraph about Pissarro's landscapes to show the development of his work through time.)

| Type | Purpose |
|---|---|
| **Chronological Order** | presents details or events in the order in which they occur |
| **Cause and Effect** | describes the relationship between what happens and why it happens |
| **Comparison and/or Contrast** | explains similarities and/or differences between people, places, objects, or ideas |
| **Order of Importance** | arranges details or reasons from the least important ones to the most important ones—or the reverse |
| **Spatial Order** | shows location of objects and places |

See **Lessons 4.3** and **4.4** for more information about improving coherence by using patterns of organization and transitions.

⏭ Using **transitions** will help give your essay **coherence.** When an essay has coherence, all paragraphs and sentences connect logically. Transitions, such as those below, create links between sentences and paragraphs.

| Ways to Connect | Examples |
|---|---|
| To show **time** | after, later, shortly, then |
| To show **cause and effect** | as a result, because, since |
| To show **comparisons** | in the same way, similarly |
| To show **contrasts** | on the contrary, however |
| To show **importance** | less important, mainly |
| To show **location** | all around, behind, under |
| To add **information** | in addition, as well, moreover |

## Exercise 1 Revising Body Paragraphs

Work with a partner to revise the paragraph below. Break it into two separate paragraphs, each with its own topic sentence. In the first paragraph, move the topic sentence to the beginning, and underline it. In the second paragraph, write a topic sentence, and underline it. Add transitions to improve coherence and clarity. Answers will vary. See sample answers in Answer Key at www.grammarforwriting.com.

Camille Pissarro

¹He used a variety of loose brushstrokes, at times in the same painting. ²Some strokes swirl around to create movement in a sky. ³Camille Pissarro painted using loose brushstrokes to create an atmosphere, or impression. ⁴Others are closer together. ⁵They show bricks in a building. ⁶*The Crystal Palace* is one of Pissarro's best and most famous works. ⁷It shows an exhibition hall of glass and iron with brick houses across the road from it. ⁸The overall impression of the scene is created with light and dark and shadows. ⁹Objects reflect each other. ¹⁰The brushstrokes in the flag and trees show a windy day. ¹¹The bright sky is filled with fluffy clouds.

## Exercise 2 Analyzing an Essay

Reread an essay you have written previously. On a separate sheet of paper, answer the questions below about it. Answers will vary.

1. How does each body paragraph support the thesis, or claim, of your essay? How did you organize each one?

2. What transitions did you use?

3. What can you do to improve your essay?

# Conclusions

The **conclusion** of an essay should summarize your main points and restate your thesis, or claim, in a new way. You'll want to do more than simply repeat what you said in the introduction.

➡️ Keep your concluding paragraph brief. Three to five sentences may be all you need.

➡️ One way to get readers involved is to show how your ideas relate to the real world. Leave your readers thinking about the importance of your topic. Try one of these strategies to write an effective conclusion.

| Some Ways to Conclude | How to Put Them into Practice |
|---|---|
| **Link to the introductory paragraph.** | Repeat a key word or phrase. |
| **Offer an opinion or suggestion.** | Point to a solution to a problem or to a course of action for the future. |
| **End with a quotation.** | Use a quotation from an expert or a work of literature. Be sure to use quotation marks and to identify the source. |
| **Include an anecdote.** | Tell an interesting story that your readers will remember. |
| **End with a question.** | Get readers involved by having them imagine an answer to a question you ask. |

## STEP BY STEP

To write your conclusion, begin with a summary.

1. Include only the most important points.
2. Do not repeat all of your examples, although you may want to mention one that is important for your thesis, or claim.
3. End with an idea your readers will remember.

Read the following examples of a weak conclusion and a strong conclusion of a persuasive essay. What makes the second paragraph a stronger conclusion than the first?

**WEAK**   To repeat what I have said before, schools are spending more time on math and reading. When budgets are cut, art is the first subject to go. The main point is that a student's education is not complete without art.

**STRONG**   Art instruction should be a part of the curriculum, yet, sadly, across the nation middle schools are reducing or eliminating art classes. For many students, art instruction is more than a frill. It brings out and develops special talents that students will put to use in their work. Let your local school board members know that budgets must include funding for art teachers and supplies.

**CONNECTING**
**Writing & Grammar**

Use quotation marks for words directly quoted from a speaker or a work of literature or music. See **Lesson 11.6.**

The words **"**Oh, say can you see by the dawn's early light**"** come from our national anthem.

Although answers will vary, students should find the first conclusion stronger than the second. They may point out the vague statements and repetition of facts about Bearden as weaknesses of the second paragraph.

## EXERCISE 1   Analyzing Conclusions

The concluding paragraphs below are from expository essays. Evaluate the effectiveness of each. On a separate sheet of paper, write a few sentences that explain your opinions.

[1]John Singer Sargent is among the best of portrait painters. [2]Wealthy and powerful people often wanted him to do their portraits, including two American presidents. [3]Although people continued to ask him to do their portraits, in his later years he became more and more interested in painting landscapes. [4]He has been quoted as saying, "Every time I paint a portrait, I lose a friend."

[1]In conclusion, Romare Bearden was an African-American artist and writer of many talents. [2]As this paper has discussed, he produced a lot of art until his death in 1988. [3]To repeat, he was born in North Carolina and died in New York City. [4]His career as an artist and writer showed his many artistic talents.

# EXERCISE 2 Writing a Conclusion

Below are thesis statements, or claims, and notes from the body of three essays. Read the statements and notes with a partner. You and your partner should each choose a different set of notes. Use some or all of the information given below to write your concluding paragraph. Then discuss and compare your paragraphs. Answers will vary. See sample answers in Answer Key at www.grammarforwriting.com.

---

**Thesis, or claim: Public libraries should display art.**

- improves our city library
- helps young artists get noticed
- should change exhibits regularly through the year
- have different exhibits of paintings, sculptures, jewelry

---

**Thesis, or claim: Sand sculptures are works of art.**

- takes skill to find sand that holds shape
- different opinions about definition and purpose of art
- takes talent to design and carve a sculpture
- can be elaborate castles or animals

---

**Thesis, or claim: Collecting sports souvenirs is fun.**

- can share collection with friends and family
- an unusual hobby
- could use programs, hats, balls, and ticket stubs to create displays
- possibly more treasured with time

---

**WRITING HINT**

Your conclusion should restate or sum up your main ideas. Avoid confusing your readers by bringing up new information or topics in your last paragraph.

# Compare-Contrast Essay

You make choices every day. For example, you may have used your money to buy a comic book instead of seeing a movie. You compared and contrasted both possibilities and made a decision.

When you write a **compare-contrast essay,** you look at and explain similarities and differences between objects, people, or ideas. Use a Venn diagram, as shown below, to gather details.

**Playing Baseball**
- time with friends
- good exercise
- excuse to get outside

**Both**
- fun
- inexpensive

**Reading a Book**
- time by myself
- exciting stories
- use of imagination

When you write a compare-contrast essay, remember to include the features below.

## Key Features

- clear introduction to the topic
- organized ideas and supporting details using compare-contrast structure
- appropriate transitions and precise language
- formal style
- conclusion that supports the comparisons and contrasts

## ASSIGNMENT

**TASK:** Write a two- to four-page **compare-contrast essay** about two characters or two famous people.

**AUDIENCE:** classmates who know little about your topic

**PURPOSE:** to inform readers about similarities and differences

# Prewriting

**Plot Your Course** Before you begin writing, you will need to choose a subject for your comparison. Here are several ideas you can use.

1. **Do research.** Read a newspaper, and go online. Go to the library. Talk to teachers, your peers, and librarians. Keep a list of possible subjects as you research.

2. **Try freewriting.** Sit down with paper and pencil, and write nonstop for two or three minutes. Jot down ideas about possible compare-contrast subjects.

3. **Brainstorm with organizers.** Use graphic organizers to arrange and narrow your thoughts. Create a Venn diagram like the one on the previous page. Or simply make a list of possible subjects and their most noteworthy traits.

**Narrow Your Subject** Once you have brainstormed a list of possible subjects, you will need to narrow, or limit, your list. Use an organizer like the one below.

**Inverted Pyramid**

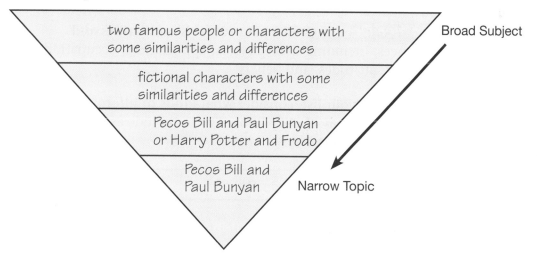

two famous people or characters with some similarities and differences — Broad Subject

fictional characters with some similarities and differences

Pecos Bill and Paul Bunyan or Harry Potter and Frodo

Pecos Bill and Paul Bunyan — Narrow Topic

## Prewriting

▶ **Make Your Point** Every good essay needs a **thesis statement,** or **claim,** which states the main idea of the essay. In a compare-contrast essay, your thesis should explain why this comparison is worth making. Follow the steps below when crafting your thesis, or claim.

For more help with thesis statements, or claims, see **Lesson 5.2.**

**R**emember

When you *compare*, you tell how two or more subjects are alike. When you *contrast*, you point out differences between subjects.

1. Your thesis should state the names of the people being compared and contrasted.

   Paul Bunyan and Pecos Bill are two characters from American folk legend.

2. Your thesis should state what you intend to compare and contrast about your subjects.

   Paul Bunyan and Pecos Bill, two characters from American folk legend, share similar physical and heroic traits.

3. Your thesis should state what the comparison suggests about a broader issue or idea.

   The physical and heroic traits shared by Paul Bunyan and Pecos Bill, two characters from American folk legend, show us what the western pioneers valued.

▶ **Gather Details** List your subjects' similarities and differences, including their physical appearances, occupations, behaviors, attitudes, and beliefs.

As you create your list, consider what kinds of information your audience may already know. Try to include as much new information as possible.

| | Pecos Bill | Paul Bunyan |
|---|---|---|
| Appearance | wears a cowboy hat and boots, uses a rattlesnake as a lasso, rides a horse | giant man, has a beard, carries an ax, has a blue ox as a companion |
| Occupation | cowboy | lumberjack |

# Drafting

**Get Organized** Use one of the methods below.

1. **Point by point** Each paragraph in the body of your essay will focus on one feature shared by both subjects. For example, one paragraph might compare and contrast Paul Bunyan's and Pecos Bill's appearances. Another paragraph might discuss both characters' accomplishments.

2. **Block method** Each paragraph in the body of your essay should focus on a single subject. First, you would write all about Paul Bunyan (appearance, occupation, accomplishments, and heroic traits). Then, you would write all about Pecos Bill, discussing the same features in the same order.

As you draft, refer to an outline, such as the one below.

### Common Transitions to Compare

also
as
in the same way
likewise
similarly

### to Contrast

but
however
in contrast
on the other hand
unlike

## Writing Model

Claim: The physical and heroic traits shared by Paul Bunyan and Pecos Bill, two characters from American folk legend, show us what the western pioneers valued.

  I. Physical appearances and occupations
    A. Bunyan—bearded lumberjack with a blue ox
    B. Bill—cowboy who rides a horse named Widowmaker and uses a rattlesnake as a lasso
 II. Behaviors and fantastical accomplishments
    A. Bunyan—lakes and the Grand Canyon
    B. Bill—cyclones and shoots stars from the sky
    C. Both—in larger-than-life ways
III. Beliefs and values
    A. Bunyan—loyal and strong
    B. Bill—courageous and unpredictable
    C. Both—do right and work hard

### Remember

When writing your essay, remember to use and maintain a formal style. Avoid slang and contractions.

**INFORMAL** They're kinda like heroes, right?

**FORMAL** They are heroes.

Specific vocabulary, such as *pioneer* and *lasso*, help explain the topic.

Outline follows point-by-point organization.

## Revising

Once you have finished drafting, you will need to revise your work. Use the Revising Questions below as you reread your draft. The model below shows revisions one writer made to one body paragraph of a draft.

When you revise, keep in mind the traits of good writing. See **Lesson 1.3.**

### Revising Questions

❏ How clearly does the thesis statement, or claim, state the subjects and purpose?

❏ How clear is the organization?

❏ Where should I add transitions to make the order clearer?

❏ How effective are the introduction and conclusion?

❏ Where can I add more details about similarities or differences?

**Writing Model**

¹Paul Bunyan and Pecos Bill have beliefs and

values that American pioneers admired. ²Paul Bunyan

is loyal and strong. ³He saves people from dangerous

situations and creates landscapes, such as the

*He takes control of natural disasters and rides mountain lions.*

Give specific examples for each subject.

Add transitions to connect sentences.

Black Hills. ⁴Pecos Bill is courageous and unpredictable.

*In addition,*

⁵Both Bunyan and Bill are good men who try always to

work hard and do the right thing. ⁶They are heroes.

# Revising

> **Review Your Essay's Parts** As you revise your work, make sure that you have included the three parts of an essay.

- **Introduction** Include your thesis, or claim; sum up your essay's main points; and grab your readers' attention. Try beginning with a quotation or an exciting or unusual fact.

- **Body** Present your supporting details and arguments in a logical order so that readers follow your ideas.

- **Conclusion** Restate your thesis and give your readers a sense of completeness. Try ending with a question, a brief summary of your main points, or a final thought or fact.

For more help with these parts of an essay, see **Lessons 5.3, 5.4,** and **5.5.**

How effective are the introduction and conclusion below?

## Introduction

¹What do our legends, folktales, and myths say about us? ²What do these stories suggest about our values and beliefs? ³The beliefs of the characters in American folktales and legends reflect American values of a certain time. ⁴<u>The physical and heroic traits shared by Paul Bunyan and Pecos Bill, two characters from American folk legend, show us what the western pioneers valued.</u>

Opening questions

Clear claim

## Conclusion

¹These two characters reflect the values of Americans. ²In their similarities and their differences, Pecos Bill and Paul Bunyan change the landscape around them. ³Both are also humorous and kind. ⁴They reflect how many Americans on the frontier thought of themselves.

Brief summary

## Editing and Proofreading

Now that you have finished revising, set aside time to edit and proofread your work. Go back and read slowly, checking for errors in grammar, spelling, punctuation, usage, and mechanics. Examine your work line by line, using resources like the spell-check program on a computer. Use this checklist to guide your work.

### CONNECTING
*Writing & Grammar*

When you compare two or more things, use the comparative form of the adjective. If the adjective has three or more syllables, use *more* or *less*. See **Lesson 9.2.**

Pecos Bill does **more outrageous** stunts than Paul Bunyan.

## Editing and Proofreading Checklist

❑ Have I checked that all words are spelled correctly?

❑ Have I capitalized the first letter of every sentence?

❑ Have I correctly used adjectives in comparisons?

❑ Have I avoided sentence fragments and run-ons?

❑ Have I indented the first line of every paragraph?

### Reflect On Your Writing

• What do you think is the most effective part of your essay?

• Which part of your essay would you still like to revise?

• What have you learned about compare-contrast essays?

## Publishing and Presenting

Use one of these ways to share your essay with others.

• **Make a collage or poster.** Use the Internet or the library to find photographs or drawings representing the people or characters you compared and contrasted. Present your work to the class.

• **Read your essay to the class.** Answer any questions they have. Before giving your presentation, practice reading it aloud.

# Chapter Review

## A. Practice Test

In the passage below, there is a question *for each numbered item*. Read the passage carefully, and circle the best answer to each question.

### Childhood Obesity

Experts say that our nation's children are getting too big for their own good. Children who are obese will likely have many health problems as adults. <u>Obesity exists in our country.</u>
**1**

Some people blame the food <u>industry. Other people</u> say parents are
**2**
responsible for their kids' choices. <u>In my opinion, it's probable that neither party is entirely correct or wrong.</u>
**3**
Both share blame for the problem.

The food industry does indeed bombard children with advertisements for unhealthy snacks, but it is the job of parents to protect their children from all sorts of dangers in the world. If a child were to get hurt crossing the street in heavy traffic, would we blame the car company? <u>Some people can eat ten hamburgers a day and still not gain weight.</u>
**4**

1. What is the main problem with the thesis, or claim?
   **A.** It needs a transition.
   **B.** It is too narrow.
   **C.** It does not make a claim about the topic; it only states the topic.
   **D.** It is a fragment.

2. What is the best replacement for the underlined section?
   **A.** industry other people
   **B.** industry. People
   **C.** industry, other people
   **D.** industry, but others

3. What is the best replacement for the underlined section?
   **A.** Both parties are completely wrong.
   **B.** Most likely, the answer lies somewhere in between.
   **C.** As a result, they're both wrong.
   **D.** There are a million reasons.

4. What change, if any, should be made to the underlined section?
   **A.** NO CHANGE
   **B.** Add a transition.
   **C.** Move it to the introduction.
   **D.** Change it so it relates to the paragraph.

On the other hand, the food industry needs to be more responsible for informing consumers about the possible dangers of its products. <u>As a nation, we need to remember the words of an old proverb: "It takes a village to raise a child."</u> **5** It is certainly wrong for food companies to compromise health to make a profit.

**5.** Where should this sentence be inserted in the essay?
**(A.)** at the beginning of the final paragraph
**B.** at the beginning of the first paragraph
**C.** at the end of the third paragraph
**D.** at the end of the fourth paragraph

## B. Evaluating Thesis Statements, or Claims

Read each thesis statement, or claim, below. Each is for a two-page essay. In the space provided, write *N* if the statement is too narrow, *B* if it is too broad, or *S* if it is strong.

_B_ **1.** Hip-hop music is popular today.

_S_ **2.** My encounter with a bear taught me about two aspects of my personality.

_N_ **3.** At 2,228 meters, Australia's highest point is Mount Kosciusko.

_S_ **4.** The movie *Avatar* was groundbreaking for three reasons.

_B_ **5.** There are many accomplished poets.

## C. Writing Introductions and Conclusions

Write a short introduction or conclusion for one topic below. Use the technique indicated in parentheses. Remember to include a strong thesis, or claim.  Answers will vary. Sample answer is shown.

**1.** benefits of healthy snacks (introduction – quotation)

**2.** similarities between two movies (conclusion – example)

**3.** advantages of life in your state (introduction – amazing fact)

**4.** exploring space (conclusion – opinion or suggestion)

**5.** benefits of doing volunteer work (introduction – example)

Doing volunteer work can help you meet people, visit interesting places, and learn new skills. Even more important, volunteering can make you feel good about yourself. The two hours I spend each week in the hospital playroom make me appreciate my life. Who could ask for a better reward?

## D. Revising a Compare-Contrast Essay

On a separate sheet of paper, revise the draft below to improve its coherence. Insert transitions, and combine sentences where needed. Delete sentences that interrupt unity, and proofread your revision carefully. Then label the three parts of the essay.

### Proofreading Symbols

| | | | |
|---|---|---|---|
| ⩗ | Delete. | ∧ | Add. |
| ⊙ | Add a period. | ⩘ | Add a comma. |
| / | Make lowercase. | ¶ | Start a new paragraph. |
| ≡ | Capitalize. | ∾ | Switch order. |

¹Would you like to live in a big city or rural area? ²I have spent time living in both places. ³ ^Therefore, I have a unique perspective on the question. ⁴The answer is that there are advantages to each.    *introduction*

⁵Big cities can be crowded and hectic. ⩗ ^,but ⁶They can also teach kids about using "street smarts." ⩗ ⁷~~This~~ is ^,which an important skill. ⁸ ^In addition, There is often more to do in a big city. ⩗ ^because ⁹There are so many different kinds of people and activities. ^For instance, you can go to museums, concerts, and restaurants from a variety of cultures.    *body*

¹⁰ ^On the other hand, Living in a rural area can teach kids about nature. ⩗ ¹¹ ^since There are so many opportunities for outdoor exͫloration.

¹²~~But be careful of bears if you go camping.~~ ^Also, life in the country can often be quieter and slower paced.

¹³Ideally, kids should be exposed to life in both kinds of places. ¹⁴ ^As a result, They will get as well-rounded an education as I did. ¹⁵~~Personally, I like cities and rural areas.~~ ^Five years in Denver and five years on a ranch in the mountains have made me who I am today.    *conclusion*

# Parts of a Sentence

# Sentences and Sentence Fragments

A **sentence** contains a subject and a predicate, and it expresses a complete thought. (See Lesson 6.2 for more about subjects and predicates.) Every sentence begins with a capital letter and ends with a period, a question mark, or an exclamation point.

SUBJECT     PREDICATE

Gloria Chavez sings Latin pop.

1. Who sings? Gloria Chavez. The **complete subject** is *Gloria Chavez.*

2. What does Gloria Chavez do? She sings Latin pop. The **complete predicate** is *sings Latin pop.*

▥➡ A **sentence fragment** is only part of a sentence. It may be missing a subject, a predicate, or both. Often you can correct a sentence fragment by adding a subject or predicate.

FRAGMENT   Went on tour in Brazil last summer. **[missing a subject]**

CORRECT   Gloria went on tour in Brazil last summer.

FRAGMENT   The Brazilian fans. **[missing a predicate]**

CORRECT   The Brazilian fans really liked her music.

▥➡ Sometimes a sentence fragment needs to be attached to the sentence next to it.

FRAGMENT   While she was on tour.
[This sentence fragment is a **subordinate clause,** a group of words that is part of a sentence and cannot stand on its own.]

REVISED   While she was on tour, Gloria signed many autographs.

---

**CONNECTING**
*Writing & Grammar*

When you correct a sentence fragment, you may need to use a comma after an introductory phrase or subordinate clause. See **Lesson 11.4.**

INCORRECT At many of her concerts. Gloria's fans like to dance.

CORRECT At many of her concerts**,** Gloria's fans like to dance.

For more about sentence fragments and subordinate clauses, see **Lessons 2.1** and **3.4.**

## EXERCISE 1 Identifying Sentences

Mark the following sentences as either *S* for sentence or *F* for sentence fragment. If you mark *F*, write whether you would add a subject or predicate to complete the sentence.

**EXAMPLE**   Is often called "Evita." **F** subject

**1.** Eva Peron was born Maria Eva Ibarguren. S

**2.** Was an intelligent girl.  F subject

**3.** Eva became a film and radio star.  S

**4.** During the 1940s in Argentina, Eva and Juan Peron.  F predicate

**5.** Became powerful people in Argentina.  F subject

## EXERCISE 2 Rewriting Sentences

**HiNT**

You may need to change the punctuation and capitalization as you correct the fragments.

If he could, **h**e would have played baseball.

Rewrite the following paragraph to correct any sentence fragments. You may add a subject or a predicate or attach a fragment to a complete sentence.

Answers will vary. See sample answer in Answer Key at www.grammarforwriting.com.

**EXAMPLE**   If he could. He would have played baseball.

If he could, he would have played baseball.

> ¹Edward James Olmos sang. ²In a rock band during the late 1960s and early 1970s. ³He starred on Broadway. ⁴And won an Academy Award nomination for *Stand and Deliver.* ⁵Olmos and his wife. ⁶Have several children. ⁷He spends much time on social causes. ⁸Mainly for the needs of children.

**Working Together**

Answers will vary. See sample answer in Answer Key at www.grammarforwriting.com.

## EXERCISE 3 Writing a Paragraph

Work with a partner. Choose a kind of music you both enjoy. Brainstorm ideas about the sound of the music and special songs and artists. Then write at least four sentences describing the music. Exchange paragraphs with another partner team, and check the paragraph for sentence fragments.

# Subjects and Predicates

Complete sentences in English have two essential parts. The **subject** tells what the sentence is about, and the **predicate** tells what the subject does, is, has, or feels. Both are needed to communicate meaning and make a complete sentence.

```
        SUBJECT              PREDICATE
┌──────────────────┐ ┌────────────────────────────┐
The gala New Year's festival is an important holiday in China.
```

▮▶ A **complete subject** is all the words in a sentence that describe the person or thing that performs the action of the sentence. A **simple subject (s)** is the main word or words in the complete subject.

```
                 s
The major celebration of the year will last for fifteen days.
└────────────────────────────┘
         COMPLETE SUBJECT
```

▮▶ A **complete predicate** is the **verb** or **verb phrase** and all the words that modify it and complete its meaning. A **simple predicate (v)** is the verb or verb phrase.

```
              v
Families gather for visits and feasts on New Year's Eve.
        └──────────────────────────────────────┘
                 COMPLETE PREDICATE
```

**Note:** In this book, the term *verb* refers to the simple predicate, and *subject* refers to the simple subject unless otherwise noted.

## EXERCISE 1  Identifying Complete and Simple Subjects

Write the complete subject of each sentence. Then underline the simple subject.

> **EXAMPLE**    The history of China is fascinating.
>
> The <u>history</u> of China

**Remember**

A verb phrase contains a main verb and one or more helping verbs. See **Lesson 8.1** for more about verb phrases and helping verbs.

## Some Common Helping Verbs

| | |
|---|---|
| am | has |
| are | have |
| be | is |
| been | may |
| being | might |
| can | must |
| could | should |
| do | was |
| does | were |
| had | would |

**HINT**

To find the subject, ask *who* or *what* is doing something or *whom* or *what* is being talked about. Subjects are never part of prepositional phrases. See **Lesson 10.2**.

1. The hardy horsemen from northern China moved south.
   The hardy <u>horsemen</u> from northern China
2. They invaded areas settled by the Han people.
   <u>They</u>
3. The largest ethnic group in China is the Han.
   The largest ethnic <u>group</u> in China
4. The achievements of the Han people are amazing.
   The <u>achievements</u> of the Han people
5. Paintings have survived from early days.
   <u>Paintings</u>

## EXERCISE 2 Identifying Complete and Simple Predicates

Write the complete predicate of each sentence. Then underline the simple predicate (including helping verbs) twice.

**EXAMPLE**   The ancient Chinese used a lunar calendar.

<u><u>used</u></u> a lunar calendar

1. Chinese years are grouped in sets of twelve.
   <u><u>are grouped</u></u> in sets of twelve
2. An animal represents each year.
   <u><u>represents</u></u> each year
3. People pay their debts before the New Year.
   <u><u>pay</u></u> their debts before the New Year
4. The dragon is a popular symbol for the Chinese New Year.
   <u><u>is</u></u> a popular symbol for the Chinese New Year
5. The eve of the New Year may start with a late feast.
   <u><u>may start</u></u> with a late feast
6. People gather with family and friends.
   <u><u>gather</u></u> with family and friends
7. Dumplings are served during the feast.
   <u><u>are served</u></u> during the feast
8. One of the dumplings contains a coin.
   <u><u>contains</u></u> a coin
9. The coin is for good luck.
   <u><u>is</u></u> for good luck
10. I found the lucky coin in my dumpling last year.
    <u><u>found</u></u> the lucky coin in my dumpling last year

Answers will vary. Students may write about watching a fireworks display or staying up late to see televised celebrations from around the world. See sample answer in Answer Key at www.grammarforwriting.com.

## Write What You Think

On a separate sheet of paper, write at least five sentences that explain your answer to the questions below. When you have finished, underline each simple subject once and each simple predicate twice.

How do you celebrate the coming of a new year? What do you do?

# Hard-to-Find Subjects

You need to know how to identify the subject in a sentence so that you can choose a verb that agrees with it in number.

▪▶ Usually, the subject comes before the verb and is easy to spot. Other times, it can be hard to find because of the word order or words that come between the subject and the verb.

| Rule | Example |
|---|---|
| The words *here* and *there* are never the subject of a sentence. (Look for the subject after the verb in such sentences.) | There are ten **students** in my dance class.<br>[Ask yourself, "Who are?" The answer is *students*.] |
| The subject is never part of a prepositional phrase. (See Lesson 10.2.) | **One** of the students loves ballet.<br>[One loves ballet.] |
| To find the subject in a question, turn the question into a statement. | How does **she** turn so quickly?<br>[She does turn so quickly.] |
| The subject *you* is not stated in a command or request. It is called the **understood subject.** | Point your toes.<br>[*You* point your toes.] |

▪▶ Sentences with *here* or *there* and questions are two examples of inverted sentences. In an **inverted sentence,** the subject follows the verb. Some sentences that begin with a phrase may also have an inverted order.

When is the ballet recital?

After the show came the loud applause.

## EXERCISE 1  Finding Subjects

Underline the subject in each sentence. Write *you* if the sentence is understood in a command or request.

**EXAMPLE**  Here is a definition of tap dance.

**1.** Did African-American enslaved people invent tap dance?

**2.** Listen to this story. you

Using inverted sentences, such as questions, adds variety to your writing. See **Lesson 10.4** for more about inverted sentences.

> **R**emember
>
> Some subjects, such as proper names, include more than one word.
>
> **Bill Robinson** was a famous African-American tap dancer.

3. Enslaved <u>people</u> on plantations sent secret messages through music.

4. Before long <u>they</u> began tapping their feet.

5. <u>Rhythms</u> from Europe and Africa led to tap.

6. There were <u>dancers</u> like Master Juba.

7. Here is a <u>program</u> from *Minstrel Misses*, a show.

8. Did these <u>performers</u> use the term "tap"?

9. Is the <u>"Shim Sham"</u> still danced today?

10. Please do not wear tap shoes on the street. you

**Working Together**

# Exercise 2 Reading a Paragraph

Work with a partner to underline the subject of each sentence. **Hint:** To find the subjects more easily, cross out the prepositional phrases. The subject is one of the remaining words.

¹<u>World War I</u> between the Allies and the Central Powers was fought in Europe. ²An <u>assassination</u> in 1914 started the war. ³There were <u>millions</u> of casualties. ⁴Then the <u>United States,</u> under President Woodrow Wilson, joined the Allies. ⁵In 1918, the <u>war</u> ended. ⁶After the war, there was a social <u>revolution</u>. ⁷<u>It</u> brought a rejection of older customs. ⁸Young <u>women</u> in the 1920s wore stockings and short skirts. ⁹Were <u>members</u> of the older generation upset? ¹⁰<u>Many</u> of them didn't like seeing young women dancing at nightclubs.

# Exercise 3 Analyzing Your Own Writing

Choose a paragraph you recently wrote for a class. As you read it, circle any inverted sentences. If there are none, rewrite one sentence so that the subject follows the verb.

Answers will vary. If time permits, have students exchange papers and discuss their use of inverted sentences.

# Compound Subjects and Verbs

A sentence may have more than one subject and more than one verb.

➠ A **compound subject** is two or more subjects with the same verb. Subjects are joined by *and, or,* or *but.* Sometimes they are joined by pairs of conjunctions, such as *either* and *or* or *neither* and *nor.*

**Plants** and **animals** fascinate me.

Either **poison ivy** or **allergies** caused this itch.

**Campers, bikers,** or **hikers** easily pick up poison ivy.

➠ A **compound verb** is two or more verbs with the same subject. Compound verbs are joined by the same conjunctions and conjunction pairs as compound subjects.

Poison ivy **creeps** along the ground or **climbs** trees.

The outer covering of the berries **dries** and **falls** away.

Insects **chew** the leaves, **make** holes in them, and **release** the poison.

➠ Use compound subjects and verbs to combine sentences and make your writing less wordy. (See Lesson 3.6.)

| SHORT SENTENCES | The muscles of insects are inside their protective shells. Their organs, too, are inside outer shells. |
|---|---|
| COMBINED SENTENCES | The **muscles** and **organs** of insects are inside their protective shells. |
| SHORT SENTENCES | Scorpions ambush their prey. Scorpions capture their prey. |
| COMBINED SENTENCES | Scorpions **ambush** and **capture** their prey. |

**Remember**

Subjects and verbs must agree in number. See **Lesson 10.3.** Most compound subjects joined by *and* take a plural verb.

Joe and Tracy **have** allergies.

When a compound subject is joined by *or,* the verb agrees with the subject closest to it.

Either Wendy or the boys **have** the bug repellent.

Either the boys or Wendy **has** the bug repellent.

## EXERCISE 1  Identifying Compound Subjects and Compound Verbs

Read the paragraph from a first-aid manual. Underline any compound subjects once. Underline any compound verbs twice.

**EXAMPLE**  <u>Ivy</u>, <u>oak</u>, and <u>sumac</u> <u><u>can</u></u> <u><u>live</u></u> and <u><u>grow</u></u> in the wild.

<sup>1</sup>Poison <u>ivy</u>, poison <u>oak</u>, and poison <u>sumac</u> can cause skin rashes. <sup>2</sup>A red <u>rash</u> and an <u>itch</u> are symptoms of contact with all three plants. <sup>3</sup>The rash usually <u><u>appears</u></u> in a few days and <u><u>may last</u></u> several weeks. <sup>4</sup><u><u>Wash</u></u> contaminated clothing, never <u><u>burn</u></u> the plants, and always <u><u>be</u></u> on the lookout for poisonous plants.

## EXERCISE 2  Combining Sentences

Combine the sentences by using a compound subject or verb.
Answers will vary. Sample answers are shown.

**EXAMPLE**  Frogs prey on spiders. Lizards and birds do, too.

*Frogs, lizards, and birds prey on spiders.*

**1.** Forests are a habitat for spiders. Jungles are habitats, too.
Forests and jungles are habitats for spiders.

**2.** Spiders prey on insects. Spiders help control insect pests.
Spiders prey on insects and help control insect pests.

**3.** Spiders' webs help spiders climb. Webs allow them to float through the air. Webs trap their prey.
Spiders' webs help spiders climb, allow them to float through the air, and trap their prey.

**4.** Spitting spiders move slowly. They are considered harmless.
Spitting spiders move slowly and are considered harmless.

**5.** Recluse spiders can be poisonous to humans. They can even cause death. Widow spiders can be poisonous and cause death.
Recluse spiders and widow spiders can be poisonous to humans and even cause death.

## EXERCISE 3  Writing a Paragraph

Working Together

Answers will vary. See sample answers in Answer Key at www.grammarforwriting.com.

Work with a partner to write at least five sentences about spiders. You can describe your feelings about them, give advice about how to get rid of them, or make up a story about one. Use at least one compound subject and one compound verb.

# Direct Objects

A **direct object (DO)** is a noun, pronoun, or group of words that tells *who* or *what* receives the action of the verb.

> **DO**
> Mr. McSwain teaches **English**. [Teaches *what? English*]

> **DO**
> Did you see **him** in school? [Did see *whom? him*]

▶ Not all sentences with an action verb have a direct object.

> The actors performed well. [*Well* is not a direct object. *Well* does not answer the question *whom?* or *what?* after the verb *performed*.]

> The speech lasted for hours. [*Hours* is not a direct object. *Hours* is the object of the preposition *for*. A direct object is never in a prepositional phrase.]

## STEP BY STEP

The cowboy was wearing green boots yesterday.

To identify a direct object:

1. Find the action verb. Only sentences with an action verb can have a direct object.
   ACTION VERB = *was wearing*

2. Ask *whom?* or *what?* after the action verb.
   Was wearing what? *boots*

3. The word that answers the question is the direct object.
   **DO**
   The cowboy was wearing green **boots** yesterday.

▶ A sentence may have more than one direct object. Sometimes, a compound direct object may follow the same verb. In sentences with more than one action verb, a direct object may follow each one.

> **DO** **DO** **DO**
> We discussed **sports**, **food**, and **movies**.

> **DO** **DO**
> He ate a **sandwich** and called his **father**.

---

**R**emember

Only sentences with action verbs can have direct objects. A sentence with a **linking verb** (such as *is*, *are*, *was*, and *were*) does not have a direct object. See **Lessons 6.6** and **8.1** for more about linking and action verbs.

We are happy. [*Happy* is not a direct object since *are* is a linking verb.]

---

**ONLINE PRACTICE**
www.grammarforwriting.com

## EXERCISE 1  Finding Examples in Literature

Underline the four direct objects in the passage below.

> **Literary Model**
>
> [1]Then he pulled a <u>handkerchief</u> out of his pocket and wiped her <u>tears</u>. [2]This gesture of tenderness undid <u>her</u> completely, and she put her <u>head</u> down on her knees and sobbed.
>
> —Excerpt from *A Wrinkle in Time* by Madeleine L'Engle

## EXERCISE 2  Identifying Direct Objects

If the underlined word in each sentence is a direct object, write *OK*. If not, write the word that is the direct object.

**EXAMPLE**   The principal dislikes phones in <u>schools</u>. *phones*

1. A ringing phone disrupts a <u>class</u> discussion frequently.
discussion
2. A loud conversation in a hall <u>corridor</u> annoys other students.
students
3. The school board banned cell phones on school <u>property</u>.
phones
4. Some students want their <u>phones</u> in case of an emergency.
OK
5. Does the <u>rule</u> take away students' rights?
rights
6. The principal took my friend's phone <u>yesterday</u>.
phone
7. My friend told his <u>dad</u>.
OK
8. My friend's parents discussed the issue last <u>night</u>.
issue
9. The Johnsons had <u>questions</u> about the rule.
OK
10. However, they understand the schools' <u>reasoning</u>.
OK

**Working Together**

## EXERCISE 3  Using Direct Objects

Sentences should each have at least one direct object. See sample answers in Answer Key at www.grammarforwriting.com.

Work with a partner to write five sentences about your school. Include at least one direct object in each sentence.

**EXAMPLE**   The cafeteria needs a coat of paint and new tables.

# Subject Complements

A noun, pronoun, or adjective that follows a **linking verb** and identifies or describes the subject is called a **subject complement.** There are two main types of subject complements: predicate nominatives and predicate adjectives.

➡ A **predicate nominative (PN)** is a noun or a pronoun that identifies the subject.

| Noun | Mr. Chang is a **florist.** [The noun *florist* tells what *Mr. Chang* is.] |
|---|---|
| | His wife was a **nurse.** [The noun *nurse* tells what his *wife* was.] |
| Pronoun | His assistants are **you** and **I.** [The pronouns *you* and *I* tell who the *assistants* are.] |
| | The first customer was **he.** [The pronoun *he* tells who the *customer* was.] |

➡ A **predicate adjective (PA)** is an adjective that describes the subject.

| Adjective | The flowers look **beautiful.** [The adjective *beautiful* tells what the *flowers* look like—beautiful flowers.] |
|---|---|
| | Do the roses seem **fresh?** [The adjective *fresh* tells how the *roses* seem—fresh roses.] |

➡ A sentence may have compound predicate nominatives or compound predicate adjectives.

Those flowers are **tulips, daisies,** and **violets.**

Do they appear **strong** and **healthy?**

---

**Remember**

A **linking verb** needs a subject complement after it in order to express a complete thought.

INCOMPLETE    She was.

COMPLETE
She was **tall.**

## Common Linking Verbs

### Forms of *to be*

| | |
|---|---|
| am | is |
| are | was |
| be | were |
| been | |

### Other Linking Verbs

| | |
|---|---|
| appear | remain |
| become | seem |
| feel | smell |
| grow | sound |
| look | taste |

See **Lesson 8.1** for more about linking verbs.

**TEST-TAKING TIP**

Sometimes a test question asks you to decide whether a word is a predicate nominative or a direct object. Look at the verb in the sentence. If it is an action verb, the word cannot be a predicate nominative. For example, see question 4 on page 154.

**Benjamin Franklin**

**Working Together**

# EXERCISE 1 Finding Predicate Nominatives

On a separate sheet of paper, write the linking verbs and the predicate nominatives in the sentences below.

**EXAMPLE**   She was the first woman senator.

*was, senator*

**1.** The congressman is the only candidate from Ohio. is, candidate

**2.** The winners were LeRoy and I. were, LeRoy, I

**3.** Age becomes an issue in some elections. becomes, issue

**4.** Television stars are sometimes candidates. are, candidates

**5.** Is Kelly the election winner? is, winner

# EXERCISE 2 Finding Predicate Adjectives

Write the linking verbs and the predicate adjectives in the sentences below.

**EXAMPLE**   Ben Franklin was patriotic.

*was, patriotic*

**1.** Today, Franklin's name is familiar to children and adults.
is, familiar

**2.** He was adventurous and interested in science.
was, adventurous, interested

**3.** Franklin grew curious about electricity.
grew, curious

**4.** He seemed always mindful of the "greater good."
seemed, mindful

**5.** People in other countries were pleased with his work abroad.
were, pleased

# EXERCISE 3 Using Subject Complements

Working with a partner, choose a hero, past or present.
Answers will vary. See sample answer in Answer Key at www.grammarforwriting.com.

**1.** On a separate sheet of paper, write a paragraph of at least five sentences about this hero.

**2.** Include at least two nouns and two adjectives as subject complements.

**3.** Share your paragraph with the class.

# Summary

Have you ever had to describe the plot of a movie or book to a friend? When you described it, you probably only related the most important details. In other words, you summarized. **Summaries** retell the main idea and key details of events, narratives, or pieces of nonfiction. Summaries often appear in longer pieces of writing.

| Summary | Purpose |
| --- | --- |
| **Book Reviews** | to retell the plot of a book |
| **Literary Analyses** | to describe key elements of a literary work |
| **Research Reports** | to explain key ideas, a complicated process, or a series of events |
| **Study Notes** | to list the key details of a topic |

Now focus on key features for writing a summary.

## Key Features

- main idea and essential information
- evidence from a nonfiction text
- logically organized ideas
- relevant facts and details
- precise language

## ASSIGNMENT

**TASK:** Write a **summary** of a long nonfiction article. Your summary should be no more than one-third of the original article's length.

**PURPOSE:** to briefly retell the main ideas

**AUDIENCE:** your family and classmates

**KEY INSTRUCTIONS:** Include at least one paraphrase.

**CONNECTING**
*Writing & Grammar*

Be sure to include the author's name, the title of the work, and where and when it appeared.

I read the article "Say No" by Laura Sanchez in *The Daily News.*

See **Lessons 11.6** and **12.2** for more about how to punctuate titles.

▶ **Get the Big Idea** ▶ First, read your source material at least twice. As you read, note the main idea and relevant supporting details. Effective summaries focus only on essential information in the text. Avoid inserting your personal opinions.

| **Essential Information** | **Not Essential** |
|---|---|
| • main ideas | • vivid descriptions |
| • important points | • examples and anecdotes |
| • key facts and statistics | • long quotations |

As you read, ask yourself these questions:

**1.** What is the writer's main idea?

**2.** Which details are needed to understand the main idea?

**3.** What details can I leave out?

If you can, annotate, or mark up, the original source. Circle the main idea, and underline relevant details.

> [1]Many parents are exasperated by how homework dominates their children's lives, even over the summer. [2]But what they do not realize is that <u>most studies find little connection between homework and achievement in elementary school and only a moderate connection in middle school.</u> ([3]Teachers routinely assign too much homework.)

▶ **Use Your Own Words** ▶ Like a summary, a **paraphrase** retells. However, a paraphrase is about as long as the original. It can be useful to paraphrase an especially important or difficult sentence. Change enough words in the sentence so that your paraphrase sounds like you. A good paraphrase of the first sentence in the source above is "Parents are overwhelmed by the amount of homework children receive, even during summer break."

**Choose Your Words Carefully** Follow the guidelines below to create an effective summary.

- **Use a thesaurus.** Your summary must be in your own words. If you are having trouble thinking of **synonyms,** or words of the same or nearly the same meaning, for the words used in your source, consult a thesaurus.

- **Be honest.** Presenting someone else's words as if they were your own is called **plagiarism.** To avoid plagiarism, use your own words. Enclose any phrases you borrow in quotation marks.

- **Be concise.** Because your summary must be about one-third the length of the original source, avoid wordiness. To do so, ask yourself, "How can I say this accurately and in the fewest possible words?"

Below are two summaries of the same source material. What makes the second one more effective?

> ¹Experts believe reading to be the most important educational task. ²Yet a Scholastic/Yankelovich study released last month found that reading for fun declines sharply after age eight. ³The number one reason according to parents: too much homework.

**WRITING HINT**

Match both the **denotations** (definitions) and **connotations** (positive or negative feelings suggested by a word) of your source's language. For example, if your source used the word *frugal*, your summary should not replace it with *cheap*. *Frugal* has a positive connotation, while *cheap* is more negative.

See **Lesson 2.6** for more about word choice.

INEFFECTIVE    Experts believe that reading is the most important educational activity. Yet, a study from last month shows that reading for fun declines after age eight. The number one reason for this is too much homework.
[This summary is too long and has too many words from the original source.]

EFFECTIVE    A study shows that reading for pleasure drops off after age eight because students have too much homework.

Be sure that all your sentences have a subject and a verb and express a complete thought. Fix sentence fragments by adding the missing subject or verb. See **Lesson 6.1.**

FRAGMENT Too much homework every night.

SENTENCE Too much homework every night **discourages students.**

**Check Your Summary** After you have finished your draft, take a few minutes to review it. You may want to reread the original source so that you remember the main idea and relevant details. Use the checklist to help you review your summary. The model below shows one writer's summary.

## WRITING CHECKLIST
### Did you...

✔ restate the main idea and include essential information?

✔ use your own words, concise language, and accurate synonyms?

✔ include at least one paraphrase and avoid fragments?

✔ check that your writing is free of grammar and spelling errors?

Title, author, and date of editorial

Main idea

Essential information

### Writing Model

¹According to writer Sara Bennett, whose article "Homework Does Not = A's" appeared in the July 3, 2006, edition of *USA Today*, elementary and middle school students are given more homework than experts recommend. ²Bennett says that while parents are often upset by the amount of homework assigned, they should know that more homework doesn't mean better grades. ³In fact, students in countries that score higher on achievement tests are generally assigned less homework than students in the United States. ⁴Bennett says that reading is the main educational activity. ⁵However, one study suggests that pleasure reading decreases after age eight because of homework.

# Chapter Review

## A. Practice Test

Read the draft and questions below carefully. The questions ask you to identify parts of sentences. Fill in the corresponding circle for your answer choice.

**(1)** Born into slavery in eastern Maryland in 1818, Frederick Douglass led a remarkable life. **(2)** When he was about eight, Douglass was sent to Baltimore to work as a houseboy for Hugh and Sophia Auld. **(3)** Mistress Auld taught him the alphabet, and Douglass asked neighborhood boys for help with reading and writing. **(4)** Even as a young boy, Douglass recognized the power of the spoken and written word and became determined to use language to make positive changes in his life and in society.

**(5)** At the age of twenty, Douglass escaped from slavery and settled in New Bedford, Massachusetts. **(6)** Soon, he became a lecturer for the Massachusetts Anti-Slavery Society. **(7)** By 1848, Douglass had written his autobiography, gone on a speaking tour in Europe, and published the first issue of a weekly newspaper, the *North Star.* **(8)** Douglass helped recruit African-American troops for the Union Army and became an advisor to Abraham Lincoln. **(9)** In addition to his work as an abolitionist, Douglass was famous for his support of women's rights. **(10)** By the time of his death in 1895, this former slave had achieved success and international fame as an abolitionist, statesman, and social reformer.

Ⓐ Ⓑ ● Ⓓ Ⓔ  **1.** What is the simple subject of sentence 1?
   A. slavery
   B. eastern Maryland
   C. Frederick Douglass
   D. remarkable life
   E. Douglass

Ⓐ Ⓑ Ⓒ ● Ⓔ  **2.** Which of the following is true of sentence 3?
   A. It is a sentence fragment.
   B. It is a run-on sentence.
   C. It has two predicate adjectives.
   D. It has two direct objects.
   E. It is an inverted sentence.

Ⓐ Ⓑ Ⓒ Ⓓ ●  **3.** Which of the following is true of sentence 5?
   A. It has two direct objects.
   B. It is a sentence fragment.
   C. It is a run-on sentence.
   D. It has a compound subject.
   E. It has a compound verb.

Ⓐ ● Ⓒ Ⓓ Ⓔ  **4.** What is *advisor* in sentence 8?
   A. the simple subject
   B. a predicate nominative
   C. a direct object
   D. part of a compound subject
   E. part of a verb phrase

Ⓐ Ⓑ Ⓒ ● Ⓔ  **5.** What is the simple predicate of sentence 9?
   A. was famous
   B. support
   C. was famous for his support
   D. was
   E. work

## B. Writing Sentences

No group of words below expresses a complete thought. Turn each group into a sentence by adding the missing sentence parts indicated in parentheses. Change punctuation, and add words as needed.
Answers will vary. Sample answers are shown.

   **1.** Couldn't go skiing. (compound subject joined by *and*)
   Lizzie and Luis couldn't go skiing.

   **2.** My basketball coach. (action verb and direct object)
   My basketball coach threw the ball.

**3.** My favorite foods. (linking verb and predicate adjective)

My favorite foods are crunchy.

**4.** Is having a pizza party. (compound subject joined by *or*)

Either Vicki or Wes is having a pizza party.

**5.** The best pets. (linking verb and predicate nominative)

The best pets are rabbits.

## C. Analyzing a Summary

Read the draft of a summary below.

**1.** Underline the simple subjects in the first two sentences.

**2.** Draw two lines under the simple predicates (verbs) in the first two sentences.

**3.** Circle nine direct objects.

**4.** Draw a box around three subject complements (predicate adjective or predicate nominative).

**5.** Draw a line through any unnecessary details and personal opinions.

¹The <u>movie</u> *Clueless* <u>is</u> a comedy based on Jane Austen's novel *Emma*. ²<u>It</u> <u>tells</u> the story of a privileged teenage girl. ³Cher is very sure of herself. ⁴Cher befriends a new girl named Tai. ⁵Tai likes Travis. ⁶However, Cher does not approve at all. ⁷Meanwhile, Cher has her own problems. ⁸At first, Cher dislikes Josh. ⁹Finally, Tai reveals her feelings for Josh. ¹⁰Then Cher recognizes her own love for Josh. ¹¹~~This scene is filmed in front of a fountain.~~ ¹²Cher finally realizes her errors in judgment. ¹³In the end, both Cher and Tai get great boyfriends. ¹⁴There is a happy ending for everyone. ¹⁵~~In my opinion, the movie is great.~~ ¹⁶~~Do you agree?~~

# Nouns and Pronouns

# Nouns

**Parts of speech,** such as nouns, verbs, and adjectives, describe how words are used in sentences. A **noun** names a person, place, thing, or idea. There are several types of nouns.

➤ A **common noun** names any person, place, thing, or idea.

> The **leader** of the **organization** works in that **city.**

A **proper noun** names a specific person, place, thing, or idea. Proper nouns always begin with capital letters.

> **Danica** works for the **Red Cross** in **Anchorage.**

➤ All nouns are either common or proper and also concrete or abstract. A **concrete noun** names a thing that you can see, hear, smell, taste, or touch.

> The **campers** saw a **wolf** near the **pond.**

In contrast, an **abstract noun** names an idea, a quality, a feeling, or a characteristic.

> Their **fear** disappeared when the **fun** began.

➤ A **collective noun** is a word that names a group of people or things. (See the list on the right.)

> Our **family** visited Alaska last year.

> One **group** of tourists saw a **herd** of buffalo.

➤ A **compound noun** consists of two or more words. Use a dictionary if you are unsure whether a compound noun is written as one word, two or more separate words, or a hyphenated word.

| | | |
|---|---|---|
| mankind | polar bear | great-aunt |
| laptop | New York | one-fourth |
| honeybee | high school | sister-in-law |

## Some Collective Nouns

| | |
|---|---|
| audience | family |
| band | group |
| class | herd |
| club | jury |
| committee | panel |
| crowd | team |

See **Lesson 11.8** for more about using hyphens.

**HiNT**

Even if a noun consists of more than one word, count it as one noun.

**Remember**

Proper nouns begin with a capital letter. Articles (*the*) and short prepositions (*of*) should not be capitalized. See **Lesson 12.1.**

the **S**tatue of **L**iberty

# Exercise 1  Finding Nouns

On a separate sheet of paper, list the twenty common and proper nouns in the passage below. Circle the proper nouns in your list.
See answers in Answer Key at www.grammarforwriting.com.

¹Evon Peter is from the Alaskan village of Vashraii K'oo. ²His goal is protection of the land. ³He opposes drilling in the Arctic Wildlife Region because of the effects it will have on our environment. ⁴His wife, Enei Begaye, is a Navajo. ⁵They co-founded Native Movement. ⁶The organization sponsors many activities and special events, including training, conferences, and workshops.

# Exercise 2  Using Nouns

Complete each sentence by adding the type of noun named in parentheses. Answers will vary. Sample answers are shown.

**EXAMPLE**    I wish I had more (<u>abstract</u>).

I wish I had more courage.

1. That girl collects (<u>common</u>) and (<u>common</u>).
That girl collects **rocks** and **shells**.
2. The (<u>collective</u>) left the (<u>common</u>) early.
The **audience** left the **park** early.
3. Shannon's face showed (<u>abstract</u>).
Shannon's face showed **excitement**.
4. Did (<u>proper</u>) see the (<u>common</u>)?
Did **Ramon** see the **truck**?
5. Stan wants to visit (<u>compound</u>).
Stan wants to visit the **Sahara Desert**.

**Write What You Think**    Answers will vary. See sample answer in Answer Key at www.grammarforwriting.com.

On a separate sheet of paper, write a persuasive paragraph that explains your answer to the following question:
Should young people be required to do community service?

1. Write at least five sentences. Use specific details to make your position clear.
2. Include at least two proper nouns. Circle them.

# Plural and Possessive Nouns

Be careful not to confuse plural nouns and possessive nouns. Although the plural and possessive forms of most nouns end with the letter -*s*, their meanings and their spellings differ.

⏩ A **plural noun** names more than one person, place, thing, or idea. In most cases, you can make a singular noun plural by adding -*s* or -*es*. (See Lesson 12.5 for other rules about forming plural nouns.)

shoe — shoe**s**          boss — boss**es**          lunch — lunch**es**

Note that most plural nouns do not have apostrophes.

INCORRECT     Big **storms'** caused many flight **delay's.**

CORRECT       Big **storms** caused many flight **delays.**

⏩ To form possessive nouns, you need to add apostrophes. A **possessive noun** names who or what owns or has something.

shoes of the woman — woman**'s** shoes

lunches of both boys — boys**'** lunches

Learn these rules for forming the possessive of any noun.

**1.** Add an apostrophe and -*s* to singular nouns.

a girl**'s** skirt          Mr. Hess**'s** car          the cat**'s** paw

**2.** Add only an apostrophe to plural nouns that end in -*s*.

both teachers**'** books      the Smiths**'** house      two dogs**'** leashes

**3.** Add an apostrophe and -*s* to plural nouns that do not end in -*s*.

the mice**'s** tails        the men**'s** team        the geese**'s** feathers

| Singular | The **bus** has new tires. |
|---|---|
| Singular Possessive | The **bus's** tires are new. |
| Plural | All the **buses** arrived early. |
| Plural Possessive | Many of the **buses'** seats are old. |

# EXERCISE 1  Using Possessives

Label each word as plural, singular possessive, or plural possessive. On a separate sheet of paper, write a sentence that includes each word. Answers will vary. Sample answers are shown.

**1.** swimmers
plural—I saw four swimmers.

**2.** shark's
singular possessive—That shark's teeth are sharp.

**3.** eagles
plural—Fred saw two eagles in flight.

**4.** eagles'
plural possessive—Both eagles' nests were empty.

**5.** boys'
plural possessive—All of the boys' bikes are red.

**6.** boy's singular possessive—That boy's name is Jason.

**7.** whales
plural—The photo shows two whales.

**8.** lifeguard's singular possessive—A lifeguard's job is hard.

**9.** reptiles' plural possessive—Many of the reptiles' cages are large.

**10.** Garcias'
plural possessive—The Garcias' new house is on First Street.

Working Together

# EXERCISE 2  Correcting Nouns

Work with a partner to find and correct errors in how plural and possessive nouns are used in the passages below. Underline any errors, and write the correct form.

¹The odd-looking bird called the dodo was only known

to human's for eighty years' before it disappeared. ²The
      humans            years

                                          sailors
bird had no natural predators before Portuguese sailor's

discovered it. ³It was not afraid of any strangers. ⁴The
                            sailors'
bird was easy prey for the sailors dogs.

   Piranhas'
¹Piranhas's jaws and teeth make them different from
                               creatures'
other underwater animals. ²These creature's appetites are
                                 zoos
huge! ³The piranhas that eat meat are seen in many zoo's.
              inches                animal's
⁴They grow to be about twelve inches' long. ⁵This animals'
desire to attack is rare. ⁶Piranhas are not the man-eater's
                                  man-eaters
that folklore suggests.

# Pronouns

**Pronouns (P)** are words that replace nouns or other pronouns.

▐▐▶ Many pronouns refer to another word in the sentence or in a preceding sentence. The **antecedent (A)** is the word the pronoun replaces.

      **A**             **P**
Many **students** read **their** books on the bus.

   **A**                  **P**
**Augie** enjoys field trips because **he** sees new places.

Some pronouns have more than one antecedent.

  **A**     **A**           **P**        **A**  **P**
**Augie** and **Ty** visited the museum. **They** saw a model **train. It** was fifty years old.

▐▐▶ The chart below shows four types of pronouns and their functions in sentences. Examples of each type are listed on the right.

| Type | Use | Examples |
|---|---|---|
| **Personal Pronouns** | to be subjects and objects | **I** will go with **you** and **them.** **We** need to leave now. |
| **Possessive Pronouns** | to show possession | **My** ticket is here. Where is **yours?** |
| **Indefinite Pronouns** | to express an unspecified person, thing, or amount | **Nobody** should smoke. **Many** are late. |
| **Demonstrative Pronouns** | to point out specific things or people | **This** is the balcony. Look at **that!** |

## Personal Pronouns

| | | |
|---|---|---|
| he | it | they |
| her | me | us |
| him | she | we |
| I | them | you |

## Possessive Pronouns

| | | |
|---|---|---|
| her | mine | their |
| hers | my | theirs |
| his | our | your |
| its | ours | yours |

## Some Indefinite Pronouns

| | |
|---|---|
| anybody | neither |
| anyone | no one |
| both | nobody |
| each | one |
| everybody | several |
| everyone | some |
| few | somebody |
| many | |

## Demonstrative Pronouns

| | |
|---|---|
| this | these |
| that | those |

**HiNT**

The antecedent for a pronoun may be in a previous sentence. One indefinite pronoun has no antecedent.

# EXERCISE 1 Identifying Pronouns and Antecedents

Underline personal, possessive, indefinite, and demonstrative pronouns in each of the following sentences. Then write the antecedent to which each pronoun refers.

**EXAMPLE**    Ed did his report on the life of Anita Castro.

his = Ed

1. Castro was a dressmaker in Los Angeles. She worked with unions to protect dressmakers' rights.
   she = Castro
2. Dressmakers worked long hours for little pay, and they worked under poor conditions.
   they = dressmakers
3. In 1934, Castro organized a strike against poor working conditions. She dedicated her life to establishing unions.
   she, her = Castro
4. Has anyone seen Ed's photograph of Castro?
   anyone
5. If the picture belongs to Ed, give it to him.
   it = picture, him = Ed

# EXERCISE 2 Finding Pronouns

Underline the twelve pronouns in the passage below. On a separate sheet of paper, tell what type each one is.

anyone (indefinite)
one (indefinite)
It (personal)
His (possessive)
He (personal)
they (personal)
their (possessive)
He (personal)
it (personal)
That (demonstrative)
Everyone (indefinite)
his (possessive)

¹Does anyone know who was one of the best right fielders ever to play baseball? ²It was Roberto Clemente. ³His team was the Pittsburgh Pirates. ⁴He married Vera Zabala, and they made Puerto Rico their home. ⁵Clemente died in an accident. ⁶He was delivering relief supplies to Nicaragua following an earthquake. ⁷The plane, which had had mechanical troubles earlier, was overloaded, and it crashed. ⁸That was such a tragedy. ⁹Everyone who knew of his courage was saddened.

# Subject and Object Pronouns

**Personal pronouns** can be used as subjects and as objects.

|  | Singular | Plural |
|---|---|---|
| **Used as Subjects** | I | we |
|  | you | you |
|  | he, she, it | they |
| **Used as Objects** | me | us |
|  | you | you |
|  | him, her, it | them |

➡ Use a **subject pronoun** as a subject or a predicate nominative.

1. A subject pronoun acts like the subject of a sentence or clause.

   **They** joined the tour in Egypt. [not *Them*]

2. A subject pronoun renames the subject and acts like the **predicate nominative** after a linking verb (such as *is*, *was*, *seem*, and *appear*).

   The guides were Ava and **she**. [not *her*]

➡ Use an **object pronoun** as a direct object or the object of a preposition.

1. As a **direct object,** an object pronoun answers the question *whom?* or *what?* after an action verb.

   The travelers saw pyramids and loved **them**. [not *they*]

2. An object pronoun follows a preposition (such as *in, to, with,* and *by*) as the **object of a preposition** in a prepositional phrase. (See Lesson 9.6 for more about prepositional phrases.)

   The bus stopped by **us**. [not *we*]

See **Lessons 6.5** and **6.6** for a review of direct objects and subject complements.

**TEST-TAKING TIP**

To decide whether to use a subject or object pronoun in a compound structure, try each part separately.

Krista and (I, me) led the tour.

(Krista and) **I** led the tour.

See item 3 in Exercise C on page 178 for a sample question.

## EXERCISE 1 Choosing Pronouns

Underline the correct pronoun(s) in each sentence.

> **EXAMPLE** Mari and (<u>she</u>, her) studied at Spelman College.

**1.** The teacher gave Tony and (we, <u>us</u>) this assignment.

**2.** Between you and (I, <u>me</u>), we don't have enough time.

**3.** You and (<u>I</u>, me) will finish it Friday.

**4.** My teachers are Dr. Lipski and (him, <u>he</u>).

**5.** Mr. River told you and (I, <u>me</u>) about Marian Wright Edelman.

**6.** (<u>She</u>, Her) and her family lived in South Carolina.

**7.** Her father taught (<u>her</u>, she) about the value of education.

**8.** (<u>She and he</u>, Her and him) did hours of community service.

**9.** The two who have finished our papers are Mari and (me, <u>I</u>).

**10.** Mari read her paper to Tony and (<u>me</u>, I).

Working Together

## EXERCISE 2 Revising a Paragraph

Work with a partner to find four errors with pronouns in the paragraph. Underline the incorrect pronouns. Then rewrite the corrected paragraph on a separate sheet of paper.
See Answer Key at www.grammarforwriting.com.

**James Baldwin**

¹In school, you and <u>me</u> are learning about James Baldwin. ²The first article that he wrote was printed in a school magazine when <u>him</u> was about thirteen. ³Our teacher told you and <u>I</u> about his early life. ⁴Richard Wright, a well-known writer, befriended Baldwin and supported him in his writing efforts. ⁵We learned about writer's block. ⁶Baldwin once suffered from it. ⁷Today two of America's greatest writers are <u>him</u> and Wright.

# Pronoun Agreement

A pronoun should agree in number with its **antecedent,** the word that the pronoun refers to. Singular pronouns refer to singular nouns. Plural pronouns refer to plural nouns.

▸ When two or more antecedents are joined by *and*, use a plural pronoun.

> The **piano** and **violin** need tuning because **they** sound terrible.

▸ When two or more singular antecedents are joined by *or* or *nor*, use a singular pronoun.

> Either **Dante** or **Joe** will play **his** guitar.

▸ When the antecedent is a compound subject that refers to only one person, use a singular pronoun.

> My cousin and best friend is practicing **her** music.

▸ A pronoun that does not refer to a specific person, place, thing, or idea is an **indefinite pronoun.** (See Lessons 7.3 and 10.5.) As the lists on the right show, some indefinite pronouns always take singular pronouns, and others always take plural pronouns.

> **One** of the girls lost **her** oboe reed. **[singular]**

> **Several** of the students did **their** homework. **[plural]**

**Note:** When the antecedent of a singular indefinite pronoun refers to males and females, use *his or her.*

> **No one** should write in **his or her** book.

▸ Depending on the word(s) they refer to, the indefinite pronouns *all*, *any*, *most*, and *some* can be singular or plural.

> **All** of the <u>music</u> is in **its** original wrapping. **[singular]**

> **All** of the <u>students</u> had **their** uniforms cleaned. **[plural]**

## Singular Indefinite Pronouns

| | |
|---|---|
| anybody | neither |
| anyone | no one |
| each | nobody |
| either | one |
| everybody | somebody |
| everyone | someone |

## Plural Indefinite Pronouns

| | |
|---|---|
| both | many |
| few | several |

### WRITING HiNT

When the use of *his or her* sounds awkward, try rewriting the sentence.

**Students** should not write in **their** books.

**No one** should write in **the** books.

## Exercise 1 Choosing Correct Pronouns

Circle the correct pronoun in the parentheses.

> **EXAMPLE** Either Jack or Josh has lost (his) their) jacket.

**1.** Mr. and Mrs. Chou are upset with (their) its) sons.

**2.** Neither Jack nor Josh remembered (his) their) own chores.

**3.** Some of the girls finished (their) her) jobs.

**4.** Everyone should make (their, his or her) bed.

**5.** Both of the boys do (his, their) own laundry.

## Exercise 2 Editing for Pronoun Use

Read the paragraph to find five incorrectly used pronouns. Cross them out. Then write the correct form of each.

> **EXAMPLE** Either Sam or Mark was there with ~~their~~ *his* friends.

**HINT**

Sometimes the object of a prepositional phrase that comes right after an indefinite pronoun gives you a clue about whether to use a singular or a plural pronoun.

Most of the **food** lost **its** freshness. [singular]

Most of the **shirts** had **their** labels. [plural]

¹Kitty and Brianna went to the teen center where ~~she~~ *they* took chess lessons. ²Kitty's parents and Brianna's parents were pleased because each of the girls enjoyed ~~their~~ *her* time at the center. ³One of the girls brought treats from ~~their~~ *her* own kitchen, and everyone at the center always had ~~their~~ *his or her* fair share. ⁴All of the seventh graders liked the center because ~~he or she~~ *they* felt welcome there.

**Working Together**

Answers will vary. See sample answer in Answer Key at www.grammarforwriting.com.

## Exercise 3 Writing with Pronouns

Work with a partner. Write a radio commercial for a community center. Make sure that all pronouns agree with their antecedents. Use at least one singular and one plural indefinite pronoun.

# Clear Pronoun Reference

Always make sure that the **antecedent** of a pronoun is clearly stated. A vague pronoun reference can confuse readers.

➡ Make sure that each personal pronoun refers clearly to one antecedent. If a pronoun could refer to more than one word, reword the sentence to make the antecedent clear, or eliminate the pronoun.

| | |
|---|---|
| UNCLEAR | When Jasmine handed her sister the dog, **she** sneezed. [Who sneezed? Jasmine, her sister, or the dog?] |
| CLEAR ANTECEDENT | Jasmine sneezed when she handed the dog to her sister. [Reword the sentence.] |
| NO PRONOUN | When Jasmine handed her sister the dog, **Jasmine** sneezed. [Substitute a noun for the pronoun.] |

➡ Be sure that pronouns like *it, this, that,* and *which* refer to a specific word or phrase. Otherwise, the meaning is unclear.

| | |
|---|---|
| VAGUE | Jasmine wants to be a kindergarten teacher because **it** interests her. [What interests her? There is no clear antecedent for *it* in the sentence.] |
| CLEAR | Jasmine wants to be a kindergarten teacher because **working with young children** interests her. [Eliminate the pronoun.] |

**WRITING HINT**

As you rewrite a sentence to correct a pronoun reference problem, avoid using a double subject.

Jasmine ~~she~~ sneezed.

Her sister ~~she~~ is allergic to cats.

## EXERCISE 1  Clarifying Pronoun References

Underline the pronoun in each sentence. Then rewrite the sentence to make the pronoun reference clear.
Answers will vary. Sample answers are shown.

EXAMPLE  Grandma and Mrs. Damian read the newspaper, but <u>she</u> forgot what the article said.

Grandma and Mrs. Damian read the newspaper, but Mrs. Damian forgot what the article said.

1. Dad and Jim walked out the door, but <u>he</u> forgot to turn off the light. Dad and Jim walked out the door, but Jim forgot to turn off the light.

2. Mom and Aunt Alice went together, but <u>she</u> didn't like the movie. Mom and Aunt Alice went together, but Mom didn't like the movie.

> **HiNT**
> These sentences can be rewritten in more than one way. The key is to make clear to whom or to what the pronoun refers. You may add, delete, or rearrange words.

3. Dad saw the movie and the play but didn't like <u>it</u>.
Dad saw the movie and the play but didn't like the movie.
4. Read the reviews and the songs, and memorize <u>them</u>.
Read the reviews and the songs. Memorize the song lyrics.
5. In the article <u>it</u> says that the play was clever.
The article says that the play was clever.

## EXERCISE 2 Rewriting Sentences

Decide whether each of the pronouns in bold has a clear antecedent. If it does, write *C*. If the pronoun reference is unclear, rewrite the sentence to correct the problem.
Students' revised sentences will vary. Sample answers are shown.

**EXAMPLE** **It** said on the Web site that researching family history is easy.

The expert said on her Web site that researching family history is easy.

1. Many businesses and Web sites have facts about family histories. **It** is very helpful. Many businesses and Web sites have information about family histories, and the sites are very helpful.
2. Families can search for information about relatives, and they can share information. **It** brings families together. Searching for and sharing information about relatives brings families together.
3. My parents do research, and **they** have learned a lot. C
4. Time and energy are needed by family history buffs. **It** is not easy. Family history buffs need time and energy because doing a family history is not easy.
5. The article on family history on the Web site was updated. **That** is useful. That useful article on family history was updated on the Web site.
6. When I read the article, I was surprised that **it** was so long. C
7. When **they** have time, my cousins should research their families. C
8. Eliza and Beth interviewed their grandfather, but **she** was disappointed with the interview. Eliza and Beth interviewed their grandfather, but Eliza was disappointed with the interview.
9. The girls met with their cousins, and **they** asked many questions. The girls asked many questions when they met with their cousins.
10. Eliza called Beth after **she** got home. After Eliza got home, she called Beth.

# Persuasive Essay

Every day you encounter persuasive arguments. Bloggers may argue their viewpoints online. Friends may try to convince you to watch a movie they enjoyed. A commercial on TV may urge you to buy a new product. Persuasive writing attempts to convince readers to share the author's opinion or to take a particular action.

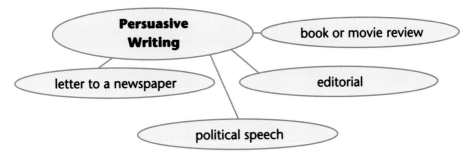

Another kind of persuasive writing is a **persuasive essay**, or **argument**.

## Key Features

- precise claim, or thesis
- logical reasons and relevant evidence as support
- words and phrases that clarify the relationships among your claims, reasons, and evidence
- discussion of opposing claims
- formal style
- conclusion that follows from the argument presented

## ASSIGNMENT

**TASK:** Write a three- to four-page **persuasive essay** about a change you would like to see in your community or your school.

**AUDIENCE:** your classmates

**PURPOSE:** to persuade readers to agree with you

# Prewriting

> **Pick a Topic** First, make a list of changes you want to see in your school and community. Since your purpose is to convince your readers of your argument, pick the change that matters most to you and can be easily supported by evidence.

Then, state your opinion in a clear **claim,** or **thesis statement,** in your introductory paragraph. Make sure the thesis statement is neither too broad nor too narrow for the length of your paper.

A claim states the main idea of your essay.
For more about thesis statements, see **Lesson 5.2.**

| | |
|---|---|
| **TOO BROAD** | Everyone must care for the environment. |
| **TOO NARROW** | Mrs. Sanchez should recycle aluminum cans. |
| **STRONG** | As a community, we can work toward a cleaner environment by planting trees and improving our recycling program. |

> **State Your Reasons and Evidence** Next, provide at least two convincing **reasons** for your claim.

| | |
|---|---|
| **REASON 1** | Trees improve air quality and surroundings. |
| **REASON 2** | Our weak recycling program does not eliminate nearly as much waste as it could. |

Then present **evidence** to support each reason.

## WRITING HINT

Avoid or explain any technical terms your audience may not know.

We must make our community green, or environmentally friendly.

| Evidence | Definition | Example |
|---|---|---|
| **Facts** | statements that can be proved true | Thirty percent of our community's garbage is recyclable. |
| **Examples** | specific cases or instances | Imagine how much more beautiful our downtown would be with more trees. |
| **Anecdotes** | brief stories or incidents | I have seen lots of unnecessary wastepaper in our school. |
| **Quotations** | an expert's spoken or written words | Dr. Ahn claims that in fifty years "the earth will change radically." |

# Prewriting

**Make Room for Opposition** Make your argument stronger by anticipating and responding to **counterarguments,** or arguments that could be used against your opinion. Jot down a counterargument and your response to it in a chart.

| My Opinion | We must improve our recycling program. |
|---|---|
| Counterargument | Improving the program will cost too much money. |
| My Response | The money we use to improve the program will be worth it over time. It is more valuable to have a healthier environment than an environment full of overflowing landfills. |

**Sound Convincing** Use at least one persuasive technique in your essay.

- **Rhetorical question** A rhetorical question is a question that is asked for effect. No answer is expected.

- **Parallel structure** Parallelism is the repetition of similar grammatical structures. (See Lesson 2.4 for examples.)

- **Repetition** Repetition is the reuse of key words or phrases.

Which persuasive techniques are used in this passage from a famous speech?

## Literary Model

¹What constitutes an American? ²Not color nor race nor religion. ³Not the pedigree of his family nor the place of his birth. ⁴Not the coincidence of his citizenship. ⁵Not his social status nor his bank account. ⁶Not his trade nor his profession. ⁷An American is one who loves justice and believes in the dignity of man.

—Excerpt from "What Is an American?" by Harold Ickes

WRITING HINT

Use an outline to organize your paper in a clear way.

Claim

I. Reason 1

  A. Evidence 1

  B. Evidence 2

  C. Evidence 3

II. Reason 2

  A. Evidence 1

  B. Evidence 2

  C. Evidence 3

For more about the parts of an essay, see **Chapter 5.**

Topic sentence

Transition

Statistic

Personal experience

Statistic

## Drafting

▶ **Organize the Body** ▶ Now organize your details into the three basic parts of an essay. Each part serves a different purpose.

1. Your **introduction** presents your topic and thesis, or claim, and should catch your audience's attention. Begin your introduction with a question, a quotation, or a fact.

2. Your **body paragraphs** present your reasons and evidence. Start your first body paragraph with a topic sentence that states your first reason. Then present evidence for that reason. You may need several paragraphs to state your evidence. Add **transitions,** such as *next* and *another reason*, to connect ideas between sentences and paragraphs.

3. Your **conclusion** restates your main points and gives your readers a sense of completeness. It should also clearly state the action you want your audience to take.

Read the body paragraph below. How effective is it?

### Writing Model

¹A stronger community recycling program will improve our environment. ²For example, think about the last time you threw out your garbage. ³How many bags were there? ⁴Now multiply that by 5,250, our town's population. ⁵That is just for one week. ⁶Consider the amount of waste we produce each year. ⁷If you are still unsure, visit the county's landfill like I did. ⁸We create one hundred tons of garbage per year. ⁹With changes, garbage production can be reduced by 30 percent.

# Revising

Now that you are done drafting, review and revise your work. Use these questions to help guide your revision. The model below shows the revisions one writer made to an introduction.

> As you revise, keep in mind the traits of good writing. See **Lesson 1.3.**

## Revising Questions

- ❏ How clear and concise is my claim?
- ❏ How convincing are my reasons and evidence?
- ❏ Where can I add persuasive techniques?
- ❏ How reasonable is my tone?
- ❏ Where can I add transitions to clarify the order?
- ❏ How strong is my response to the counterargument?

### Writing Model

¹Over the next fifty years, the earth will be ^radically changed by pollution. ²Imagine seeing a dense fog of unclean air and garbage lining the streets. ^Is that the type of world you want to live in? ³What can we do? ⁴As a community, we can work toward a cleaner environment by planting trees and improving our recycling program.

^First, ⁵We must plant trees. ⁶Trees clean the air by taking in carbon dioxide and releasing oxygen. ⁷Too much carbon dioxide is polluting our air.

Grab your reader's attention.

Use persuasive techniques, such as rhetorical questions.

Use transitions between sentences and paragraphs.

## Editing and Proofreading

After revising, review your draft one last time to correct any errors in grammar, usage, punctuation, and mechanics.

## Editing and Proofreading Checklist

❏ Have I checked that all words are spelled correctly?
❏ Have I capitalized the first letter of every sentence?
❏ Have I ended each sentence with a period, an exclamation point, or a question mark?
❏ Are any words missing or run together?
❏ Have I avoided run-on sentences?
❏ Is every paragraph indented?

**Proofreading Symbols**

Ϥ Delete.
⊙ Add a period.
# Add a space.
/ Make lowercase.
¶ Start a new paragraph.
≡ Capitalize.

### Writing Model

¹We must remember that the earth needs us to take care of it. ²The solution is not about taking action, we take action already by throwing garbage away instead of recycling it. ³The solution is about taking the right action. ⁴Our lack of trees and our abundance of garbage are harming the earth. ⁵Do we want to save our earth, or Do we want to turn it into a dying planet? ⁶We all must dedicate ourselves to solving this problem. ⁷If we do not, who will?

## Editing and Proofreading

**Avoid Pronoun Errors** Pronouns are words that stand in for nouns. Some examples include *he, she, it, they, them, us,* and *we.* Pronouns must refer to a clear **antecedent,** or the word or words they replace.

NOT CLEAR    When I asked Jon and Lennie about joining the environmental club, **he** told me to fill out the proper forms.

CLEAR    When I asked **Jon and Lennie** about joining the environmental club, **Jon** told me to fill out the proper forms.

> For more help with pronoun reference, see **Lesson 7.6.**

## Publishing and Presenting

Use one of the suggestions below to present your paper.

1. **Give a speech.** Turn your essay into a speech. Transfer all of your main ideas and supporting details onto note cards. Use these note cards to prompt you during your speech. Be sure to practice your pacing, tone, and gestures before you present.

2. **Submit an editorial.** Send your essay to your school's student newspaper or to a community newspaper that accepts outside editorials. Before you submit it, check to make sure your essay is the right length and follows other publication guidelines.

3. **Have a discussion.** Discuss your essay with a family member. How convincing is your argument to him or her? What suggestions does he or she have for improving it?

Consider adding your essay to your **writing portfolio.** Ask:

1. How does this essay reflect my best possible effort?
2. How does this essay show my progress as a writer?

> **Reflect On Your Writing**
>
> - Which part of your essay—the introduction, body, or conclusion—do you think is most effective? Why?
> - Which part of your essay did you have the most trouble writing? Why?

# Chapter Review

## A. Practice Test

Read each sentence below carefully. If you find an error, choose the underlined part that must be changed to make the sentence correct. Fill in the circle for the corresponding letter. If there is no error, fill in circle *E*.

EXAMPLE

Ⓐ Ⓑ Ⓒ ● Ⓔ   <u>Many</u> experts say <u>that</u> students who identify <u>their</u> learning
 A            B                    C

styles get more out of <u>her</u> education.   <u>No error</u>
                         D                    E

Ⓐ Ⓑ ● Ⓓ Ⓔ   **1.** <u>The concept of</u> learning styles became popular <u>with</u> the
            A                                          B

publication of <u>Howard Gardners</u> book <u>*Frames of Mind*</u>.
                    C                        D

<u>No error</u>
 E

Ⓐ Ⓑ Ⓒ ● Ⓔ   **2.** <u>Some</u> <u>people</u> are visual <u>learners</u> <u>because we learn</u> best from
            A     B            C        D

pictures and diagrams.   <u>No error</u>
                          E

Ⓐ Ⓑ Ⓒ ● Ⓔ   **3.** Auditory <u>learners</u> benefit <u>more from</u> things <u>they</u> can hear.
                      A             B              C

Music and sound play a big role in <u>its lives</u>.   <u>No error</u>
                                      D              E

When you are asked to identify sentence errors, you must judge every word in context. Always read the *whole* sentence before making your choice, even if you think you see an error right away.

Ⓐ●ⒸⒹⒺ **4.** <u>Athletes</u> may have trouble communicating with artists
　　　　　　A

　　　　because <u>his learning</u> style <u>is</u> visual <u>rather than</u> physical.
　　　　　　　　　B　　　　　　C　　　　　　D

　　　　<u>No error</u>
　　　　　E

●ⒷⒸⒹⒺ **5.** My <u>friend and me</u> sometimes have <u>misunderstandings</u>
　　　　　　　　A　　　　　　　　　　　　　　B

　　　　due to <u>our</u> different learning <u>styles.</u>　<u>No error</u>
　　　　　　C　　　　　　　　　　D　　　　E

ⒶⒷ●ⒹⒺ **6.** <u>All</u> of <u>Sue's</u> books are <u>audiobook's</u> because <u>Sue</u> is an
　　　　　A　　　B　　　　　　C　　　　　　D

　　　　auditory learner.　<u>No error</u>
　　　　　　　　　　　　E

Ⓐ●ⒸⒹⒺ **7.** <u>Some</u> <u>kids</u> learning <u>styles</u> can change <u>over</u> time.
　　　　　A　　B　　　　　C　　　　　　D

　　　　<u>No error</u>
　　　　　E

ⒶⒷ●ⒹⒺ **8.** Al says <u>we are</u> both visual <u>learners</u> because <u>him</u> and <u>I</u>
　　　　　　　　A　　　　　　　B　　　　　C　　　D

　　　　prefer movies to books.　<u>No error</u>
　　　　　　　　　　　　　　E

ⒶⒷⒸⒹ● **9.** <u>I think</u> <u>I am</u> a verbal learner because reading, writing,
　　　　　A　　　B

　　　　and <u>talking are</u> what help <u>me</u> learn best.　<u>No error</u>
　　　　　　C　　　　　　　　D　　　　　　E

ⒶⒷⒸ●Ⓔ **10.** <u>No matter</u> what <u>your</u> learning style is, <u>you</u> <u>and him</u> can
　　　　　　A　　　　　B　　　　　　　　C　　D

　　　　find a way to succeed.　<u>No error</u>
　　　　　　　　　　　　　E

## B. Identifying Nouns

Read each sentence below. Label each underlined noun with all of the following terms that apply.

$PR$ = proper      $CO$ = collective      $PL$ = plural      $PS$ = possessive

1. <u>Parents</u> [PL] often determine what is safe and appropriate for their <u>children</u> [PL] to watch on television by relying on some <u>group's</u> [CO, PS] guidelines.

2. This <u>system's</u> [PS] problem is that "safe" and "appropriate" are extremely subjective <u>terms</u> [PL].

3. For example, <u>Mary Jackson's</u> [PR, PS] opinion may differ from another's on a documentary about <u>World War II</u> [PR].

4. <u>Mrs. Jackson</u> [PR] might find it too violent for her <u>sons</u> [PL] to watch, while <u>Mr. Rosenberg</u> [PR] thinks it's an important history lesson for his <u>daughter's</u> [PS] <u>friends</u> [PL].

5. Families must watch television together to truly assess a <u>station's</u> [PS] programming for <u>kids</u> [PL].

## C. Choosing and Identifying Pronouns

Read each sentence below. Underline the correct word in parentheses. Then label its function: $S$ for subject, $PN$ for predicate nominative, $O$ for object, or $PS$ for possessive.

_S_ 1. My sister and (me, <u>I</u>) decided to make dinner for our mom last night.

_O_ 2. I told (<u>her</u>, she) that we should make something simple, like spaghetti.

_O_ 3. My sister baked a soufflé for Lennie and (we, <u>us</u>).

_PN_ 4. The best cooks are Jill and (<u>I</u>, me).

_PS_ 5. I smiled when the (ovens, <u>oven's</u>) timer buzzed.

## D. Correcting Pronoun Reference

Each sentence below contains a pronoun whose antecedent is unclear. Underline the unclear pronoun. Then, rewrite the sentence to make the pronoun reference clear. Answers may vary. Sample answers are shown.

1. Hannah told Rachel that <u>she</u> could adopt a cat.
   Hannah said that Rachel could adopt a cat.
2. Rachel discussed cat care with Hannah before <u>she</u> went to the shelter.
   Before Rachel went to the shelter, Hannah discussed cat care with her.
3. Hannah gave Rachel a few tips as <u>she</u> looked at the cats in front of them.
   As Rachel looked at the cats in front of them, Hannah gave her a few tips.
4. Rachel liked the black cat best because <u>she</u> was friendly.
   Because the black cat was friendly, Rachel liked her best.
5. In the shelter, <u>it</u> advises visitors to stay quiet.
   The shelter rules advise visitors to stay quiet.

## E. Revising a Persuasive Paragraph

Rewrite the draft below on a separate sheet of paper. Correct any noun or pronoun errors. Also fix any errors in grammar, usage, punctuation, mechanics, and spelling. Add a counterargument and response at a logical point in the paragraph.

Answers will vary. See sample answer in Answer Key at www.grammarforwriting.com.

[1]Principal tate is considering cutting our schools budget for arts education in order to provide student's with more test-prep materials. [2]These would be a big mistake. [3]Everyone should have the best education they can. [4]In order to live fully in the world, students' need to be exposed to culture in the form of music, art, theater, and dance. [5]If Principal Tate cuts the art budget, no one will leave School prepared to appreciate and understand the world around them.

# Verbs

# Verbs

Every sentence has at least one verb. **Verbs** are words that express an action or a state of being.

▮▶ The easiest **action verbs** to identify show an action you can see: *kick, throw, skate, climb, pounce.* Other action verbs show an action that takes place in your mind: *think, like, enjoy, wonder.*

Action verbs **(v)** often take a direct object **(DO)**. (See Lesson 6.5 for more about direct objects.)

>      V          DO
> The skater **won** the gold medal.

▮▶ **Linking verbs (LV)** do not express action. They join the subject with a subject complement **(sc)**, a word that identifies or describes the subject. (See Lesson 6.6 for more about subject complements.)

>              LV   SC
> The quarterback **was** tired.

Notice both kinds of verbs in the passage below.

### Literary Model

Miss Saunders <u>is</u> a motion machine this morning. She <u>sets</u> down her briefcase, <u>throws</u> her black bag into the closet up front, <u>slaps</u> her hands together like giant paddles, and <u>tells</u> everybody to get quiet.

—Excerpt from *The Skin I'm In* by Sharon G. Flake

▮▶ Many sentences contain a verb phrase. A **verb phrase** has a **main verb (MV)** and at least one **helping verb (HV)**.

>      HV     MV
> The runner **may have fallen** behind during the last lap.
> HV       MV            MV
> **Will** the coach **change** his mind and **call** us?

## Some Linking Verbs

| | |
|---|---|
| am | look |
| appear | seem |
| are | smell |
| become | sound |
| feel | taste |
| grow | was |
| is | were |

### Remember

The same verb can be a linking verb in one sentence and an action verb in another.
>         LV     SC
> That **smelled** sweet.
>      V    DO
> We **smelled** smoke.

Point out that "to get" in the last sentence is an infinitive, or a verb form that often begins with the word *to* and is followed by a verb. Students will learn more about infinitives in Lesson 8.6.

## Some Helping Verbs

| | | |
|---|---|---|
| be | did | is |
| been | do | were |
| being | does | will |
| can | have | |

## EXERCISE 1 Recognizing Verbs

Read the following sports article. Underline all of the verbs, including any helping verbs in a verb phrase.

> ¹Austrian Markus Stockl <u>is</u> a great athlete. ²He <u>set</u> a new world speed record in the downhill mountain bike class. ³Stockl <u>crushed</u> his own record by 14.3 mph. ⁴He <u>flew</u> down a snow slope in Chile and <u>hit</u> a speed of 130.7 mph. ⁵Videos of his record-breaking run <u>have flooded</u> the Internet, and sports chat rooms <u>have been filled</u> with talk about him. ⁶His skills <u>are</u> amazing.

## EXERCISE 2 Identifying Verbs

Label each verb in the following sentences as an *action verb* or a *linking verb*.

**EXAMPLE**   The air smelled fresh as the climbers were arriving.

smelled (linking verb), were arriving (action verb)

1. The rock climber seemed strong as she moved to the cliff.
   seemed (linking verb), moved (action verb)
2. Her partner had sprained his ankle.
   had sprained (action verb)
3. The climbers' voices sounded weak, but they were smiling.
   sounded (linking verb), were smiling (action verb)
4. Did they worry when the rain started?
   Did worry (action verb), started (action verb)
5. The two climbers looked pale and gasped for air.
   looked (linking verb), gasped (action verb)

**Working Together**

## EXERCISE 3 Writing a Dialogue

Answers will vary. Students' dialogues should have at least five action verbs and five linking verbs. See sample answer in Answer Key at www. grammarforwriting.com.

With a partner, choose a sports event, and create a dialogue between two television announcers. Use at least five linking verbs and five action verbs to describe the players and action.

**EXAMPLE**   <u>Announcer 1:</u> The team is on the field.

<u>Announcer 2:</u> The Wildcats win the coin toss.

# Regular and Irregular Verbs

Every verb has four basic forms, or **principal parts.**

| Present | I **play** basketball. |
|---|---|
| Present Participle | I **am playing** on the school team. |
| Past | I **played** with energy. |
| Past Participle | I **have played** in every game. |

Note that helping verbs are used with present participle and past participle forms. (See Lesson 8.1 for more about helping verbs.)

➠ There are two kinds of verbs: regular and irregular. A **regular verb** is a verb whose past and past participle are formed by adding -*ed* or -*d* to the present. The present participle of regular verbs is formed by adding -*ing* to the present.

| Present | Present Participle (Use with *am, is, are, was, were.*) | Past | Past Participle (Use with *has, had, have.*) |
|---|---|---|---|
| walk | (is) walk**ing** | walk**ed** | (had) walk**ed** |
| jump | (is) jump**ing** | jump**ed** | (had) jump**ed** |

➠ Unlike regular verbs, **irregular verbs** do not form their past and past participle forms by following this rule. The past and past participle forms of irregular verbs are formed in a variety of ways.

In some cases the past and past participle forms are the same.

| Present | Past | Past Participle |
|---|---|---|
| say | said | (had) said |
| win | won | (had) won |

However, sometimes the forms of irregular verbs are different.

| Present | Past | Past Participle |
|---|---|---|
| go | went | (had) gone |
| take | took | (had) taken |

**WRITING HINT**

You will need to change the spelling of some verbs when you add -*ing* or -*ed* endings.

like ➞ liking

worry ➞ worried

drop ➞ dropped

For more about spelling rules, see **Lesson 12.4.**

## HiNT

Never use a helping verb with the past tense.

INCORRECT The storm **had began** on Tuesday.

CORRECT The storm **began** on Tuesday.

Never use a participle form without a helping verb.

INCORRECT We **seen** lightning.

CORRECT We **have seen** lightning.

GRAMMARIAN

WOOF
WOOFS
WOOFING
WOOFED

v. harris

http://www.CartoonStock.com

## Exercise 1 Identifying Verb Forms

Write *present participle*, *past*, or *past participle* for the verb underlined in each sentence.

EXAMPLE    Ken <u>got</u> the story idea from his uncle. **past**

**1.** One of Ken's uncles is <u>hiking</u> in Alaska. present participle

**2.** He and a friend <u>brought</u> camping gear and sturdy shoes. past

**3.** Both of them <u>swam</u> in the lake. past

**4.** By Friday they had <u>caught</u> many fish in a river. past participle

**5.** That night, they <u>built</u> a fire and cooked the fish. past

## Exercise 2 Choosing Correct Verbs

Draw a line under the correct verb form in the parentheses.

**1.** They (fallen, <u>had fallen</u>) asleep under a starry sky.

**2.** Suddenly, Ken's uncle (heared, <u>heard</u>) a rustling nearby.

**3.** A bear (<u>was eating</u>, had ate) their leftovers.

**4.** Panic (<u>came</u>, had came) over Ken's uncle.

**5.** He should (have knew, <u>have known</u>) better.

**6.** The campers (breaking, <u>had broken</u>) the first rule for survival.

**7.** Why hadn't you (<u>taken</u>, took) the food away?

**8.** In the quiet night, they had (became, <u>become</u>) careless.

**9.** Suddenly, a tree limb (<u>fell</u>, falled) to the ground with a crash.

**10.** The startled bear (known, <u>knew</u>) it was time to lumber off.

## Write What You Think
Answers will vary. See sample answer in Answer Key at www.grammarforwriting.com.

On a separate sheet of paper, write your reaction to one of the quotations below. Use and underline three participle forms.

"If you can dream it, you can do it." —Walt Disney

"A person who has never made a mistake has never tried anything new." —Albert Einstein

# More Irregular Verbs

LESSON

8.3

There is no single rule to help you learn how to form the **principal parts** of **irregular verbs.** You can look up the forms of these verbs in a dictionary, but it's good to learn the common spellings because you will use them often when you write.

Below are some common irregular verbs.

| Present | Present Participle (Use with *am, is, are, was, were.*) | Past | Past Participle (Use with *has, had, have.*) |
|---------|---------------------------------------------------------|------|----------------------------------------------|
| become | (is) becoming | became | (had) become |
| break | (is) breaking | broke | (had) broken |
| choose | (is) choosing | chose | (had) chosen |
| come | (is) coming | came | (had) come |
| drive | (is) driving | drove | (had) driven |
| give | (is) giving | gave | (had) given |
| grow | (is) growing | grew | (had) grown |
| know | (is) knowing | knew | (had) known |
| leave | (is) leaving | left | (had) left |
| make | (is) making | made | (had) made |
| ride | (is) riding | rode | (had) ridden |
| run | (is) running | ran | (had) run |
| see | (is) seeing | saw | (had) seen |
| show | (is) showing | showed | (had) shown |
| speak | (is) speaking | spoke | (had) spoken |
| stand | (is) standing | stood | (had) stood |
| swim | (is) swimming | swam | (had) swum |
| teach | (is) teaching | taught | (had) taught |
| think | (is) thinking | thought | (had) thought |
| wear | (is) wearing | worn | (had) worn |
| write | (is) writing | wrote | (had) written |

See **Lesson 8.2** for more about irregular verbs and their principal parts.

**R**emember

Remember that a present participle is formed by adding *-ing* to the present form of the verb.

Anne Frank's bravery and hope **continue** to impress people. **[present]**

Anne Frank's bravery is **continuing** to make an impression. **[present participle]**

See **Lesson 12.4** to review spelling changes you may need to make to form a present participle.

Verbs

**R**emember

Note the irregular forms of *to be*.

**Present**

| I am | we are |
|---|---|
| you are | you are |
| he is | they are |

**Past**

| I was | we were |
|---|---|
| you were | you were |
| he was | they were |

The present participle is *being*. The past participle is *been*.

# Exercise 1 Using Irregular Verbs

On a separate sheet of paper, rewrite each sentence. Use the correct past, present participle, or past participle form of the verb in parentheses. Do not add or delete any other words.

**EXAMPLE** The picture (show) a wheelbarrow from China.

*The picture showed a wheelbarrow from China.*

1. Long ago, the Chinese (make) a plow of cast iron.
Long ago, the Chinese made a plow of cast iron.
2. A fourth-century helicopter toy (lead) to today's helicopters.
A fourth-century helicopter toy led to today's helicopters.
3. Chinese warriors (ride) horses into battle.
Chinese warriors rode horses into battle.
4. Schools in China have (teach) about Confucius.
Schools in China have taught about Confucius.
5. Students in ancient China (write) essays to pass exams.
Students in ancient China wrote essays to pass exams.
6. The Chinese population has (grow).
The Chinese population has grown.
7. The world's population is (grow) rapidly.
The world's population is growing rapidly.
8. China's population has (rise) to more than 1.3 billion people.
China's population has risen to more than 1.3 billion people.
9. Many people have (think) that overpopulation causes problems.
Many people have thought that overpopulation causes problems.
10. We were (speak) about this yesterday in history.
We were speaking about this yesterday in history.
11. Carey (bring) in an article about world population.
Carey brought in an article about world population.
12. I have (think) a lot about this issue.
I have thought a lot about this issue.
13. Have you (choose) a topic for your history report?
Have you chosen a topic for your history report?
14. Mrs. Clark (give) us a list of ideas.
Mrs. Clark gave us a list of ideas.
15. The librarian is (come) to our class to discuss research.
The librarian is coming to our class to discuss research.

Working Together

# Exercise 2 Writing with Irregular Verbs

Talk with a partner about your families—siblings, grandparents, cousins, and so on. Write five sentences using at least three forms of different irregular verbs.

Answers will vary. See sample answers in Answer Key at www.grammarforwriting.com.

**EXAMPLE** I grew up as the youngest of four children.

# Verb Tense

The **tense** of a verb shows when an action takes place.

▐▶ Verbs have three simple tenses.

**1.** The **present** shows action happening now or repeatedly.

    She **runs** each afternoon.

**2.** The **past** shows action that happened in the past.

    I **ran** yesterday for the first time.

**3.** The **future** shows action that will happen in the future.

    I **will run** tomorrow. I **shall complete the race in an hour.**

▐▶ Verbs have three perfect tenses.

**1.** The **present perfect** shows action already completed.

    I **have run** enough for today.

**2.** The **past perfect** shows action that happened before another past action or time.

    I **had run** before it began to snow.

**3.** The **future perfect** shows action that will be completed before another future action or time.

    By next Tuesday, I **will have run** six miles.

▐▶ Do not switch from one verb tense to another unless you need to show a change in time. Keep tenses consistent.

| | |
|---|---|
| FAULTY | Habib **takes** piano lessons and **practiced** a lot. |
| CORRECT | Habib **took** piano lessons and **practiced** a lot. |
| CORRECT | Habib **takes** piano lessons and **practices** a lot. |

**R**emember

Notice that you need helping verbs to form some of the six verb tenses shown above. See **Lessons 8.1** and **8.2** for more about helping verbs and verb forms.

# EXERCISE 1 Keeping Tenses Consistent

Underline the verb in each sentence that is consistent in tense with the other verb in the same sentence.

    **EXAMPLE**   Tricks are hurtful, and they (<u>seem</u>, seemed) cruel.

1. Bullies tease others because they (liked, <u>like</u>) the power.

2. One bully followed me home and (pushes, <u>pushed</u>) me.

3. Then his friend (laughs, <u>laughed</u>) and took my book.

4. My friends (<u>asked</u>, ask) me how I was feeling.

5. My parents faced bullies when they (are, <u>were</u>) young, too.

## EXERCISE 2 Correcting Verbs

Rewrite the e-mail. Correct six verbs that are in the wrong tense.
Answers may vary. See sample answer in Answer Key at www.grammarforwriting.com.

**EXAMPLE**   When I see the e-mail, I was happy.

*When I saw the e-mail, I was happy.*

| **To:** | mlmcnulty@internet.com |
| --- | --- |
| **From:** | jvaladez@internet.com |
| **Subject:** | Important news |

Dear Martin,

   ¹Guess what happened? ²A letter for me comes yesterday. ³I will pick up the mail, and there it was. ⁴When I open the envelope and looked at the note inside, I get so excited. ⁵The letter was from my school, and it will say that I receive this year's Leadership Prize at a special ceremony next week. ⁶That will be so much fun!

Your friend,

Juan

# Active and Passive Voice

In a sentence with a verb in the **active voice,** the subject performs an action. In a sentence with a verb in the **passive voice,** the subject receives the action of the verb.

■▶ In the passive voice, the verb phrase always includes a form of the helping verb *be,* such as *am, is, are, been, was,* or *were,* and the past participle of the main verb.

ACTIVE    Scientists **see** new species of fish every week.
[The subject, *scientists*, performs the action.]

PASSIVE    New species of fish **are seen** by scientists.
[The subject, *species*, receives the action.]

■▶ Use the passive voice when the doer of the action is unknown or unimportant. Also use passive voice to emphasize the action or the receiver of the action.

Several photos **were taken.**
[The writer does not know who took the photos.]

The coins **were** carefully **unearthed** by divers.
[The writer emphasizes the unearthing of the coins, not who unearthed them.]

■▶ In general, use the active voice to save words and make your writing livelier. Notice how the passage below contains strong verbs to show the excitement of a soccer game.

## Literary Model

¹Victor <u>called</u> for the ball, and Shandra <u>got</u> it to him with a mighty heave. ²He <u>fought</u> his way out of a pack at midfield and <u>sprinted</u> straight for the Palmetto goal. ³Two defenders <u>sandwiched</u> him and <u>threw</u> him off balance, but his momentum <u>carried</u> him on. ⁴The fullback <u>hit</u> him with a forearm to the shoulder that <u>sent</u> him sprawling forward, sliding through the mud.

—Excerpt from *Tangerine* by Edward Bloor

> To review helping and main verbs, see **Lesson 8.1.**

As you revise, eliminate wordiness by rewriting sentences that are in the passive voice. Sentences in the active voice use fewer words. See **Lesson 2.5.**

The species was classified by researchers. (6 words)

Researchers classified the species. (4 words)

Verbs

## EXERCISE 1  Revising Headlines

Rewrite the headlines so that the verbs are in the active voice
and in the present tense.

**EXAMPLE**   New Ship Is Launched by Cruise Line

*Cruise Line Launches New Ship*

1. Views of the Andes Are Photographed by Students
   Students Photograph Views of the Andes
2. Spectacular River Trips Are Enjoyed by Rafters
   Rafters Enjoy Spectacular River Trips
3. Discount Airfares Are Offered by All Airlines
   All Airlines Offer Discount Airfares
4. Thousands of Tickets Were Lost by Computer System
   Computer System Loses Thousands of Tickets
5. The Race Has Been Won by the Atlanta Team
   The Atlanta Team Wins the Race

> **Remember**
>
> Present tense verbs
> show actions that
> are happening now
> or repeatedly. See
> **Lesson 8.4.**
>
> I **take** a walk
> every day.

## EXERCISE 2  Using the Active Voice

Read the following travel article. On a separate sheet of paper,
revise it to change eight verbs in passive voice to active voice.
See answer in Answer Key at www.grammarforwriting.com.

**EXAMPLE**   Goals should be set by young people.

*Young people should set goals.*

[1]A flight around the world was made by Dan Dominguez and Chris Wall. [2]The value of hard work was shown by the two young men. [3]The 22-year-olds started their journey in 2000, and five continents were flown across by them. [4]Their goal had been achieved.

[5]Pilots' licenses were earned in 1996 by Wall and Dominguez. [6]After a five-week flight from Texas to Alaska that year, they vowed to circle the globe. [7]A small two-engine plane was bought by them two years later. [8]Their flight around the world was supported by sponsors. [9]Their amazing adventure was appreciated by thousands of people.

Working Together

## EXERCISE 3  Writing in the Active Voice

Work with a partner to create five sentences in the passive voice
about the achievements of students you know. Then exchange
your sentences with the ones written by another partner team.
Replace the passive verbs with active ones.

Answers will vary. See
sample answers in
Answer Key at www.
grammarforwriting.com.

# Verbals and Verbal Phrases

**Verbals** are verb forms that act like other parts of speech. There are three types of verbals: participles, gerunds, and infinitives.

➠ A **participle** is a verb form that acts like an adjective and ends in *-ing* or *-ed*.

> The **tired** boaters battled the **blowing** storm. [adjectives]

A **participial phrase** is a group of words that includes a participle and the other words that complete its meaning.

> Ann, **hoping for the best,** calmed the others. [adjective]

➠ A **gerund** is a verb form that acts like a noun and ends in *-ing*. Like a noun, a gerund is used as a subject, a predicate noun, a direct object, or an object of a preposition.

> **Boating** is their favorite sport. [subject]
>
> Carla's favorite sport is **sailing.** [predicate noun]
>
> Both families enjoy **swimming.** [direct object]
>
> I got paid for **babysitting.** [object of a preposition]

A **gerund phrase** is a group of words that includes a gerund and all the other words that complete its meaning.

> **Paddling in rough water** takes muscle power. [noun]

➠ An **infinitive** is a verb form that almost always begins with the word *to* and functions as a noun, an adjective, or an adverb.

> They wanted **to win.** [noun, the direct object]
>
> Sean wants more food **to eat** right now. [adjective]
>
> The surfer is fun **to watch.** [adverb]

An **infinitive phrase** is a group of words that includes an infinitive and the other words that complete its meaning.

> **To be with friends on a boat** is fun. [noun]

**CONNECTING**
*Writing & Grammar*

Use participial phrases to add vivid descriptive detail to your sentences.

**Amazed by the sound,** the small boy stared at the waves **crashing on the beach**.

See **Lesson 2.3** for more ideas about how to add details to sentences.

**Remember**

Some verbal phrases may contain one or more prepositional phrases. See **Lesson 9.6.**

**Pointing to his left,** Ray waved. [participial phrase]

The boys wanted **to dock by the house with the flag.** [infinitive phrase]

**Sailing to the island** was fun. [gerund phrase]

## Verbs

Copyright © 2014 by William H. Sadlier, Inc. All rights reserved.

**HINT**

Look carefully at how words that end in *-ing* are used in a sentence. They may be participles, gerunds, or verbs.

The **running** water was cold. [participle—adjective]

**Running** is my favorite hobby. [gerund—noun]

They were **running** slowly. [verb]

### EXERCISE 1  Identifying Verbals

Identify the underlined word(s) as a participle, gerund, or infinitive.

**EXAMPLE**   The <u>flowering</u> bush attracted bees. *participle*

1. The <u>wilting</u> flowers needed water badly. participle
2. My favorite of the <u>colored</u> bushes is the purple smoke. participle
3. <u>To survive</u>, plants need sunlight. infinitive
4. <u>Choosing</u> which plants <u>to buy</u> was hard. gerund, infinitive
5. Uncle John enjoys <u>gardening</u>. gerund

### EXERCISE 2  Finding Verbal Phrases

Underline the verbal phrase in each sentence. Write *P* for participial, *G* for gerund, or *I* for infinitive. If a sentence has no verbal phrase, write *none*.

**EXAMPLE**   <u>Singing in the choir</u> is her hobby. *G*

1. <u>Volunteering in a hospital</u> can be very rewarding. G
2. I am taking yoga classes. none
3. Mrs. Margolis loves <u>to paint on her porch</u>. I
4. <u>Cooking both of the dinners</u> took time. G
5. Jenna, <u>singing classic tunes</u>, entertains the seniors. P

Working Together

### EXERCISE 3  Using Verbal Phrases

Complete each sentence. Add the kind of phrase in parentheses.
Answers will vary. Sample answers are shown.

**EXAMPLE**   <u>Raking the leaves</u> takes time. (gerund)

1. My dad likes <u>to swim in the ocean</u>. (infinitive phrase)
2. Did you see the box <u>stuffed with paper</u>? (participial phrase)
3. <u>Playing chess</u> is Karl's hobby. (gerund phrase)
4. <u>Standing by the cliff,</u> I felt nervous. (participial phrase)
5. <u>To go to the beach</u> is my ideal vacation. (infinitive phrase)

# Instructions

Can you think of a day when you didn't read instructions? You probably cannot. Even performing a task as ordinary as making popcorn requires you to read instructions. **Instructions** are a kind of expository writing. They describe the materials and steps needed to complete a task.

### Kinds of Instructions

- recipes
- homework assignments
- street directions
- equipment manuals
- test directions

When you write instructions, remember to include the following features.

## Key Features

- clear purpose
- list of materials
- chronological order with transitions
- specific steps
- clear, concise language
- visuals to clarify steps as needed

## ASSIGNMENT

**TASK:** Write one- to two-page **instructions** for a task you know how to do well.

**PURPOSE:** explain the steps involved

**AUDIENCE:** people who have never done the task before

**KEY INSTRUCTIONS**: Include a photograph or diagram of the finished product at the end of your instructions.

**Pick Your Talent** You probably have lots of talents. Brainstorm about the things you know how to do well, and record them in a list or chart, such as the one below. Once you have finished, choose the one you can write instructions for in the most detail.

| Sports | I can play volleyball and hockey. |
|---|---|
| Cooking | I can make apple pies and fruit salads. ✓ |
| Building | I can make card houses, and I can build a birdhouse. |
| Hobby | I can play the guitar. |
| Special Talent | I know how to swing dance, and I'm taking a hip-hop dance class right now. I can also do handstands. |

**Picture the Steps** Next, create a list of all the steps needed to complete the task. Then, underline the materials needed. Make a separate list of them, and include it at the beginning of your instructions.

Readers won't know to preheat the oven while they prepare the apples and crust.

**Writing Model**

Preheat the oven to 400 degrees.
1. Peel, core, and slice five cups of Granny Smith
   ∧
   apples. Place them in a large mixing bowl.
2. Add one cup of sugar, a tablespoon of cinnamon,
   and one tablespoon of butter to the apples.
3. Add two cups of flour to a second bowl.

Since you know the task well, you might take some steps for granted. Remember, your audience has never completed this task before and will need to be told *every* step. Take time to review your steps and add any information.

> **Use the Right Order** The order in which the steps are given is just as important as the content of the steps themselves.

1. Use **chronological order** to list every step in the order it should be performed.

2. Add **transitions** to help your readers follow the steps. Some transition words that indicate chronological order include *first, next, before, after, then,* and *last.*

3. Create a Sequence Chart to help you plot your instructions. Be sure to use transition words with each step.

For more about chronological order and transitions, see **Lessons 4.3** and **4.4.**

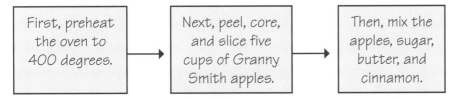

| First, preheat the oven to 400 degrees. | → | Next, peel, core, and slice five cups of Granny Smith apples. | → | Then, mix the apples, sugar, butter, and cinnamon. |

> **Keep It Simple and Clear** As you draft your instructions, use numbered lists and visuals (such as a diagram) to clarify steps that might be particularly difficult to explain or that might easily confuse readers.

While visuals can help clarify your instructions, your language must still be exact and to the point. Use clear and concise language in your instructions. Avoid wordiness and imprecise language, such as *a little bit* or *a lot.*

**WRITING HINT**

Always explain or define any terms your audience may not know.

**UNDEFINED** Only use **baking apples** in your pie.

**DEFINED** Only use baking apples, such as Granny Smiths or other tart apples, in your pie.

**Writing Model**

teaspoon
¹Last, add one ~~splash~~ of white vinegar to the

ingredients ~~that you have made~~ in your bowl.

until there are no lumps
²Then mix it ~~really well~~. ³When you are done mixing,

one cup of
spread ~~some~~ flour on a flat surface.

Fix imprecise language.

Avoid wordiness.

Be specific.

## CONNECTING
### Writing & Grammar

In your instructions, use active voice (when the subject performs the action). Passive voice (when the subject receives the action) can be wordy and unclear. See **Lesson 8.5.**

PASSIVE Now, the egg whites **are blended.**

ACTIVE Now, **blend** the egg whites.

**Check Your Draft** Use the checklist to review your instructions. Below is the first part of a draft.

### WRITING CHECKLIST
#### Did you...

✔ include a list of materials?

✔ describe a clear end result and use clear, concise language?

✔ present specific steps in chronological order and use transitions?

✔ add a photo or diagram and write one to two pages?

**Writing Model**

List of materials at the beginning

Clear transitions

Easy-to-follow steps

**Materials:** ¹You will need three mixing bowls, baking apples, sugar, cinnamon, flour, vegetable shortening, salt, an egg, water, white vinegar, a pie tin, and butter.

²To make a delicious apple pie, begin by preheating the oven to 400 degrees. ³<u>Next,</u> peel, core, and slice five cups of baking apples, such as Granny Smiths or other tart apples. ⁴Place these apples in a large mixing bowl. ⁵<u>Then,</u> add one cup of sugar, a tablespoon of cinnamon, and a tablespoon of butter. ⁶Mix well.

⁷Now prepare the crust. ⁸In a second large mixing bowl, combine two cups of flour with two-thirds of a cup of vegetable shortening. ⁹Then, add one tablespoon of salt. ¹⁰In a separate small bowl, beat together one egg, three tablespoons of very cold water, and one teaspoon of white vinegar.

# Chapter Review

## A. Practice Test

Read each sentence below carefully. Decide which answer choice best replaces the underlined part, and fill in the circle of the correct letter. If you think the underlined part is correct, fill in the circle for choice *A*.

EXAMPLE

Ⓐ Ⓑ Ⓒ ⬤ Ⓔ   On July 20, 1969, the first human being <u>have walked on the moon.</u>
(A) have walked on the moon.
(B) will have walked on the moon.
(C) has walked on the moon.
(D) walked on the moon.
(E) to be walking on the moon.

Ⓐ Ⓑ Ⓒ Ⓓ ⬤  **1.** When Neil Armstrong <u>taked his first step on the surface, he talked</u> about taking "one giant leap for mankind."
(A) taked his first step on the surface, he talked
(B) had taken his first step on the surface, he will talk
(C) had took his first step on the surface, he talked
(D) took his first step on the surface, he has talk
(E) took his first step on the surface, he talked

Ⓐ Ⓑ Ⓒ ⬤ Ⓔ  **2.** A camera <u>has recorded every move he makes, so people across America could be watching</u> on their TV screens.
(A) has recorded every move he makes, so people across America could be watching
(B) has been recording every move he made, so people across America could watched
(C) recorded every move he maked, so people across America could watch
(D) recorded every move he made, so people across America could watch
(E) will have recorded every move he makes, so people across America will watch

Ⓐ⬤Ⓒ Ⓓ Ⓔ  **3.** The astronauts <u>have wore space suits that are controlling air and temperature to ensure</u> their safety.

(A) have wore space suits that are controlling air and temperature to ensure

(B) wore space suits that controlled air and temperature to ensure

(C) weared space suits that controlled air and temperature to ensure

(D) worn space suits to control air and temperature to ensure

(E) wear space suits that had controlled air and temperature to be ensuring

Ⓐ Ⓑ⬤Ⓓ Ⓔ  **4.** The reduced gravity on the moon <u>makes the astronauts bounced</u> off the surface with each step.

(A) makes the astronauts bounced

(B) made the astronauts will bounce

(C) made the astronauts bounce

(D) had make the astronauts bounce

(E) made the astronauts have bounce

Ⓐ Ⓑ Ⓒ⬤Ⓔ  **5.** They <u>leaved an American flag on the moon to have marked</u> the historic accomplishment.

(A) leaved an American flag on the moon to have marked

(B) lefted an American flag on the moon to mark

(C) left an American flag on the moon marked

(D) left an American flag on the moon to mark

(E) are leaving an American flag on the moon to be marking

## B. Choosing the Correct Verb

Underline the correct verb in each sentence below.

**1.** My uncle Sean (<u>became</u>, become) interested in space at an early age.

**2.** He (knowed, <u>knew</u>) that he wanted to study astronomy in college.

**3.** After receiving his degree, he (<u>built</u>, had build) his career as an astronomy professor.

**4.** Uncle Sean (<u>taught</u>, teached) at the state university until last year.

**5.** This year, he (gived, <u>gave</u>) a speech about black holes to my science class.

## C. Identifying Verbals

Underline the verbal or verbal phrase in each sentence below. In the space provided, label it *P* for participle or participial phrase, *G* for gerund or gerund phrase, or *I* for infinitive or infinitive phrase.

<u>I</u> **1.** It had always been my dream <u>to go on a cruise.</u>

<u>P</u> **2.** <u>Thrilled</u>, I stepped on board the ship.

<u>G</u> **3.** I enjoyed <u>sailing from port to port.</u>

<u>P</u> **4.** <u>Staring at the ocean</u>, I relaxed on the upper deck.

<u>G</u> **5.** <u>Coming back home</u> was very hard to do.

## D. Revising Instructions

On a separate sheet of paper, rewrite the following instructions on teaching a puppy to sit. Put the steps in order, and change passive voice to active voice. Fix any errors in verb tenses.

Answers may vary. See sample answer in Answer Key at www.grammarforwriting.com.

> [1]Finally, replace treats with simple praise, such as "good dog." [2]Give your puppy a treat. [3]First, you have said "sit" and gently press down on your puppy's back so that he had been in the sitting position. [4]Repeat this process several times. [5]Each time give your puppy a treat. [6]After at least five trials, say "sit" without pressing down on your puppy's back. [7]If your puppy sits, reward him with a treat. [8]If he does not sit, say "sit" again and gently help him to sit. [9]Then start over by saying "sit" again. [10]Once your puppy has learned that he will be rewarded, following directions will be easy. [11]If your puppy is misbehaving, firmly say your puppy's name, and say "no."

# Adjectives, Adverbs, and Other Parts of Speech

# Adjectives and Adverbs

Adjectives and adverbs modify, or describe, other words in a sentence.

� arrow An **adjective** modifies a noun or pronoun. It tells *what kind*, *which one*, *how much*, or *how many*.

| What kind? | Which one? | How much? | How many? |
|---|---|---|---|
| **Spanish** art | **new** easels | **some** talent | **two** friends |
| **barking** dogs | **this** painting | **more** work | **several** shows |

Sometimes an adjective comes after the word it modifies. Note that more than one adjective can modify the same noun.

> **That clever, young** painter is **famous.**
> [The predicate adjective *famous* describes *painter*.]

▶ The words *a*, *an*, and *the* are the most commonly used adjectives. They are called **articles.** The words *a* and *an* point to any member of a general group. *The* points to someone or something in particular.

> **An** easel would be useful. **The** easel is over there.

▶ An **adverb** modifies a verb, an adjective, or another adverb. Adverbs answer the questions in the chart below.

| When? | Where? | How? | To what extent? |
|---|---|---|---|
| now | there | patiently | almost |
| tomorrow | inside | quickly | quite |

Adverbs may come before, after, or between the words they modify. Many adverbs end in *-ly*.

> Norway's **most** famous painting, *The Scream*, was recovered **finally**, **almost** three months after it was stolen from a museum.

> Officials have **happily** announced that the **extremely** valuable painting was recovered **yesterday.**

## Remember

Predicate adjectives follow a linking verb, such as *is* or *are*, and describe the subject of the sentence.

Munch's paintings are **haunting.**

See **Lesson 6.6** for more about predicate adjectives.

## WRITING HINT

Overusing the adverb *very* can make your writing boring and vague. Try to choose more vivid, precise language to express your meaning.

ORIGINAL That very old museum is very big.

REVISED That ancient museum is larger than our school.

**HiNT**

Look for one proper adjective. Proper adjectives are formed from proper nouns and begin with a capital letter. See **Lesson 12.1.**

# EXERCISE 1 Identifying Adjectives

Underline each adjective in the following sentences from a folktale. Write the word (noun or pronoun) each adjective modifies. Do not include *a, an,* or *the.*

See answers in Answer Key at www.grammarforwriting.com.

**EXAMPLE** A man once had a <u>fine</u> house. (*house*)

¹Now, <u>this</u> <u>Romanian</u> man was <u>fortunate</u> to have a handsome, loving son. ²Life was certainly <u>easy</u> for the <u>lucky</u> boy. ³"Hans needs experience with <u>ill</u> luck," said the man to himself. ⁴He began giving the son <u>difficult</u> jobs. ⁵Then, <u>one</u> day Hans went into the <u>deep</u> forest for timber.

# EXERCISE 2 Identifying Adverbs

Underline each adverb in the following sentences. Write the word (verb, adjective, or other adverb) each adverb modifies.

See answers in Answer Key at www.grammarforwriting.com.

**EXAMPLE** One winter was <u>terribly</u> cold. (*cold*)

¹One day Paul Bunyan <u>suddenly</u> spotted a little ox. ²He laughed <u>heartily</u> when he saw the appealing animal. ³He took the spunky critter home and <u>quickly</u> warmed him by the fire. ⁴The ox <u>soon</u> turned a <u>very</u> strange shade of blue. ⁵Paul <u>promptly</u> named him Babe the Blue Ox. ⁶Babe grew huge, and the camp laundry was <u>later</u> hung between his horns. ⁷It dried <u>fast</u> because the wind blew <u>extremely</u> <u>fiercely</u> at that height.

# EXERCISE 3 Writing a Description

Answers will vary. See sample answer in Answer Key at www.grammarforwriting.com.

Study the picture on the left, and brainstorm a list of adjectives and adverbs that describe Paul Bunyan or Babe. Write a paragraph of at least five sentences, using at least three adjectives and two adverbs. Underline the adjectives, and circle the adverbs.

# Comparing with Adjectives and Adverbs

When you make comparisons, you use many forms of adjectives and adverbs. These are called **degrees of comparison.**

▥▶ Use the **positive** degree when you're describing one thing. Use the **comparative** degree when you compare two things. Use the **superlative** degree when you compare three or more things.

POSITIVE — I talk **fast** when I'm nervous.

COMPARATIVE — Blake talks **faster** than I.

SUPERLATIVE — Sophia talks the **fastest** of all my friends.

Rules for forming the comparative and superlative degrees of most adjectives and adverbs are shown below. You may need to change the spelling of a word when adding *-er* or *-est.* (See Lesson 12.4 for spelling rules.)

> **Remember**
>
> Avoid double comparisons. Use either *more* (or *most*) or *-er* (or *-est*), but not both.
>
> Today's game was ~~more~~ **faster** than yesterday's game.

| Modifiers | How to Form | Examples |
|---|---|---|
| **One Syllable** | Add *-er* or *-est.* | soon, soon**er**, soon**est** <br> thin, thin**ner**, thin**nest** |
| **Two Syllables** | Add *-er* or *-est,* or use *more* or *most.* | quiet, quiet**er**, quiet**est** <br> heavy, heav**ier**, heav**iest** <br> softly, **more** softly, **most** softly |
| **Three or More Syllables** | Add *more* or *most.* | generous, <br> **more** generous, <br> **most** generous <br> mysteriously, <br> **more** mysteriously, <br> **most** mysteriously |

## Irregular Degrees of Comparison

| | | |
|---|---|---|
| good <br> well | } better | best |
| bad <br> badly <br> ill | } worse | worst |
| many <br> much | } more | most |
| little | less | least |
| far | farther | farthest |

▥▶ Some adjectives and adverbs form their degrees of comparison irregularly, as the list on the right shows. It is best to memorize these irregular degrees of comparison.

Copyright © 2014 by William H. Sadlier, Inc. All rights reserved.

**Remember**

To show decreasing comparisons, use *less* (comparative degree) or *least* (superlative degree).

My shampoo is **less** expensive than yours.

Craig visits the **least** often of all my cousins.

# EXERCISE 1 Forming Degrees of Comparison

Write the forms for the comparative and superlative degrees of the following modifiers. Use each word in a sentence.

Answers will vary. See sample answers in Answer Key at www.grammarforwriting.com.

**EXAMPLE** light, **lighter, lightest**

> This bag is lighter than that one. The tiny bag is the lightest.

**1.** little    **3.** difficult    **5.** athletic    **7.** helpful    **9.** talented

**2.** boldly    **4.** quick    **6.** many    **8.** sweetly    **10.** bad

# EXERCISE 2 Making Comparisons

Complete each of the following sentences by writing the correct comparative or superlative form in the parentheses.

**EXAMPLE** Of the two athletes, Will was the <u>**more excellent**</u> player (excellent).

**1.** Three years ago, Will met one of the __best__ tennis players in the state. (good)

**2.** During the school year, he played __more frequently__ than during the summer. (frequently)

**3.** Will had a __more powerful__ serve than his coach had. (powerful)

**4.** Will was becoming one of the __most famous__ young tennis players in the area. (famous)

**5.** Each year, he developed __more__ confidence in his playing. (much)

# EXERCISE 3 Writing a Comparison

Answers will vary. See sample answer in Answer Key at www. grammarforwriting.com.

Choose three things, such as three sports, three meals, or three comic strips. List ways that the things are alike. Decide which of the three you like best and why. Then write a paragraph in which you compare the things. Use at least three comparative or superlative forms in your paragraph.

# Adjective or Adverb?

Writers sometimes misuse adjectives and adverbs because they are not certain which part of speech is needed or what the adjective or adverb form of a particular word is.

➥ Ask yourself, "What kind of word do I want to modify?" Choose an **adjective** to modify a noun or a pronoun. Choose an **adverb** to modify a verb, an adjective, or another adverb.

> The Incas (successful, **successfully**) built amazing tombs.
> [*Successfully* is an adverb. It modifies the verb *built*.]

➥ Use adjectives, not adverbs, after linking verbs. **Predicate adjectives** follow linking verbs and describe the subject. (See Lessons 6.6 and 8.1 to review predicate adjectives and linking verbs.)

> Those Incan statues looked (**beautiful**, beautifully).
> [The predicate adjective *beautiful* describes the noun *statues*.]

➥ Some pairs of adjectives are easily confused.

**1.** Use *real* as an adjective. Use *really* as an adverb.
> That vase has **real** value. It is **really** old.

**2.** Use *bad* as an adjective. Use *badly* as an adverb.
> She felt **bad**. Her report on Incan art was **badly** written.

**3.** Use *good* as an adjective. Use *well* as an adverb most of the time. (When it refers to health, *well* is an adjective.)
> **Good** art helps people understand a culture **well**.
>
> Do you feel **well** enough to finish the painting?

See **Lesson 9.1** for more about the questions that adjectives and adverbs answer.

*Chapter 9 • Adjectives, Adverbs, and Other Parts of Speech* **205**

**ONLINE PRACTICE**
www.grammarforwriting.com

## EXERCISE 1 Explaining Correct Usage

The two adverbs in sentence b make it correct. The adverb *badly* describes the verb *played*. It tells *how* the team played. The adverb *really* describes the adverb *badly*. Adjectives like *real* and *bad* cannot describe verbs or adverbs.

Suppose a friend asks you which of the following sentences is correct.

**a.** Our team played real bad.

**b.** Our team played really badly.

Explain in several sentences which one is correct and why.

## EXERCISE 2 Choosing Adjectives or Adverbs

**Remember**

Use an adjective, never an adverb, after a linking verb.

The opening seemed **mysterious.** [not *mysteriously*]

Read each of the following sentences about author Esmé Raji Codell. Underline the adjective or adverb that will make each sentence correct.

**EXAMPLE** Codell is very (<u>good</u>, well) at writing children's books.

**1.** She writes (regular, <u>regularly</u>) for several magazines and has an (extreme, <u>extremely</u>) interesting Web site.

**2.** One of her (<u>brilliant</u>, brilliantly) books, *Sahara Special*, (rightful, <u>rightfully</u>) won several awards.

**3.** Sahara is a (real, <u>really</u>) lonely girl who (slow, <u>slowly</u>) learns to express her true feelings.

**4.** Codell is (<u>happy</u>, happily) to get letters from children and tries to answer her mail (quick, <u>quickly</u>).

**5.** One reason Codell's books are (good, well) is that her characters sound (<u>realistic</u>, realistically).

**Working Together**

## EXERCISE 3 Writing from Notes

Answers will vary. Students should use both adjectives and adverbs in the two paragraphs. Some popular authors include Gary Soto, Walter Dean Myers, Gary Paulsen, Ann Martin, M. E. Kerr, and Lensey Namioka.

Work with a partner, and choose an author whom you both like. Jot down the reasons that you enjoy his or her work.

**1.** From your notes, write at least two paragraphs.

**2.** Use at least one adjective or adverb in each sentence to make your sentences more interesting.

# Double Negatives

⟫ A negative word has the meaning "no." Using two negative words where only one is needed is called a **double negative.** Avoid using double negatives when you speak or write.

## Common Negative Words

| barely | neither | no | nobody | not | nowhere |
|--------|---------|-----|--------|---------|----------|
| hardly | never | no one | none | nothing | scarcely |

INCORRECT    I **barely** got **no** sleep. [double negative]

CORRECT    I **barely** got any sleep. [one negative word]

⟫ Many double negatives occur in sentences in which one of the negative words is a contraction such as *can't, doesn't,* or *don't.* These words contain *n't,* the shortened form of the word *not.*

INCORRECT    They **don't** want to go **nowhere** tonight.

CORRECT    They **don't** want to go anywhere tonight.

⟫ Double negatives can usually be corrected in more than one way. Choose the way that sounds most natural to you.

INCORRECT    We don't see nobody in the office.

CORRECT    We don't see anybody in the office.

CORRECT    We see nobody in the office.

Have you ever heard the phrase "Two wrongs don't make a right"? Well, one reason to avoid double negatives is that two negatives do make a positive in English. Double negatives can confuse readers. For example, the sentence "I don't owe you no money" means "I do owe you some money."

# EXERCISE 1 Identifying Double Negatives

Underline the negative words in the following sentences.
If a sentence contains a double negative, rewrite it correctly.
Write *C* if the sentence is correct.

Answers will vary. Sample answers are shown.

   **EXAMPLE**    I have<u>n't</u> <u>never</u> owned a cat.

          *I have never owned a cat.*

**1.** My brother could<u>n't</u> <u>hardly</u> walk our new puppy.
      My brother could hardly walk our new puppy.
**2.** Do<u>n't</u> <u>never</u> let the puppy out without a leash.
      Don't ever let the puppy out without a leash.

**3.** I didn't see <u>no one</u> I knew at puppy training class.
    I didn't see anyone I knew at puppy training class.
**4.** We couldn't <u>hardly</u> find room at the park to train.
    We could hardly find room at the park to train.
**5.** I can't believe the time it takes to train a pet.
    C
**6.** The trainer didn't say <u>nothing</u> about leashes.
    The trainer said nothing about leashes.
**7.** Our puppy didn't ever bark at the other dogs in class.
    C
**8.** Didn't <u>nobody</u> bring a treat for his or her dog?
    Did nobody bring a treat for his or her dog?
**9.** Our neighbor's dog couldn't <u>barely</u> walk up the stairs.
    Our neighbor's dog could barely walk up the stairs.
**10.** Didn't Mom get <u>nothing</u> for the puppy's birthday?
    Didn't Mom get anything for the puppy's birthday?
**11.** My friend Robyn doesn't like dogs.
    C
**12.** <u>None</u> of my cousins wants one <u>neither</u>.
    None of my cousins wants one either.
**13.** They haven't wanted <u>no</u> pets.
    They haven't wanted any pets.
**14.** I know <u>no one</u> who has a pet snake.
    C
**15.** <u>Nothing</u> couldn't be more frightening!
    Nothing could be more frightening!

## EXERCISE 2 Editing an Editorial

On a separate sheet of paper, revise the editorial to eliminate all the double negatives. Answers will vary. See sample answer in Answer Key at www.grammarforwriting.com.

> [1]If you scarcely have time for your homework, you don't have no time for a pet. [2]Many people will not see no purpose in training a dog or cat, but it is important. [3]Some pets scratch furniture, but others don't do nothing destructive. [4]Some animals, like lively puppies, don't never want to be ignored. [5]You can't barely walk in the front door without a greeting.

**Working Together**

Answers will vary. See sample answer in Answer Key at www.grammarforwriting.com.

## EXERCISE 3 Writing Rules

Work with a partner to write a list of three or four rules for playing a game. Use at least three negative words, but make sure you don't use double negatives.

# Misplaced Modifiers

A **modifier** is a word, a phrase, or a clause that makes the meaning of another word or group of words more exact. The meaning of a sentence can change depending on where you place a modifier. For example, how are the meanings of these sentences different?

**Almost** three pounds of meat spoiled. [*Almost* modifies three.]

Three pounds of meat **almost** spoiled. [*Almost* modifies spoiled.]

⬛➡ A **misplaced modifier** is in the wrong place. It seems to modify the wrong word in a sentence. As a result, the meaning isn't clear.

MISPLACED   A young mother pushed the stroller **in a pair of jeans.** [Is the baby stroller really wearing a pair of jeans?]

CORRECT   A young mother **in a pair of jeans** pushed the stroller.

⬛➡ To correct a misplaced modifier, move it as close as possible to the word you intend it to modify.

MISPLACED   We watched the rocket shoot into space **with our aunt and uncle.**

CORRECT   **With our aunt and uncle,** we watched the rocket shoot into space.

MISPLACED   I saw Saturn's rings **using a telescope.**

CORRECT   **Using a telescope,** I saw Saturn's rings.

## EXERCISE 1 Correcting Sentences

Rewrite each sentence to correct the misplaced modifier.

EXAMPLE   Columbus saw Haiti sailing the Atlantic.

*Sailing the Atlantic, Columbus saw Haiti.*

**1.** Columbus met the native people exhausted from the voyage.

**2.** In 1492, we watched a movie about Columbus landing in Haiti.

**3.** There are scenes of explorers who have sailed in that film.

CONNECTING
Writing & Grammar

To fix a misplaced modifier, you may decide to move a phrase or a clause to the beginning of a sentence. If so, use a comma to set off the introductory group of words.

Wearing a pair of jeans**,** a young mother pushed the stroller.

See **Lesson 11.4** to review this comma rule and others.

1. Exhausted from the voyage, Columbus met the native people.
2. We watched a movie about Columbus landing in Haiti in 1492.
3. In that film are scenes of explorers who have sailed.

**4.** Navigating rough seas, I watched the small ships.
I watched the small ships navigating rough seas.
**5.** The scene interested me on the island.
The scene on the island interested me.

## EXERCISE 2 Editing a Paragraph

Correct five misplaced modifiers in this paragraph. Rewrite the paragraph on a separate sheet of paper.
See Answer Key at www.grammarforwriting.com.

¹Toussaint L'Ouverture led the Haitian Revolution, energetic and hardworking, against slavery. ²When Spain and Britain threatened to divide his native island, an excellent military leader, Toussaint sided with the French. ³The French governed the island and promised to abolish slavery. ⁴From Santo Domingo for safety Toussaint sent his family away. ⁵Toussaint surrendered when the French wanted the island back and agreed to retire. ⁶Yet where he died the French captured him and sent him to prison.

**Working Together**

## EXERCISE 3 Using Modifiers

Many sentences with misplaced modifiers are unintentionally funny. Write two sentences that make you laugh because modifiers are misplaced. Show your sentences to a partner, and ask him or her to explain the humor and write the sentences correctly. Answers will vary. See sample answers in Answer Key at www.grammarforwriting.com.

EXAMPLE  *Growling at the stranger, Mia noticed her dog.*
*[It seems as if Mia, not her dog, is growling.*
*Correction: Mia noticed her dog growling at the*
*stranger.]*

# Prepositions and Prepositional Phrases

A **preposition** is a word that shows direction or location.

➠ A preposition (**P**) is always part of a **prepositional phrase,** a group of words that begins with a preposition and ends with a noun or pronoun. The noun or pronoun is the **object of the preposition (o).** All modifiers of the object (or objects) are part of the prepositional phrase.

P   O      O

She is filled **with fear and worry.**

In the passage below, notice the details that the prepositional phrases add.

## Some Common Prepositions

| | |
|---|---|
| about | down |
| across | during |
| after | for |
| against | from |
| along | in |
| among | like |
| around | near |
| as | of |
| at | onto |
| before | out |
| behind | over |
| below | past |
| beneath | toward |
| beside | under |
| between | until |
| beyond | up |
| by | with |

### Literary Model

¹<u>On the telephone</u>, I hear Doña Segura's shaky voice asking me <u>in Spanish</u> if Papi can come see <u>about a smell</u> <u>like gas</u> <u>in her apartment.</u> ²Everyone else is away <u>for the day</u>. ³She is blind. ⁴She does not even know that it is dark. ⁵Abuela nods. ⁶I know she will go stay <u>with Doña Segura.</u>

⁷Papi, already dressed <u>for his day</u> <u>of freedom</u>, listens <u>to me</u> tell Doña Segura that she will be right up.

—Excerpt from *Call Me María* by Judith Ortiz Cofer

➠ A prepositional phrase is used as an adjective or an adverb to modify a word in the sentence. In the model, "On the telephone" is an **adverb phrase** that modifies *hear*. (It answers the question *where?*) The prepositional phrase "like gas" in the first sentence is an **adjective phrase** that modifies *smell*. (It answers the question *what kind?*)

➠ A preposition may be compound, or made up of more than one word.

She stood **in front of** the phone. [adverb phrase]

Nobody **aside from** us is worried. [adjective phrase]

## Some Compound Prepositions

| | |
|---|---|
| ahead of | due to |
| along with | in addition to |
| aside from | in front of |
| because of | in spite of |

# EXERCISE 1 Finding Prepositional Phrases

Underline the prepositional phrase(s) in each sentence. Circle the object(s) of each preposition. The first one is done for you.

**Literary Model**

¹Alexander found himself in a New York airport in the midst of a crowd with suitcases and bundles, pushing by him shoving and stepping on his heels ²They looked like robots, half of them with a cell phone clamped to one ear and talking into the air like crazy people.

—Excerpt from *City of the Beasts* by Isabel Allende

# EXERCISE 2 Revising Sentences

Underline the misplaced prepositional phrase in each sentence. Then rewrite the sentence correctly. Students' revisions may vary. Sample answers are shown.

**EXAMPLE** The musician in the song liked the words.

The musician liked the words in the song.

1. The guitarist about love can play the song.
   The guitarist can play the song about love.
2. The harmonica around this school is a popular instrument.
   The harmonica is a popular instrument around this school.
3. The singer wore a scarf on the album cover around his neck.
   On the album cover, the singer wore a scarf around his neck.
4. About dreams, Roberto sang a song.
   Roberto sang a song about dreams.
5. The drummer was playing enthusiastically with curly hair.
   The drummer with curly hair was playing enthusiastically.

# EXERCISE 3 Using Phrases

Write a sentence that uses the prepositional phrase(s) as listed below. (See Lesson 9.1 to review the differences between adjectives and adverbs.) Answers will vary. Sample answers are shown.

1. in front of the dark curtain (as an adverb)
   The soloist wearing white stood in front of the dark curtain.
2. with the microphone (as an adjective)
   The little girl with the microphone is my sister.
3. under the hot lights (as an adverb)
   She sang under the hot lights.

# Conjunctions and Interjections

▐▶ A **conjunction** joins words or groups of words. The words *and, but, or, nor, for, so,* and *yet* are **coordinating conjunctions.** Use them to connect words or word groups of equal importance.

> Manny **or** Pedro will help us.
> [*Or* joins two subjects.]

> The cars stop **and** start.
> [*And* joins two verbs.]

> Anna ran across the bridge **and** up the hill.
> [*And* joins two prepositional phrases.]

> The taxi is fast, **yet** the train is more fun.
> [*Yet* joins two independent clauses.]

▐▶ **Correlative conjunctions** are word pairs. They join words or word groups that are used in the same way, such as two subjects or two prepositional phrases.

> **Whether** the Panthers **or** the Sharks will win is unclear.

> The teams competed **not only** in a pitching battle **but also** in a hitting contest.

▐▶ An **interjection** is a word or phrase that expresses emotion. If an interjection expresses strong emotion, it may stand by itself before or after a sentence. An exclamation point follows it.

> **Hooray!** That ball was hit out of the ballpark.

▐▶ If an interjection expresses mild emotion, join it to a sentence with a comma.

> **Oh,** I didn't know the game was that close.

### Some Correlative Conjunctions

both...and
either...or
neither...nor
not only...but also
whether...or

### Some Common Interjections

| | |
|---|---|
| aha | oh no |
| cool | oops |
| ha | ouch |
| hey | well |
| hooray | wow |
| oh | yikes |

## EXERCISE 1  Identifying Conjunctions

Underline the conjunctions in each of the following sentences. Then write what each conjunction combines: subjects, verbs, independent clauses, or prepositional phrases.

> **EXAMPLE**    Stonehenge puzzles <u>and</u> amazes us. *verbs*

ONLINE PRACTICE
www.grammarforwriting.com

TEST-TAKING TIP

1. Stones <u>and</u> rocks were used to make the giant monument. subjects

2. Ben <u>not only</u> visited <u>but also</u> researched Stonehenge. verbs

3. Builders of Stonehenge may have lived in a nearby village, <u>for</u> archaeologists found evidence of houses. independent clauses

4. Stonehenge <u>and</u> the village have stone avenues. subjects

5. Stonehenge was used <u>both</u> for religious ceremonies <u>and</u> for other reasons. prepositional phrases

# Exercise 2 Using Conjunctions and Interjections

Write an appropriate conjunction or interjection to complete each sentence.
Answers will vary. Sample answers are shown.

EXAMPLE    The creature has pearly eyes <u>*and*</u> crooked teeth.

1. The creature looks scary, <u>but</u> don't call it a monster.

2. Scientists had an underwater camera <u>and</u> took photos.

3. <u>Either</u> Mr. Wu <u>or</u> Mrs. Ford saw a shark.

4. <u>Well</u>, I believe the deep ocean has been in darkness for 2 billion years.

5. <u>Wow</u>! I can't believe what I'm seeing.

Working Together

# Exercise 3 Writing an Interview

Work with a partner. Interview each other about scientific or historical mysteries and discoveries. Write your interview using the format below. Use at least two interjections and two conjunctions. Underline them.
Answers will vary. Sample answers are shown.

QUESTION:    What discovery interests <u>or</u> amazes you?

ANSWER:    <u>Well,</u> I liked reading about King Tut's tomb.

Question: Why are you curious about Mars <u>or</u> Venus?
Answer: <u>Wow!</u> That's an easy question. Maybe we'll discover life on Mars <u>or</u> send an astronaut to Venus.
Question: <u>Oh,</u> do you really think there might be life on the planet?
Answer: I'm not sure, <u>but</u> I hope so.

# Book Review

When you are undecided about whether to watch a new movie, what do you do? You probably seek the opinion of a friend who has seen it, or you may look for a review on a blog, in a magazine, or in a newspaper. You can easily find reviews about movies, music, and products that people buy.

In a **book review,** a writer states his or her opinion of a book and supports it with specific examples from the text. A book review goes beyond just summarizing a book. It also gives a strong positive or negative evaluation.

**Book reviews evaluate...**
- theme
- style
- characters
- setting
- plot

When you write a book review, remember to include the following.

## Key Features

- clear thesis, or claim, that includes a recommendation about the book
- specific details, including text evidence
- brief summary of the text
- clearly organized introduction, body, and conclusion
- your feelings about the book

## ASSIGNMENT

**TASK:** Write a two- to three-page **book review.**

**AUDIENCE:** a person unsure about whether to read the book

**PURPOSE:** to persuade others of your evaluation of the work

# Prewriting

▶ **Choose a Book** ▶ First, select the book you want to review.

**1.** Make a list of books you've read recently.

**2.** For each book, think about three things you liked and three things you didn't like.

**3.** Choose the book you have the strongest opinions about. Keep in mind that you'll need to support your opinions with specific examples from the text. Select a book you remember well or can easily reread.

Next, take a few minutes to collect your thoughts about the book. Answer the questions below to help jog your memory.

- Which character had the most impact on me?

- Which event was the most memorable?

- Which parts were most fascinating? Which were easy to skip over?

▶ **Form Your Recommendation** ▶ Use the thoughts you gathered to formulate a **thesis statement (claim),** or the main idea of your review. Your thesis statement should clearly state whether you recommend the book or not and give the overall reason for your opinion.

Look at the two versions below. What makes the first one weak? Why is the second one strong?

> WEAK    *The Adventures of Tom Sawyer* is not that bad. I liked some of the characters.

> STRONG   *The Adventures of Tom Sawyer* is a wonderful book that will fascinate any reader. Unlike some of the adults, the young characters are often clever and always exciting.

---

**WRITING HINT**

Focus your book review on one or two aspects of the work, such as characters and theme.

---

For more help with writing a thesis, or claim, see **Lesson 5.2.**

# Prewriting

**▶ Gather Your Reasons and Evidence ▶** Next, provide at least two reasons for your recommendation. Support each reason with evidence from the text. Remember that you must present enough evidence to effectively convince your readers to read or avoid reading the book. Use a Web, such as the one that's started below, to gather details.

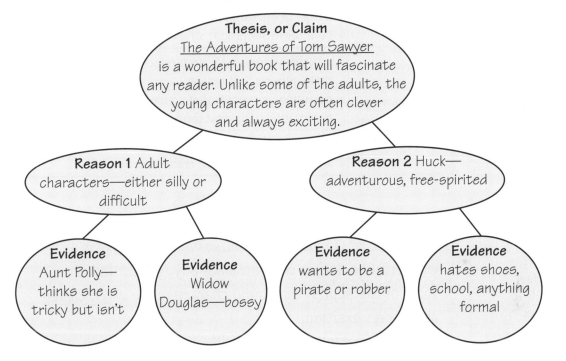

**▶ List the Basics ▶** Summarize the most important details.

| Title and Author | *The Adventures of Tom Sawyer* by Mark Twain |
|---|---|
| Setting | Missouri in the nineteenth century |
| Characters | Tom Sawyer, Huck Finn, Aunt Polly, Becky Thatcher, Joe, Widow Douglas |
| Plot | Huck and Tom search for hidden treasure. |

## Drafting

**Organize the Body** Include all three parts of an essay. Use an outline, such as the one below, to guide your drafting.

| Essay Part | Includes |
|---|---|
| Introduction | • the title and author of the work<br>• a quotation or fact to draw your reader in<br>• a brief one-paragraph summary of the book's plot<br>• your thesis statement, or claim |
| Body | • a body paragraph for each reason and evidence that supports that reason<br>• transitions, or words that connect one sentence or paragraph to the next (*also, first, most important*) |
| Conclusion | • brief summary of the main ideas you presented<br>• a final thought for your readers to consider |

**CONNECTING**
*Writing & Grammar*

When you write about a literary work, use the present tense.

Tom **is** tricky and funny.

**Writing Model**

Thesis, or Claim: *The Adventures of Tom Sawyer* is a wonderful book that will fascinate any reader. Unlike some of the adults, the young characters are often clever and always exciting.

I. Many adults are either silly or difficult.
   A. Aunt Polly thinks she is tricky but really isn't.
   B. Widow Douglas is bossy and annoying.
II. Huck is adventurous and totally free-spirited.
   A. Huck hates shoes, school, and anything formal.
   B. He wants to be a pirate or robber.
   C. He chooses to be poor rather than rich.
III. Tom is smarter than most people around him.
   A. He always outsmarts adults, like his Aunt Polly.
   B. He tricks his friends into whitewashing a fence.

# Revising

Next, use the Revising Questions to improve your draft. The model below shows one writer's changes to a body paragraph.

## Revising Questions

❑ How clear and strong is my thesis, or claim?

❑ What important details should I add to my summary? What details should I delete?

❑ Where can I add text evidence?

❑ How can I clarify the organization?

❑ How well have I expressed my feelings about the book?

As you revise, keep in mind the traits of good writing. See **Lesson 1.3.**

### Writing Model

¹I really enjoyed reading about Tom because he is a smart trickster. ²~~The~~ For example, The book begins with one of Tom's funny tricks. ³Aunt Polly catches him eating jam, which she strictly told him not to eat. ⁴He distracts her by shouting that a mouse is behind her. ⁵When Aunt Polly turns around, Tom sneaks out of the house. ⁶In one of my favorite episodes, Tom is forced to whitewash his aunt's fence. ⁷Instead of doing the chore, Tom fools his friends into whitewashing it for him by pretending to like the work. ⁸Tom seems to accomplish the impossible with his cleverness.

Include transitions to link ideas.

Add personal feelings.

## Remember

Always check the accuracy of your information, such as the proper spelling of character names, by referring to the book.

## Editing and Proofreading

Next, slowly read your draft several times, each time looking for a different item on the checklist below. Use proofreading symbols to mark your corrections.

### Editing and Proofreading Checklist

❑ Have I checked that all words are spelled correctly?

❑ Does each sentence end with a period, a question mark, or an exclamation point?

❑ Have I avoided misplaced modifiers?

❑ Are any words missing or run together?

CONNECTING
Writing & Grammar

▶ **Avoid Misplaced Modifiers** ▶ As you edit and proofread your paper, look for any misplaced modifiers. A **modifier** is a word or phrase that describes another word or phrase. Modifiers should be as close as possible to the word or phrase they modify. Otherwise, the sentence can be confusing.

For more help with misplaced modifiers, see **Lesson 9.5.**

MISPLACED    Twain claimed that adults should try to remember the adventures they had as children **in his book.**
[Here the modifier *in his book* is misplaced because it is too far away from the word it modifies: *claimed*. To correct this problem, move the modifier.]

CORRECT    Twain claimed **in his book** that adults should try to remember the adventures they had as children.

CORRECT    **In his book,** Twain claimed that adults should try to remember the adventures they had as children.

[1]*The Adventures of Tom Sawyer* is one of my favorite

books, and I strongly recommend it to anyone who hasn't

read it. [2]Some people may think that the book was written

too long ago to offer anything they can relate to, but

many of the characters are like kids today. [3]they are smart

and adventureous. [4]I enjoyed reading about Huck's carefree

personality, and I was impressed by Tom's clever tricks.

[5]Next to the characters I became wrapped up in the book

and felt as if I were there. [6]Because the young characters

are so unforgettable, readers will enjoy reading this

classic novel.

**Proofreading Symbols**

| | |
|---|---|
| ℣ | Delete. |
| ∧ | Add. |
| # | Add a space. |
| / | Make lowercase. |
| ≡ | Capitalize. |
| ⊙ | Add a period. |

## Publishing and Presenting

Finally, choose a way to share your paper with someone else.

- **Present it.** Present your book review to the class. Before you present, practice reading it aloud.

- **Post it.** Add images to your review, such as photos of the author or drawings of the characters. Post your work in the classroom or library.

- **E-mail it.** Send your review to a friend or family member who has read the book. Ask this person to share his or her opinion of the book with you.

**Reflect On Your Writing**

- What part of this assignment did you enjoy most? Why?

- How easy was it for you to find supporting text evidence?

## A. Practice Test

In the passage below, there is a question *for each numbered item.* Read the passage carefully, and circle the best answer.

### Dealing with Cliques

Jenny and Marie used to be best friends, but now <u>they are never seen together, hardly</u>. That's because Jenny
<sub>1</sub>
joined a clique, and she is now one of the <u>more popularest kids</u>. Meanwhile,
<sub>2</sub>
Marie feels sad, confused, and left out.

If this scenario sounds familiar to you, you know how painful and difficult it can be to cope with cliques. <u>The first step is understanding</u> how
<sub>3</sub>
cliques work. Not all groups of friends are cliques. <u>People naturally form groups based on common qualities and interests, and this is not a bad
<sub>4</sub>
thing</u>. A group becomes a clique when it draws lines between those on the inside and the outside. Certain social rules must be followed in order to belong. <u>Near all kids think they would rather be on the inside than the outside, but it's important to
<sub>5</sub>
remember that life inside a clique can be hard</u>.

1. What is the best replacement for the underlined part?
   **A.** NO CHANGE
   **B.** aren't hardly seen together
   **C.** they aren't never seen
   **D.** they are hardly ever seen together

2. What is the best replacement for the underlined part?
   **A.** NO CHANGE
   **B.** most popular kids
   **C.** lessest popular kids
   **D.** most populatest kids

3. What is the best replacement for the underlined part?
   **A.** NO CHANGE
   **B.** The step first is understanding
   **C.** The first step in understanding
   **D.** The step is firstly

4. What is the object of the preposition in this sentence?
   **A.** qualities and interests
   **B.** qualities
   **C.** this
   **D.** interests

5. What word is used incorrectly?
   **A.** but
   **B.** hard
   **C.** inside
   **D.** Near

People in cliques are often anxious about what others think about them. Their position is always subject to change in the group, and

**6**

often, they must hide parts of their personalities to conform. In fact, the group leader, or "queen bee," can be under so much pressure that she is the scaredest member of all.

**7**

If you're a guy, you may think that cliques are a girl's problem. Well, cliques concern you, too. Boys often

**8**

form cliques around a particular sport, style of clothing, or taste in music—and they can be just as mean as girls.

The bestest way to fight against

**9**

clique culture is to avoid it. By staying away from cliques, you can be free of peer pressure and be friends with everyone. After all, no one can have too many friends, so why limit your choices? If you're being bullied or teased by the members of a clique, it may help you to remember that they are probably as insecure as you are, if not more so. If you choose friends who make you feel well about

**10**

yourself, you can't go wrong.

6. What is the best replacement for the underlined part?
   **A.** NO CHANGE
   **B.** Always, their position is subject in the group to change
   **C.** In the group subject to change, their position is always
   **(D.)** Their position in the group is always subject to change

7. What is the best replacement?
   **A.** NO CHANGE
   **B.** of all members, she is the more scared
   **(C.)** she is the most scared member of all
   **D.** of all, she is the more scared member

8. Which item appears here?
   **A.** a demonstrative adjective
   **(B.)** an interjection
   **C.** a coordinating conjunction
   **D.** a positive adjective

9. What is the best replacement for the underlined part?
   **A.** NO CHANGE
   **(B.)** best way to fight against
   **C.** more better way to fight
   **D.** most best way against

10. Which change should be made?
    **A.** NO CHANGE
    **B.** Change the second *you* to *us*.
    **C.** Change *well* to *the better*.
    **(D.)** Change *well* to *good*.

## B. Using Modifiers

Underline each word to be modified, and circle the correct modifier in parentheses. Label the modifier *ADJ* for adjective or *ADV* for adverb.

<u>ADV</u> **1.** The presence of "reality" shows has (great, (greatly)) <u>increased</u> in the landscape of American television.

<u>ADV</u> **2.** These shows are <u>produced</u> ((cheaply) cheap), which networks seek.

<u>ADJ</u> **3.** <u>It</u> is ((clear) clearly) to most viewers that these shows are not realistic.

<u>ADJ</u> **4.** The <u>stories</u> appear ((realistic) realistically).

<u>ADV</u> **5.** By ((cleverly) clever) <u>splicing</u> film, editors create dramatic moments.

## C. Completing Sentences

Complete each sentence below by writing the correct comparative form of the word in parentheses.

**1.** Zemika is the ___best___ speller in our class. (good)

**2.** She is studying ___harder___ for this year's bee than she did last year. (hard)

**3.** She can memorize words ___more rapidly___ than I can. (rapid)

**4.** Zemika is ___more___ determined to win than Theo. (much)

**5.** Of all of us, she has the ___greatest___ chance of winning. (great)

## D. Rewriting Sentences

Rewrite each sentence below to correct the misplaced modifier(s). You may add, change, or remove words as necessary.   Answers will vary. Sample answers are shown.

**1.** In 1921, in Alameda, California, was born Yoshiko Uchida.
Yoshiko Uchida was born in 1921 in Alameda, California.

**2.** Her parents passed their love on to her of reading.
Her parents passed their love of reading on to her.

**3.** When Yoshiko was a young girl, to an internment camp, her father was sent.
When Yoshiko was a young girl, her father was sent to an internment camp.

**4.** In the internment camp, Yoshiko was forced sadly to join her father.
Sadly, Yoshiko was forced to join her father in the internment camp.

**5.** Yoshiko wrote about her culture and experiences as a famous author.
As a famous author, Yoshiko wrote about her culture and experiences.

## E. Editing a Book Review

Correct the draft below. If you need to move words, circle them and draw an arrow to where they belong. Then answer the questions.

Students' answers will vary. Sample answers are shown.

### Proofreading Symbols

| | |
|---|---|
| ɣ Delete. | / Make lowercase. |
| ∧ Add. | ¶ Start a new paragraph. |
| ⊙ Add a period. | ☰ Capitalize. |

¹The Sisterhood of the Traveling Pants was pretty good by Ann Brashares. ²There are four main characters, ~~but~~ *and* their names are Lena, Bridget, Carmen, ~~or~~ *and* Tibby. ³Over one summer the story takes place, ~~so~~ *and* you get to hear the separate experiences of each character. ⁴The girls are some of the ~~more~~ *most* likeable in any novel I've ever read. ⁵I hardly ~~never~~ *ever* like the way in novels teen girls are portrayed. ~~and~~ *but* this book ~~was~~ *is* an exception.

¶ ⁶The girls have very different backgrounds and appearances, *but* they find a pair of pants that fits them all perfect*ly.* in a thrift shop. ⁸The pants are obvious*ly* special. ⁹the girls decide they will share them. ¹⁰As each girl with the pants gets a turn, she has ~~much~~ *many* important experiences.

1. Students' answers may mention a weak thesis and/or recommendation, a lack of text evidence to support the writer's points, and many errors in grammar.

2. Students may suggest the writer state a stronger opinion of the book, beginning and concluding the review with a clear recommendation. They may also suggest that the writer back up his or her opinion with specific text references and details, develop the point about themes in more detail, and proofread far more carefully.

**1.** What aspects of this part of a book review are the weakest? Why?

**2.** What suggestions for improvement would you give to the writer?

# Subject-Verb Agreement

# Agreement of Subject and Verb

The **verb (v)** of a sentence should agree in number with the **subject (s)**.

▶ Use a singular verb with a singular subject. A **singular** subject names one thing, person, place, or idea.

> s     v
> That library **book tells** about dinosaurs.
> s     v
> The **author is** a scientist from Japan.

Singular verbs in the present tense usually end in *-s*. However, verbs used with the singular pronouns *I* and *you* do not usually end in *-s*.

> s     v
> The **exhibit features** a skeleton.
> s v     s  v
> **I like** the display of fossils, but **I have** several questions.
> s     v
> **You seem** excited about the field trip.

▶ Use a plural verb with a plural subject. A **plural** subject names more than one thing, person, place, or idea.

> s     v
> Several **charts list** important facts and dates.
> s     v
> The colorful **drawings are** interesting.

▶ Some sentences include **verb phrases,** verbs that consist of a main verb and at least one helping verb. (See Lesson 8.1.) The first helping verb **(HV)** in the verb phrase must agree with the subject.

> HV
> The guide **was** answering many questions.
> HV
> Kevin **does** not know the dinosaur's name.
> HV
> My teachers **have** been reading the brochures.

> For more about subjects and verbs, see **Lessons 6.2, 6.3,** and **6.4.**

## Some Common Helping Verbs

| | |
|---|---|
| am | has |
| are | have |
| been | is |
| can | may |
| do | was |
| does | were |

## EXERCISE 1 Choosing Correct Verbs

Underline the subject of each sentence. Then circle the verb in the parentheses that agrees with the subject.

**EXAMPLE** Computer <u>skills</u> (are) is) extremely important.

**Remember**

Most nouns that end in -*s* are plural. However, some plural nouns (such as *women*) do not end in -*s*. See **Lesson 12.5** for more about plural nouns.

1. Modern <u>families</u> (use, uses) the Internet in many ways.

2. The <u>Internet</u> (is, are) a source of information and entertainment.

3. The online <u>world</u> (present, presents) many risks.

4. Many <u>parents</u> (talk, talks) to their children about Internet safety.

5. <u>Children</u> (is, are) not the only ones at risk.

6. <u>Adults</u> (have, has) problems with dishonest people online, too.

7. My <u>grandparents</u> (is, are) having several problems.

8. <u>They</u> (does, do) not realize the risk of identity theft.

9. <u>You</u> (needs, need) to keep your personal information private.

10. <u>I</u> (have, has) read a book about computer crime.

**Working Together**

## Exercise 2 Editing a Paragraph

Work with a partner to correct subject-verb agreement errors in the following paragraph. Find the five verbs that do not agree with their subjects, and correct them. Write your corrected paragraph on a separate sheet of paper.

**HiNT**

A sentence may have more than one incorrect verb.

**Writing Model**

¹CD sales ~~has~~ *have* been slumping since 2000. ²One reason for this slump is that people download songs from the Internet for free. ³Many teens share music with their friends. ⁴Music industry leaders ~~is~~ *are* upset with the loss of money and ~~is~~ *are* proposing new laws. ⁵A new guide tells parents the legal issues about downloading music. ⁶Parents have been sued because their children ~~has~~ *have* downloaded music. ⁷Music companies ~~does~~ *do* not want to offend their customers. ⁸This issue is complicated.

# Phrases Between Subject and Verb

A subject is often separated from its verb by one or more prepositional phrases. A **prepositional phrase (P)** is a group of words that begins with a preposition and ends with an object, either a noun or pronoun.

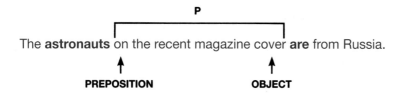

P

The **astronauts** on the recent magazine cover **are** from Russia.

PREPOSITION          OBJECT

▶ The subject of a sentence is never part of a prepositional phrase. The verb must agree with the subject, not with the object in a prepositional phrase.

The square **button** under the speed controls **blinks** constantly.
[*Blinks* agrees with the singular subject *button*, not with *controls*.]

The **commanders** of the mission during the summer **have** flown before.
[*Have* agrees with the plural subject *commanders*, not with *mission* or *summer*.]

## Some Common Prepositions

| | |
|---|---|
| about | into |
| above | near |
| across | of |
| along | off |
| around | on |
| at | over |
| below | through |
| between | to |
| by | under |
| during | until |
| for | upon |
| from | with |
| in | without |
| inside | |

## STEP BY STEP

The rings around the middle of Saturn (is, are) beautiful.

To check agreement when a phrase comes between the subject and the verb:

1. Cross out or cover up any prepositional phrases.
   The rings ~~around the middle of Saturn~~ (is, are) beautiful.

2. Decide whether the subject is singular or plural.
   SUBJECT        *rings*      [plural]

3. Choose the verb that agrees with the subject.
   VERB           *are*        [plural]

The rings around the middle of Saturn **are** beautiful.

For more on prepositional phrases, see **Lesson 9.6.**

### EXERCISE 1 Choosing the Correct Verb

Circle the verb in parentheses that agrees with the subject.

**EXAMPLE** Folk songs around the world (is, (are)) about ordinary people.

1. The subjects of folk songs ((range), ranges) from war to love.

2. The topic of civil rights ((comes), come) up in many American folk songs.

3. A folk song from the Civil War years ((was), were) "Down by the Riverside."

4. Huddie Ledbetter, with other African-American musicians, ((was), were) an important influence on folk music.

5. Other big names in folk music (is, (are)) Pete Seeger and Joan Baez.

6. One of Woody Guthrie's most famous songs ((is), are) "This Land Is Your Land."

7. The sounds of bluegrass music (reminds, (remind)) me of Guthrie's songs.

8. People around the world (enjoys, (enjoy)) folk music.

9. The appeal of many folk songs ((is), are) their simple melodies.

10. My interest in folk songs ((grows), grow) each year.

### EXERCISE 2 Writing a Paragraph

Think about kinds of music, foods, or movies that you enjoy.
Answers will vary. See sample answer in Answer Key at www.grammarforwriting.com.

1. On a separate sheet of paper, write a paragraph of at least five sentences about one of those topics. Use present tense verbs.

2. Use one or more prepositional phrases between the subject and verb in at least three sentences.

3. Circle each verb, and check subject-verb agreement.

**EXAMPLE** The title of one of my favorite songs (is) "The Luckiest."

# Compound Subjects

A **compound subject** consists of two or more subjects that share the same verb and are joined by a conjunction.

▌▶ Subjects joined by *and* usually take a plural verb.

> Pears, peaches, **and** grapes **taste** sweet.
>
> Tran **and** Sue **have** a vegetable garden.

A compound subject that names only one thing or person takes a singular verb.

> That famous chef and author **is** going to read from her book.
> [One person is meant.]
>
> Peanut butter and jelly **fills** me at lunch.
> [One dish is meant.]

▌▶ Singular subjects joined by *or* or *nor* take a singular verb.

> The soup, the bread, **or** the salad **is** served first.
>
> Neither lettuce **nor** celery **has** many calories.

▌▶ When a singular and a plural subject are joined by *or* or *nor*, the verb agrees with the subject closest to it.

> Milk, cheese, **or** peas **are** on sale. [plural]
>
> Peas, milk, **or** cheese **is** on sale. [singular]

**WRITING HINT**

Combine sentences by using compound subjects to eliminate wordiness and improve your sentence fluency.

**ORIGINAL** Onions cost an extra 25 cents. Pickles also cost 25 cents more.

**REVISED** Onions and pickles each cost an extra 25 cents.

See **Lessons 3.6** and **6.4** for more about compound subjects.

## EXERCISE 1 Combining Sentences

On a separate sheet of paper, combine the following groups of sentences into a single sentence with a compound subject.

**EXAMPLE**  *The Simpsons* is an award-winning animated comedy.
*King of the Hill* is an award-winning animated comedy.

<u>The Simpsons</u> and <u>King of the Hill</u> are award-winning animated comedies.

**1.** SpongeBob SquarePants lives at the bottom of the ocean. His friend Patrick lives there, too.
SpongeBob SquarePants and his friend Patrick live at the bottom of the ocean.

**ONLINE PRACTICE**
www.grammarforwriting.com

**2.** Homer Simpson has three children. Marge Simpson has three children.
Homer and Marge Simpson have three children.

**3.** Either *Family Ties* was on TV in the 1980s, or *I Love Lucy* was on TV in the 1980s.
Either *Family Ties* or *I Love Lucy* was on TV in the 1980s.

**4.** My brother watches cartoons every Saturday. I watch cartoons every Saturday. So does my sister.
My brother, my sister, and I watch cartoons every Saturday.

**5.** The new reality show is not popular. The new cooking programs are not popular either.
Neither the new reality show nor the new cooking programs are popular.

## EXERCISE 2 Choosing Correct Verbs

Underline the subject(s) in each sentence. Circle the verb in parentheses that agrees with the subject. **Hint:** Not every sentence has a compound subject.

**EXAMPLE** My mother and father (likes, like) to watch old movies.

**1.** Neither Sam nor his parents (enjoy, enjoys) horror films.

**2.** Both plot and characters (matters, matter) to me.

**3.** Some movies (has, have) been based on books.

**4.** A British actress and an American actress (are, is) getting terrific reviews.

**5.** The author and producer (speak, speaks) her mind.

**6.** Either the costumes or the title song (deserve, deserves) an award.

**7.** Neither TV stars nor movie stars (makes, make) terrific role models.

**8.** Both adults and children (like, likes) action films.

**9.** A good plot or talented actors (are, is) important.

**10.** Many foreign films of the last year (was, were) dramas.

# Inverted Sentences

In most sentences, the subject comes before the verb.

> The **book includes** Civil War photographs.

➨ In an **inverted sentence,** the subject follows the verb or part of the verb phrase. The chart below shows three kinds of sentences in which the subject often follows the verb.

| Sentence that... | Example |
|---|---|
| Begins with *here* or *there* | Here **is** one **picture.** |
| Begins with one or more phrases | Next to the trees **stands President Lincoln.** |
| Is a question | When **were** the **photos taken?** |

Because the subjects in inverted sentences are in an unusual position, make an extra effort to check that the verb agrees with the subject. To find the subject of an inverted sentence, reword it so that the subject precedes the verb.

INVERTED    There **is Lincoln. Was** he **addressing** the soldiers?

REWORDED    **Lincoln is** there. **He was addressing** the soldiers.

## EXERCISE 1  Identifying Agreement Errors

Most of the sentences below contain errors in subject-verb agreement. If a verb does not agree with its subject, circle it, and write the correct form. If a sentence is correct, write *C*.

EXAMPLE    Here (is) some books about Frederick Douglass. *are*

**1.** In Maryland is Douglass's birthplace. c

**2.** (Was) Douglass's mother and father slaves? were

**3.** There('s) many letters from Douglass to Lincoln. are

**4.** (Have) Lee or Sean read any of Douglass's speeches? Has

**5.** Here (are) the map of the Underground Railroad stops. is

**R**emember

Use the contractions *here's* (*here is*) and *there's* (*there is*) only with singular subjects.

INCORRECT There's the soldiers.

CORRECT There's the soldier.

CORRECT There are the soldiers.

**HINT**

Some of the sentences may have a compound subject. To review compound subjects, see **Lesson 10.3.**

**Working Together**

# EXERCISE 2 Editing a Report

Read the report below with a partner, and find three verbs that do not agree with their subjects. Cross out the incorrect verbs, and write the correct forms.

### Writing Model

    Have
¹H̶a̶s̶ many people heard of Susan B. Anthony? ²The political activist was born in 1820. ³Early in her life, Anthony developed a sense of fairness and justice. ⁴She traveled and lectured across the country to promote women's rights. ⁵She also campaigned against slavery. ⁶Here was a woman with a keen mind. ⁷Working with
                was
her in many states w̶e̶r̶e̶ a dear friend named Elizabeth Cady Stanton. ⁸They campaigned for laws to give women and African-Americans the right to vote. ⁹However, the Republicans did not support the amendment as promised.
                                        were
¹⁰Not until after Anthony's death w̶a̶s̶ women granted the vote.

# EXERCISE 3 Writing Sentences

On a separate sheet of paper, write five sentences about the photograph. Use verbs in the present tense. Include at least three inverted sentences. Check to be sure each subject agrees with its verb.

Answers will vary. Students should use at least three inverted sentences. See sample answers in Answer Key at www.grammarforwriting.com.

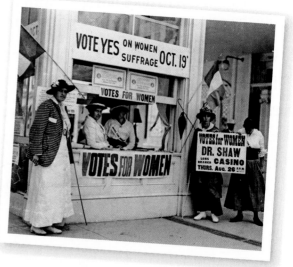

# Other Agreement Problems

▥▶ A **collective noun** is a word that names a group. (See the list on the right.) A collective noun takes a singular verb when it refers to the group as a single unit. It takes a plural verb when it refers to the group's individual members or parts.

SINGULAR　The **committee has made** its decision.
[The committee as one unit has decided.]

PLURAL　The **family have arrived** at the reunion in small groups.
[The individual members of the family arrived.]

▥▶ An **indefinite pronoun** does not refer to a specific person, place, thing, or idea. Some indefinite pronouns are always singular and take singular verbs. Others are always plural and take plural verbs. (See the lists on the right.)

SINGULAR　**Neither** of us **is** late. **Has either** of them **arrived?**

PLURAL　**Both** of the girls **are** here. **Few** of the rooms **are** open.

▥▶ Depending on their meaning in a sentence, the indefinite pronouns *all, any, most,* and *some* may be either singular or plural. The object of a preposition that follows the pronoun can often help you determine whether to use a singular or plural verb.

SINGULAR　**Some** of the music **seems** too loud.
[*Some* refers to the singular word *music*.]

PLURAL　**Some** of my friends **are** here.
[*Some* refers to the plural word *friends*.]

▥▶ Words and phrases that express an amount (a fraction, a measurement, a number, a length of time) take a singular verb when they refer to a single unit. They take a plural verb when they refer to a number of individual units.

SINGULAR　**Four dollars** is the cost.
[single unit]

PLURAL　**My four dollars are** in the box.
[individual units]

## Some Collective Nouns

| | |
|---|---|
| audience | crowd |
| band | family |
| class | group |
| club | jury |
| committee | team |

## Some Singular Indefinite Pronouns

| | |
|---|---|
| anybody | neither |
| anyone | no one |
| each | nobody |
| either | one |
| everybody | somebody |
| everyone | someone |

## Plural Indefinite Pronouns

| | |
|---|---|
| both | many |
| few | several |

# EXERCISE 1 Choosing Correct Verbs

Underline the subject of each sentence. Then circle the verb in the parentheses that agrees with the subject.

**HINT**

In several of the sentences, the subject follows the verb. See **Lesson 10.4** for more about inverted sentences.

**EXAMPLE**    <u>All</u> of my friends (is, (are)) reading *The Giver.*

1. <u>Neither</u> of my sisters (have, (has)) read it.

2. The <u>class</u> ((are), is) writing their book reviews in groups.

3. <u>Each</u> of us (enjoy, (enjoys)) Lois Lowry's novels.

4. <u>Many</u> of the characters ((have), has) unusual names.

5. When ((is), are) the new <u>book</u> going to be published?

6. Two <u>hours</u> (are, (is)) the amount of time I read each night.

7. On several pages ((is), are) a <u>picture</u>.

8. <u>Each</u> of the chapters ((includes), include) a photo.

9. (Is, (Are)) <u>any</u> of Lowry's books set in the past?

10. The first <u>half</u> (are, (is)) what I've read so far.

# EXERCISE 2 Writing Sentences

Write a sentence using each of the subjects listed below. Write your sentences on a separate sheet of paper, and use the present tense. Answers will vary. Sample answers are shown.

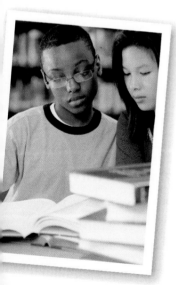

**EXAMPLE**    jury (singular)

The jury is announcing its verdict.

1. team (plural)   The team practice
their separate plays.

2. band (singular)
My band practices each morning.

3. months (singular)
Five months is the time it took to learn the song.

4. years (singular)
Ten years is a decade.

5. everyone
Is everyone happy?

**Write What You Think**   Sentences will vary. See sample answer in Answer Key at www.grammarforwriting.com.

Answer the question below in five sentences. Use at least one collective noun and one indefinite pronoun.

What kind(s) of books do you and your friends like to read most?

# Writing Prompt Response

Test preparation involves more than studying names, dates, and facts. To be fully prepared, you must understand the kinds of questions you may commonly be asked, such as writing prompts. A **writing prompt** may ask you to analyze, explain, describe, argue, or compare and contrast.

| Task | Expectation |
|------|-------------|
| Analyze an issue or passage. | Examine the parts of a whole. |
| Explain or describe a topic. | Provide information and details. |
| Argue a point. | Take a position on an issue, and provide persuasive supporting reasons and evidence. |
| Compare and contrast people, things, or events. | Show similarities and differences. |

When you respond to a writing prompt, remember to include the following key features.

## Key Features

- key words from the prompt
- introduction, body, and conclusion
- clear thesis that states your overall analysis and identifies the literary elements you will focus on
- text evidence that supports your thesis, or claim
- logical organization with transitions that show how your evidence supports your analysis
- formal style

## ASSIGNMENT

**TASK:** Write a four- to five-paragraph **response to a literary analysis writing prompt.**

**PURPOSE:** to provide a clear and complete answer to a prompt

**AUDIENCE:** your teacher

▶ **Understand the Prompt** ▶ Read the prompt slowly at least twice. Underline key words that tell you what to do and what is expected of you.

Form
Purpose
Topic

**PROMPT:** Choose a poem you have read that has a distinct form or structure. What is the role of the structure in the poem, and how does it affect the poem's message? Write a brief <u>literary analysis essay</u> in which you <u>analyze how the poem's structure contributes to its overall meaning.</u>

▶ **Write a Thesis Statement, or Claim** ▶ A good **claim:**

A thesis statement, or claim (see **Lesson 5.2**), is the main idea of your response.

**1.** appears in the introduction

**2.** relates clearly to the topic

**3.** states your main idea concisely

Include key words, or briefly restate the prompt to help keep you on track and prepare your reader for what is to come.

**Writing Model**

¹From the first line of "Paul Revere's Ride," Henry Wadsworth Longfellow turns an important historical event into an engaging story. ²The poem begins "Listen, my children, and you shall hear," and from then on, it follows a simple rhyme scheme and quick, predictable rhythm. ³Throughout "Paul Revere's Ride," <u>the narrative form and the simple rhythm and rhyme scheme emphasize the speed and suspense of the ride and create a memorable story for readers and listeners.</u>

Thesis statement, or claim

▶ **Back Up Your Response** ▷ Next, gather evidence from the text to support your thesis, or claim. Use a chart to organize the supporting details you will present.

| Quotation | Effect |
|---|---|
| "One, if by land, and two, if by sea; And I on the opposite shore will be," | simple rhyme and rhythm make poem easy to remember |
| "A hurry of hoofs in a village street" | regular rhythm and alliteration increase pace and tension |

Be sure to offer a variety of text evidence. Include direct quotations and paraphrases, and draw your own conclusions as you analyze the poem.

▶ **Organize Your Response** ▷ Now it's time to draft your response. Remember, your response will consist of three main parts.

- **Introduction** Include your thesis statement, or claim, and grab your reader's attention.

- **Body** Present details in support of your thesis. Organize your body logically, and include **transition** words and phrases.

- **Conclusion** Sum up your main ideas, and restate your thesis.

Use an informal outline to guide your writing.

**Writing Model**

1. Introduction
2. Body
   A. First and last stanzas of poem: structure makes historical event interesting and memorable
   B. Revere's ride: structure and sound effects emphasizes the pace and suspense of the events of the ride
3. Conclusion

**WRITING HINT**

Use transitions (such as *therefore, as a result,* and *however*) to help your reader follow your thinking throughout your literary analysis. For more about transitions and paragraph organization, see **Lessons 4.4 and 4.5.**

**WRITING HINT**

Most of the writing tests you take will be timed. Budget your time so that you can spend a few minutes prewriting at the beginning and a few minutes proofreading at the end. See **Chapter 1.**

**CONNECTING**
Writing & Grammar

Be sure to check your sentences for subject-verb agreement. Remember that compound subjects joined by *and* take a plural verb.

**Rhyme** and **rhythm** both **draw** readers into the story.

See **Lesson 10.3** to review compound subjects.

**Check Your Response** ➤ Use this list to check your work.

## WRITING CHECKLIST
### Did you...

✔ include key words from the prompt and write a clear thesis, or claim?

✔ present a variety of text evidence, such as quotations?

✔ write a well-organized response in a formal style?

✔ proofread for errors in grammar, punctuation, and spelling?

Attention-getting introduction
Transition

Thesis statement, or claim

Direct quotation

**Writing Model**

¹From the first line of "Paul Revere's Ride," Henry Wadsworth Longfellow turns an important historical event into an engaging story. ²For example, the catchy rhyme and rhythm draw readers into the story. ³Throughout "Paul Revere's Ride," the narrative form and the simple rhythm and rhyme scheme emphasize the speed and suspense of the ride and create a memorable story for readers and listeners.

⁴As a narrative poem, the opening of "Paul Revere's Ride" must set up the story and engage the audience. ⁵In the opening lines, "Listen, my children, and you shall hear / Of the midnight ride of Paul Revere," Longfellow addresses his audience directly and introduces Paul Revere.

# Chapter Review

## A. Practice Test

Read each sentence below carefully. Decide which answer choice best replaces the underlined part, and fill in the circle of the corresponding letter. If you think the underlined part is correct, fill in the circle for choice *A*.

**EXAMPLE**

Ⓐ Ⓑ Ⓒ Ⓓ Ⓔ   <u>An orchestra have different families</u> of instruments.
(A) An orchestra have different families
(B) An orchestra has different family
(C) An orchestra has different families
(D) Orchestras has different families
(E) Orchestras have different family

Ⓐ Ⓑ Ⓒ ● Ⓔ   **1.** <u>Do the orchestra play</u> pieces by Mozart?
(A) Do the orchestra play
(B) Do the orchestra plays
(C) Does the orchestra plays
(D) Does the orchestra play
(E) Does the orchestras play

Ⓐ Ⓑ Ⓒ Ⓓ ●   **2.** One of the most famous <u>orchestras in America are the Boston Pops</u>.
(A) orchestras in America are the Boston Pops
(B) orchestra in America are the Boston Pops
(C) orchestras in America, the Boston Pops
(D) orchestra in America is the Boston Pops
(E) orchestras in America is the Boston Pops

**TEST- TAKING TIP**

If you're stuck on a question, move on. Circle the question number so you'll remember to come back to it after you've answered the questions you know.

**3.** The oboe <u>and the clarinet belongs to the woodwind</u> family.
   (A) and the clarinet belongs to the woodwind
   (B) and the clarinet belong to the woodwind
   (C) or the clarinets belongs to the woodwind
   (D) nor the clarinet belong to the woodwind
   (E) and all the clarinets belongs to the woodwind

ⒶⒷ⬤ⒹⒺ **4.** Either <u>the violins or the viola produce</u> the highest sound.
   (A) the violins or the viola produce
   (B) the violin or the viola produce
   (C) the violins or the viola produces
   (D) the violins or the viola which produces
   (E) the viola or the violins produces

⬤ⒷⒸⒹⒺ **5.** <u>Everybody in the audience is</u> cheering loudly.
   (A) Everybody in the audience is
   (B) Everybody in the audience are
   (C) There's the members of the audience
   (D) All of the audience members is
   (E) In the audience, the people is

## B. Choosing the Correct Verb

Read each sentence below. Underline the verb in parentheses that agrees with the subject.

**1.** Laws regarding cell phone use (varies, <u>vary</u>) from state to state.

**2.** Some states (<u>ban</u>, bans) all drivers from using cell phones.

**3.** Both New York and Connecticut (has, <u>have</u>) enacted laws banning the use of handheld cell phones while driving.

**4.** In California there (<u>is</u>, are) a law prohibiting all drivers from using cell phones, except when they (is, <u>are</u>) in emergency situations.

**5.** One hundred dollars (are, <u>is</u>) the fine for breaking cell phone laws in some states.

## C. Proofreading a Writing Prompt Response

Read the writing prompt and part of a sample response below. Correct any errors in subject-verb agreement. Then on a separate sheet of paper, answer the questions that follow. Answers will vary. Sample answers are shown.

**PROMPT:** We all have special places we like to go. Where is your favorite place? Write several paragraphs describing the place in detail. Include at least three reasons that the place is special to you.

¹There is [are] many special places I love, but my favorite place, without a doubt, are [is] my family's kitchen.

²When my brother and I comes [come] home from school at the end of a long day, the smell of our father's cooking always cheer [cheers] us up. ³Rice and beans are my favorite side dish, but my brother prefer [prefers] mashed potatoes. ⁴Either tamales or tortilla soup are [is] on our family's menu every Sunday.

⁵A second reason I love the kitchen are [is] the conversations my family members have there. ⁶In the kitchen, each of us find [finds] out what the others did during the day. ⁷No matter how busy our lives gets [get], the kitchen is a place where we catches [catch] our breath and enjoys [enjoy] one another's company.

1. What are the major problems with this student's response?
   The introduction should have more than one sentence. The writer omitted a conclusion, gave only two reasons, and included irrelevant facts about foods instead of vivid descriptive details.
2. If you were to give this student test-taking advice, what would you tell him or her?
   The writer should read the prompt more carefully, stay focused on the thesis, describe the place better, and leave time to proofread.

# Punctuation

# End Marks

**End marks** are periods, question marks, and exclamation points. They indicate not only where a sentence ends, but whether it is a statement, a question, a command, or an exclamation.

1. Use a **period (.)** at the end of a **declarative sentence** that makes a statement.

   Sleeping and eating are important activities.

   Most teens need at least eight hours of sleep a night.

Also use a period at the end of most **imperative sentences** that give a command or make a request.

   Please turn off the computer. [request]

   Get to bed now. [command]

2. Use an **exclamation point (!)** at the end of an **exclamatory sentence** that expresses strong feeling. Avoid using too many exclamation points. They will lose their effectiveness with frequent use.

   Lia exclaimed, "I'll never finish my paper before dinner!"

An exclamation point is also used at the end of an interjection if the word or phrase expresses strong emotion. (See Lesson 9.7 to review interjections.)

   Oh, no!   Oops!   Whew!   Wow!

3. Use a **question mark (?)** at the end of an **interrogative sentence** that asks a direct question. It is not used after an indirect question, which states what is being asked without giving the exact words and ends with a period.

   Should I go to bed at the same time every night?

   I wondered whether I was getting enough sleep.

---

**WRITING HINT**

To help your reader recognize your tone, or attitude, you may use an exclamation point after a strong command.

Call the police at once!

---

**Remember**

Place a question mark or exclamation point *inside* the closing quotation marks only when the quotation itself is a question or an exclamation.

I asked, "Have you seen Shay?"

Who said, "Give me liberty, or give me death"?

See **Lesson 11.6** for more about punctuating quotations.

## EXERCISE 1 Using Correct End Marks

Add the correct end mark, and write *declarative, imperative, interrogative,* or *exclamatory* to identify each sentence.

**1.** I know who wrote *Moby-Dick*⊙ declarative

**2.** Why didn't the teacher ask me for the answer? interrogative

**3.** Is that the book about Captain Ahab and a whale? interrogative

**4.** Believe it or not, that whale took off Captain Ahab's leg! exclamatory

**5.** Tell me more about the story⊙ imperative

## EXERCISE 2 Rewriting Sentences

On a separate sheet of paper, rewrite the following sentences. Follow the directions, and use the correct end mark.
Answers may vary slightly.

**1.** Whales are mammals. (Change to interrogative.)
Are whales mammals?

**2.** Can you write an essay about whales for science class? (Change to imperative.)
Write an essay about whales for science class.

**3.** Is the blue whale the largest animal on the earth? (Change to declarative.)
The blue whale is the largest animal on the earth.

**4.** How exciting would it be to see a blue whale in the ocean? (Change to exclamatory.)
It would be exciting to see a blue whale in the ocean!

**5.** A blue whale can weigh more than a hundred tons. (Change to interrogative.)
Can a blue whale weigh more than a hundred tons?

## EXERCISE 3 Writing About a Photograph

Find an interesting photograph of animals from a magazine or Web site. Write five sentences describing or responding to the picture. Use each kind of sentence at least once. Do not use end punctuation. Then get in groups of three or four, and display all photographs. Read the sentences aloud, match them to the photographs, and add the correct end mark. Answers will vary.

See **Lesson 3.1** to review the four kinds of sentences.

# Abbreviations

A shortened form of a word or phrase is an **abbreviation.** Use periods at the end of most abbreviations.

| Type | Examples |
|---|---|
| Initials in names | J. D. Millstein    Gloria A. Wills <br> John L. Jones |
| Titles with names | Mr.  Mrs.  Ms.    Jr. <br> Dr.  M.D. Ph.D.  Sr. |
| Organizations | Assn.  Inc.  Co.  Corp. |
| Addresses | Ave.  Blvd.  Rd.  St. |
| Calendar items | Fri.  Sun.  Dec.  Jan. |
| Times | A.M.  P.M.  A.D.  B.C. |
| Other | ft.    in.  N.  min. <br> tsp.  hr.  vs.  etc. |

➟ Some abbreviations do not use periods. They include **acronyms,** or abbreviations formed from the first or first few letters of several words. Some acronyms are pronounced as words. Others are pronounced letter by letter.

| | | | |
|---|---|---|---|
| mph | UN | NATO | TV |
| km | FBI | DVD | PIN |

➟ Usually it's best to avoid abbreviations in formal writing. Do not abbreviate a title unless it is used before or after a proper name. Avoid using A.M. or P.M. when an exact time is not specified.

INCORRECT    My appointment with the **Dr.** is in the A.M.

CORRECT    My appointment with the **doctor** is in the **morning.**

> **Remember**
>
> If you are unsure whether to use a period with an abbreviation, check a dictionary. Note that the U.S. Postal Service uses two-letter state abbreviations with no periods.
>
> TX    FL    NJ

## Exercise 1  Punctuating Abbreviations

Read the sentences below, and insert periods where needed in the abbreviations. If the sentence is correct as written, write *C*. **Note:** You do not need to spell out any of the abbreviations.

**EXAMPLE**    Jaime A. Escalante was born in Bolivia.

1. Mr. Escalante taught math at a troubled high school in Los Angeles, CA, from 1974 to 1991.

2. Garfield High is located at E. Sixth St. and Vancouver Ave.

3. Escalante once worked for Burroughs Corp., a large computer manufacturer.

4. Escalante's classes often started at 7:30 A.M.

5. Students sometimes worked until 5 or 6 P.M.

6. Escalante tutored students on weekends and rewarded good students with NBA tickets. *C*

7. Dr. Henry Gradillas was the principal of Garfield High.

8. Gradillas left Garfield High in the 1980s to earn his Ph.D.

9. Jaime Escalante's story was made into a movie that was distributed by Warner Bros. Pictures.

10. After Mr. Escalante retired from teaching, he hosted a TV series.

## Exercise 2  Writing an E-mail

On a separate sheet of paper, write an e-mail to a friend.
Answers will vary. See sample answers in Answer Key at www.grammarforwriting.com.

1. Write at least five sentences about your favorite teacher, your favorite class, or your best day ever.

2. Use at least two abbreviations in the e-mail.

---

**Remember**

When an abbreviation with a period comes at the end of a sentence, do not use a second period.

Students often stayed until 6 P.M.

However, do use a question mark or an exclamation point following an abbreviation.

Who is Julia Martin, Ph.D.?

---

# Commas in Compound Sentences and Series

A **comma (,)** is a punctuation mark that signals a separation of ideas or a slight pause.

▶ Use a comma before *and, or, nor, but, for, so,* and *yet* to join independent clauses in a compound sentence.

> Discarded corncobs are waste**, but** one day they may be a source of fuel.

> Gasoline is expensive**, and** prices are rising.

▶ Use a comma to separate words in a series of three or more items. Place a comma after every item except for the last one.

> Companies must develop ways to **harvest, store,** and **transport** corncobs.

> **Corn oil, sweeteners,** or **feed** for livestock may also be produced by ethanol plants.

▶ Use a comma to separate two or more adjectives that come before and modify the same noun. If it makes sense to use *and* between the adjectives, use a comma.

> Gasoline is a **liquid, colorless** fuel. [*liquid and colorless*]

Do not use a comma if the first adjective modifies the second adjective. Also avoid using a comma if adding *and* between the adjectives sounds awkward.

> The future may bring a **new electric** car. [not *new and electric*]

## EXERCISE 1 Adding Commas

Add any missing commas in the following sentences. Write *C* if no commas are needed.

> **EXAMPLE**    On August 24, A.D. 79, Mount Vesuvius erupted**,** and the Italian volcano blew its top.

**1.** The towns of Pompeii Herculaneum and Stabiae were destroyed.

> **Remember**
>
> Use a comma in a compound sentence but not with a compound verb.
>
> Ethanol is made from corn**, and** it may be an alternative fuel.
>
> Ethanol **lowers** gasoline prices and **reduces** pollution.
>
> See **Lessons 3.5, 3.6,** and **6.4** to review compound sentences and verbs.

**HiNT**

Remember not to use a comma after the *and* that comes before the last item in a series.

The eruption was quick, devastating, and unexpected.

2. They were buried and they remained hidden for hundreds of years.

3. One eyewitness, Pliny the Younger, wrote several long letters. c

4. Pliny the Younger was a statesman writer and orator.

5. Historians have analyzed and studied his letters. c

6. Pliny the Younger wrote about many subjects but he is best known for his accounts of the eruption of Vesuvius.

7. He described a cloud stretching to the ground dust emerging and the sky darkening.

8. Confused terrified residents tried to escape.

9. People cried moaned and shouted.

10. The smoky, dark air was frightening. c

# EXERCISE 2 Proofreading a Passage

Read the historical account below. Use proofreading symbols to add or delete commas.

**Proofreading Symbols**

∧ Add a comma.
Ɏ Delete.

¹It was a particularly hot, windy and dry night on October 8, 1871. ²Some said the Chicago Fire started when a cow kicked over a lantern but they may have been wrong. ³The fire resulted in losses and caused the deaths of about 300 people. ⁴The flames engulfed many buildings but the fire eventually burned itself out. ⁵A neighbor of Mrs. O'Leary named "Peg Leg" Sullivan may have been responsible. ⁶Another theory pointed to a meteor shower but neither of these theories has been proved.

# Other Comma Uses

Use these additional rules for **commas** when you write.

| | Rule | Example |
|---|---|---|
| **Introductory Words, Phrases, or Clauses** | Use a comma to set off a word or word group that introduces a sentence. | For Little League pitchers, rules limit the number of pitches in a game. |
| **Interrupters, Parenthetical Expressions** | Use a comma to set off additional information that isn't necessary. | It is stressful, in fact, to play any sport year-round. |
| **Direct Address** | Use a comma to set apart the noun that names a person being addressed. | Please explain, Dr. Andrews, why young athletes face unusual risks. |
| **Nonessential Clauses** | Use a comma to set off a subordinate clause that adds extra (nonessential) information to a sentence. | Sports injuries, which are common, sideline many young athletes. |
| **Nonessential Appositive Words and Phrases** | Appositives rename a noun. Set them apart with commas if they add extra information. | Mike Mussina, a Yankees pitcher, has served on the Little League Board of Directors. |
| **Date and Year** | Use a comma to separate the date and year and after the year if the date is in the middle of a sentence. | The first Little League game was played on June 6, 1939, in Pennsylvania. |
| **Direct Quotations** | Use a comma to separate a direct quotation from the rest of the sentence. | "Mike Mussina," a fan said, "is one of the all-time greats." |

## CONNECTING
### Writing & Grammar

To decide if a word group is nonessential, ask yourself, "Can I omit it without changing the main idea of the sentence?" If the answer is *yes*, set it off with commas.

Last night's game, **which I saw on TV,** was exciting. [The clause adds extra information.]

If the answer is *no*, do not set it off with commas.

The player **whom I like** struck out. [The essential clause identifies which player.]

## EXERCISE 1 Proofreading Sentences

Circle the number of the correctly punctuated sentence.

1. "Where" Janet asked "is my bat?"

2. In May 2008, the high school banned non-wood bats in baseball games. "The reason," said the coach, "is safety."

**3.** When the high school banned non-wood bats in baseball games the coach was pleased.

**4.** At a recent meeting however, the issue came up again.

**5.** Steve asked, "John when did the rules change?"

## Exercise 2 Proofreading a Column

Add fourteen missing commas in the advice column below.

**EXAMPLE** I have a problem**,** Ms. Mannerly.

¹*My little brother, a nine-year-old pest, is always getting me in trouble.* ²*However, my parents blame me for everything.* ³*Please, Ms. Mannerly, give me some advice!*
—Upset Older Brother

⁴Well, Older Brother, you are not alone. ⁵In fact, I hear from kids all the time with the same complaint. ⁶Alice Sparks, a psychologist, has written a book on the subject. ⁷You have, I assume, tried to talk to your brother. ⁸For now, the best thing may be to stay clear of him as much as possible. ⁹The responsibilities of being an older brother, which may seem unfair, will make you more patient in the long run.

**Write What You Think** Answers will vary. See sample answer in Answer Key at www.grammarforwriting.com.

Write an editorial of at least six sentences about a problem that is affecting your school, your sports team, or your community. Explain the reasons that the problem is bothering you, and suggest possible ways to solve it. Include one introductory word or phrase and one interrupter.

# Semicolons and Colons

**Semicolons (;)** and **colons (:)** are punctuation marks that signal a pause. Use them correctly by following a few rules.

⏩ A semicolon joins sentences or parts of a sentence.

1. Use a semicolon to join independent clauses in a **compound sentence** when you do not use a coordinating conjunction. Sometimes you may use a transition after the semicolon.

   The bake sale will be in the auditorium; parents should bring items to the side door.

   Lisa Kahn has some free time now; therefore, she will coordinate the sale.

2. If an item in a series already has a comma, use semicolons to separate the items.

   The teaching advisors are Ms. Dubov, nutrition; Mr. Fernandez, art; and Mrs. Henry, drama.

⏩ A colon signals that something will follow.

1. Use a colon to introduce a list of items at the end of a complete sentence.

   The school will sell homemade baked goods: muffins, rolls, cakes, and bread.

   Do not use a colon when the list follows the main verb of a sentence or a preposition.

   The volunteers are Tina, Tom, and Zoe.

2. Use a colon between the hour and the minutes and after the greeting in a business letter or an e-mail.

   10:15 A.M.          9:00 P.M.          Dear Ms. Wright:

3. Use a colon before a formal or long quotation.

   Consider Mark Twain's view: "Part of the secret of success in life is to eat what you like and let the food fight it out inside."

**WRITING HINT**

Avoid using a semicolon to join unrelated ideas. The parts of a compound sentence should express thoughts that are closely related to each other.

See **Lessons 3.5** and **3.6** for more about compound sentences.

**Remember**

Use a comma after the greeting in a friendly letter or before a short quotation.

Dear Aunt Ruth,

She announced, "We raised more than ninety dollars."

## EXERCISE 1 Adding Semicolons and Colons

Add semicolons and colons to the following sentences. If a sentence is correct, write *C*.

**HINT**

If you use a transition, such as *finally, therefore, however, also,* or *then,* after a semicolon in a compound sentence, follow it with a comma.

Some young writers make it big**;** **however,** some never achieve much success.

**EXAMPLE**   Getting a book published is difficult**;** therefore, not many people are successful writers.

**1.** Teens have published best-selling books**;** however, some never publish anything again.

**2.** These one-time authors fade away**;** many are later forgotten.

**3.** There are a few well-known novelists who began writing in their teens**:** Helen Oyeyemi, author of *The Icarus Girl***;** Mary Shelley, author of *Frankenstein***;** and Christopher Paolini, author of a fantasy series.

**4.** Writers need imagination, a good story to tell, and a lively writing style. C

**5.** Reading from 8**:**30 in the morning until 9**:**15 that night, Sam finished S. E. Hinton's book yesterday.

## EXERCISE 2 Writing About a Chart

Write four sentences about the following chart. Use either a semicolon or colon in each sentence.
Answers will vary. See sample answers in Answer Key at www.grammarforwriting.com.

**EXAMPLE**   S. E. Hinton was a literary success at a young age; her book was published when she was a teen.

| Author | Nationality | Book | Age |
|---|---|---|---|
| S. E. Hinton | American | *The Outsiders* (1967) | written when she was 16 |
| Helen Oyeyemi | Nigerian/British | *The Icarus Girl* (2005) | written before she was 19 |
| Christopher Paolini | American | *Eragon* (2003) | begun when he was 15 |
| Mary Shelley | British | *Frankenstein* (1818) | begun when she was 18 |

# Quotation Marks

**Quotation marks (" ")** are a form of punctuation used to set off the words of a speaker and certain kinds of titles.

➠ Use quotation marks around a **direct quotation,** or a person's exact words.

>    Tom said, "I'm entering the science fair this year."

>    "I'm entering the science fair," Tom said, "to win."

➠ Use quotation marks to enclose the titles of short works.

| | |
|---|---|
| POEMS | "Hidden" |
| SONGS | "The Star-Spangled Banner" |
| SHORT STORIES | "The Tell-Tale Heart" |
| PARTS OF BOOKS | Chapter 2, "New Beginnings" |
| ARTICLES | "The Other America" |

## Punctuation with Quotation Marks

| Rule | Example |
|---|---|
| Always put periods and commas inside the quotation marks. | "I saw a UFO," said Jerome. |
| Use commas to set off the speech tags in the middle of a divided quotation. | "Stay in your seats,"the pilot said, "and keep your seat belts fastened until we land." |
| Question marks and exclamation points go inside the closing quotation marks if the quotation is a question or exclamation. | "I was amazed!" cried the passenger. |
| Question marks and exclamation points go outside the closing quotation marks if the whole sentence is a question or exclamation. | Which American astronaut said, "Houston, we have a problem"? |

> **R**emember
>
> When a **speech tag** (such as "he said") divides a quotation, enclose each part of the quotation in quotation marks. Do not capitalize the first word of the second part of a divided quotation unless it begins a new sentence.
>
> "I'll lend you the book," Maria said, "when I finish it."

# EXERCISE 1  Inserting Quotation Marks

Insert quotation marks where they are needed. If the sentence is correct, write *C*.

**1.** Chapter 6 of *Treasure Island* is titled "The Captain's Papers."

**2.** Which character in the novel kept repeating "pieces of eight"?

**3.** "The Sinking Ship" is a fable by Robert Louis Stevenson.

**4.** Mrs. Vasquez says that she likes books about the sea. c

**5.** "Who is your favorite author?" the students asked their teacher.

# EXERCISE 2  Editing Dialogue

Use proofreading symbols to correct the dialogue below. Refer to the chart on the previous page to help you add or delete punctuation marks in the dialogue below.

**HINT**

Start a new paragraph when there is a change of speakers.

¹The phone rang three times. ²"Hello," said a young female voice. ³"Who's calling?"

"This is Ken Davis," I said. ⁵"May I speak with Sarah?"

⁶"This is Sarah," said the voice at the other end.

⁷"Sarah," I said, "you left your science notebook on the school bus, so I took it home to keep it safe."

⁸"Wow!" Sarah exclaimed. ⁹"I'm so glad you called!"

**Working Together**

# EXERCISE 3  Using Quotation Marks

Work with a partner to write a dialogue between two people who are trying something new, such as a hobby or sport. Use direct quotations, and include at least one question, one exclamation, and one divided quotation. Answers will vary. See sample answer in Answer Key at www.grammarforwriting.com.

# Apostrophes

**Apostrophes (')** are used to show possession, to show where letters or numbers have been left out, and to form certain plurals.

▫▶ Use an apostrophe to show ownership or possession.

| Possessives | Rule | Examples |
|---|---|---|
| **Singular nouns** | Add an apostrophe and -s. | brother**'s** bike<br>book**'s** cover |
| **Plural nouns that end in -s** | Add only an apostrophe. | babies**'** cribs<br>horses**'** stalls |
| **Plural nouns that do not end in -s** | Add an apostrophe and -s. | women**'s** rights<br>children**'s** clothing |
| **Indefinite pronouns** | Add an apostrophe and -s. | everyone**'s** taxes<br>nobody**'s** problem |

▫▶ Use an apostrophe and an -s to form the plurals of letters, words, and numbers.

    five c**'s**        many and**'s**        five 9**'s**

▫▶ Use an apostrophe in place of a missing letter to form a **contraction.** The apostrophe shows where a letter or letters are left out when two words are combined.

    should + not = shouldn**'t**        she + will = she**'ll**

An apostrophe is also used to show the missing numbers in the contraction of a year.

    class of 2012 = class of **'**12

**HINT**

Plural nouns that end in -*s* do not have an apostrophe unless they are also possessive.

**Anteaters** have sticky tongues.

**Anteaters'** sticky tongues help them catch their prey.

For more about plurals and possessives, see **Lesson 7.2.**

# EXERCISE 1 Using Apostrophes

On a separate sheet of paper, write the sentences correctly. The number of errors in apostrophes is in parentheses.

1. A new jacket, introduced in Britain in 07, gives parents updates on a teens' whereabouts every ten seconds. (2) A new jacket, introduced in Britain in '07, gives parents updates on a teen's whereabouts every ten seconds.

2. Its useful for tracking a young persons movements, especially one who participates in extreme sports. (2) It's useful for tracking a young person's movements, especially one who participates in extreme sports.

3. One woman said she didnt think that anybodys teen would agree to wear the jacket. (2) One woman said she didn't think that anybody's teen would agree to wear the jacket.

4. Theres one problem with the jackets basic design: if you take off the jacket, its useless. (3) There's one problem with the jacket's basic design: if you take off the jacket, it's useless.

5. Another device intended for toddlers safety is made to be sewn into childrens clothing. (2) Another device intended for toddlers' safety is made to be sewn into children's clothing.

# EXERCISE 2 Using Apostrophes

First, rewrite each phrase below with a possessive or a contraction. Then write a sentence using each of the following phrases in a sentence. Answers will vary. See sample answers in Answer Key at www.grammarforwriting.com.

1. the team of men

2. the idea of no one

3. stripes of a zebra

4. in 1985

5. do not

**Working Together**

# EXERCISE 3 Writing Sentences

**Types of Cafeteria Food Eaten by Students**

Work with a partner to write five sentences with apostrophes about the graph above.

Answers will vary. See sample answers in Answer Key at www.grammarforwriting.com.

# Other Marks of Punctuation

➡ Use **parentheses ( )** to set off words that explain or define another word.

>  Both team captains **(**Jamal and Ty**)** got trophies.

➡ **Hyphens (-)** are used for a variety of reasons.

**1.** To join compound adjectives that come before a noun:

>  chocolate-covered raisins      a two-way street

When compound adjectives come after a noun, they usually are *not* hyphenated.

>  The raisins are chocolate covered.

**2.** To join compound numbers between twenty-one and ninety-nine and fractions:

>  twenty-three      a three-fourths majority

**3.** To join certain compounds:

>  ex-wife      self-employed      all-inclusive

**4.** To divide words, if necessary, at the end of a line:

>  help-ing      sil-ly      com-pu-ter

> **Remember**
>
> Always divide a word between syllables. Never divide a one-syllable word.

➡ **Dashes** are used to show a break in thought or to set off an explanation.

| Uses for Dashes | Example |
| --- | --- |
| Signal an abrupt break in thought or speech | Do we want to eat breakfast—I hope there's time—before leaving? |
| Signal an explanation or a list with commas | Orange vegetables—carrots, sweet potatoes, pumpkins—are a good source of vitamin C. |

# EXERCISE 1  Adding Punctuation

Read the sentences below.

**1.** On a separate sheet of paper, revise each sentence.

**2.** Add dashes and hyphens where needed.

**EXAMPLE**  Sojourner Truth she took that name later in life was born a slave.

Sojourner Truth—she took that name later in life—was born a slave.

**1.** Sojourner a self-taught woman spoke Dutch and English.

**2.** She worked for the Van Wagener family taking their name briefly but later moved to New York City.

**3.** Our library has twenty two books and photos of her.

**4.** I have read one third of her autobiography.

**5.** An ex slave, Sojourner was also dedicated to women's rights.

**6.** She addressed a women's rights convention in Ohio in the mid 1800s.

**7.** At the Ohio convention, she gave her well known speech, "Ain't I a Woman?"

**8.** In the post Civil War period, she traveled frequently.

**9.** She fought against discrimination on streetcars and won quite an achievement for a woman and former slave.

**10.** She died in 1883 I do not remember where.

Sojourner Truth

# EXERCISE 2  Writing Paragraphs

Write one or two paragraphs about an important historical figure. Include at least one hyphen, one dash, and a set of parentheses.

Answers will vary. Encourage students to gather information from books, magazines, and online. See sample answer in Answer Key at www.grammarforwriting.com.

# Research Report

Have you ever forgotten a fact, such as a person's name, while discussing your favorite sports team or movie? What did you do? You probably went online and searched for this information. In other words, you researched.

Throughout your school years, teachers will ask you to write research reports. A **research report** is a type of writing that answers a question about a topic by presenting information collected from a variety of sources.

When you write a research report, remember to include the following features.

## Key Features

- strong, clear thesis, or claim
- multiple print and digital sources
- relevant information from credible primary and secondary sources
- clear order and transitions
- paraphrases, quotations, and summaries of sources used
- in-text citations and a list of Works Cited

## ASSIGNMENT

**TASK:** Write a four- to five-page **research report** about communication and technology.

**AUDIENCE:** your classmates and teacher

**PURPOSE:** to explain a topic

## Prewriting

**▶ Find Your Topic ▶** Before you begin writing, brainstorm a list of possible topics about communication and technology. To narrow your list, try doing active things, such as:

- performing preliminary research online or at the library
- discussing topics with an expert, parent, or teacher
- reading newspapers or magazines
- listening to other students discuss their topics

Then, choose a topic that:

- you are curious to learn more about
- is neither too broad nor too narrow for a four- to five-page paper
- has several reliable sources of information you can easily find

**▶ Remember ▶**

As you do more research, you can revise and refine your thesis, or claim. For more help with thesis statements, see **Lesson 5.2.**

**▶ Think About Your Point ▶** Once you have started researching your topic, begin to draft a **thesis statement,** or the claim of your report. Think of your thesis statement as a question that you will answer with the rest of your report.

Make sure your claim fits the length of the assignment. If it is too narrow, you'll have difficulty finding enough research material to support it. If it is too broad, your paper will lack focus.

| | |
|---|---|
| **TOO BROAD** | Text messaging is used around the world. |
| **TOO NARROW** | Abbreviations are often used in text messages. |
| **STRONG** | Some educators believe text messaging improves students' writing, while others fear that it weakens it. |

# Prewriting

> **Gather Sources and Take Notes** > As you continue to research your topic, use an electronic database or an online search engine. Collect several primary and secondary sources from credible print and digital sources. You may need to refocus the question guiding your research, depending on what you find.

| **Primary sources** are firsthand accounts. | letters, diaries, interviews, historical documents, speeches |
| --- | --- |
| **Secondary sources** are secondhand accounts based on primary sources. | encyclopedias, history textbooks, biographies, analyses of literature |

Gather a variety of relevant details, such as facts, statistics, and expert opinions. Take notes by summarizing, paraphrasing, or quoting.

- A **summary** restates only the main ideas and key details from the source. It is much shorter than the original text.

- A **paraphrase** restates the ideas in the source, but it is usually the same length as the original.

- A **quotation** copies the exact words of the source and places them inside quotation marks.

> **Track Sources** > Take **notes** on your sources, including the author, title, publication information, and relevant details. Create numbered **source cards,** such as the one below, or use a computer to keep track of your notes. You'll use these notes to create a Works Cited list. (See page 266.)

(See page 266.)

Text Messaging and School                                                    3

Text-messaging shortcuts are creeping more and more into

students' formal writing. (page 42)

Number of source that this detail refers to

Detail and page that it appears on

# Drafting

**Organize the Body** Follow the guidelines below.

See **Chapter 5** for more information about writing introductions, conclusions, and body paragraphs.

- Your **introduction** and **conclusion** are doorways. Your readers enter and exit the report through them. Make sure your introduction grabs your readers' attention with an unusual fact, interesting anecdote, or brief story. Your conclusion should restate your thesis, or claim, and give your readers a sense that your report is complete.

- The **body** supports your claim. Every paragraph should include a **topic sentence,** which states the main idea for that paragraph. All details in a paragraph should support the topic sentence.

- The order of body paragraphs and the order of sentences within each paragraph should be clear and easy to follow. Connect sentences and paragraphs with **transitions,** such as *first* and *mainly*.

Refer to an outline, such as the one below, as you draft.

## Writing Model

Thesis, or Claim: The rise of text messaging has raised a debate among educators. Some educators believe text messaging improves students' writing, while others fear that it weakens it.

Use Roman numerals for each main idea.

Indent, and use a capital letter for each supporting detail.

Use either complete sentences or phrases in an outline.

    I. Text messaging may strengthen writing skills.
       A. Because of text messaging, students write more.
       B. "Textspeak" abbreviations help students take notes in class.
    II. Text messaging may lead to poor writing.
       A. Abbreviations and slang appear in school papers.
       B. Studies show a drop in students' grammar and spelling skills.

# Revising

Use the Revising Questions to review your draft. The model below shows revisions made to part of a body paragraph.

As you revise, keep in mind the traits of good writing. See **Lesson 1.3.**

## Revising Questions

❏ How clear is my thesis statement, or claim?

❏ How effectively did I use details from both primary and secondary sources?

❏ How effectively and accurately did I paraphrase, summarize, or quote sources?

❏ Where can I add transitions to clarify order?

❏ How strong are my introduction, body, and conclusion?

¹Think of the five most common abbreviations you use when you send a text message. ²You probably would find it strange if someone used those abbreviations when he or she spoke to you. ³However, the shorthand used in text messaging is no longer just found on cell phones or online. ⁴It is beginning to appear in formal writing, such as academic papers. ⁵For example, A recent article stated that "students are turning in papers with abbreviations and symbols like &. "(Jan 3) ⁶This trend weakens students' writing is not good.

Add transitional words to link ideas.

Add in-text citation. Be specific.

## Revising

**Avoid Plagiarism** Failing to **cite,** or name, your sources is plagiarism. **Plagiarism** is the stealing of other people's words or ideas. Here are some general rules to follow to avoid plagiarism.

1. The source for any fact that is not common knowledge must be documented. A fact is considered common knowledge if it is almost universally known. For example, the fact that George Washington was the first president of the United States is considered common knowledge for American readers.

2. Cite your sources in the body of your report with an **in-text citation.** This rule is true regardless of whether you used a quotation, a paraphrase, or a summary.

   Some teachers encourage students to use "textspeak" in appropriate settings, such as note-taking and informal writing (Swirsky 5).

3. Include a **Works Cited** list at the end of your report. This list identifies the sources you cited in your report. For the correct format to use, ask your teacher. The Modern Language Association (MLA) format is shown below.

List sources in alphabetical order by the author's last name.

If an entry runs over a line, indent the following lines by one-half inch.

Double-space the entire list.

### Works Cited

Alvarez, Eve. "Text Talk's Toll." *Tech Trends*

   3 Oct. 2008. Web. 18 Oct. 2012.

Holmes, Jake. "Pupils Use 'Text Speak.'" *Student News*

   19 Jan. 2008: 1. Print.

Ian, Shana B. "The Effect of Text Messaging on

   Students' Writing." *Publishing Times* 19 Oct. 2009:

   1–8. Print.

## Editing and Proofreading

Next, slowly reread your report, looking for any errors in grammar, usage, mechanics, or spelling. Use the Editing and Proofreading Checklist as a guide.

### Editing and Proofreading Checklist

❑ Have I checked that all words are spelled correctly?
❑ Have I used quotation marks and apostrophes correctly?
❑ Have I correctly used end punctuation?
❑ Have I indented the first line of every paragraph?

▸ **Check Direct Quotations** Check that you used correct punctuation in your quotations.

1. When you quote a source exactly, set it in quotation marks. Always put the end mark after the citation, never before.

   According to an article in *Publishing Times*, teens claim that they **"**use text-speak naturally**"** (Ian 1)**.**

2. Place a comma before the quotation if a speech tag precedes it.

   According to Lee**,** "Many teachers find the trend alarming" (Ian 2).

3. Place a comma inside the closing quotation marks if a speech tag follows the quotation.

   Text messaging "makes writing a daily habit for some teens**,**" Swirsky explains (15).

> For more help with commas and quotation marks, see Lessons **11.4** and **11.6.**

## Editing and Proofreading

**Writing Model**

¹A report from 2007 indicated that the ability of students to use grammar successfully was on the decline. ²According to the report's author∧"students are unduly reliant on short sentences, simple tenses and a limited vocabulary⊙"(Sorrel 10)⊙³The author's claim that this is the result of text messaging is based on thousands of student writing samples.

**Remember**

Use visual aids, such as charts or graphs, to present complicated information or data. Make sure your visuals are clear and relate to your ideas.

## Publishing and Presenting

Now that you've finished your report, use one of these ways to share it with others.

- **Post it.** Post your report on the Internet. Create a link to any online source that you cited in your report.

- **Make a documentary.** Interview your classmates about the subject of your research report. Ask for their opinions. Share your findings with the class.

- **Present it.** Show photographs, diagrams, charts, and any objects related to the subject that will enhance your presentation. Invite another class to hear the presentation.

**Reflect On Your Writing**

- Which part of your report is most effective?
- Which part of your report did you have the hardest time writing? Why?
- What have you learned as a researcher?

# Chapter Review

## A. Practice Test

Read each sentence below. Decide which answer choice best replaces the underlined part, and fill in the circle of the corresponding letter. If you think the underlined part is correct, fill in the circle for choice *A*.

EXAMPLE

Ⓐ Ⓑ Ⓒ Ⓓ Ⓔ    <u>Madam CJ. Walker was a self made</u> African-American businesswoman.
(A) Madam CJ. Walker was a self made
(B) Madam C. J. Walker was a self made
(C) Madam. CJ Walker was a self made
(D) Madam C. J. Walker was a self-made
(E) Madam CJ' Walker was a self—made

Ⓐ ● Ⓒ Ⓓ Ⓔ  **1.**  <u>Walker whose birth name was Sarah Breedlove was born in 1867.</u>
(A) Walker whose birth name was Sarah Breedlove was born in 1867.
(B) Walker, whose birth name was Sarah Breedlove, was born in 1867.
(C) Walker, who's birth name was Sarah Breedlove, was born in 1867.
(D) Walker, whose birth name was Sarah Breedlove was born in, 1867.
(E) Walker whose birth name, was Sarah Breedlove, was born in 1867.

Proofread answer choices carefully for errors in punctuation. If someone is quoted, be sure that the speaker's exact words are enclosed in quotation marks.

ⒶⒷⒸⒹ**Ⓔ** 2. <u>Breedlove had five siblings</u> Louvenia, Alexander, James, Solomon, and Owen, Jr.
(A) Breedlove had five siblings
(B) Breedlove had: five siblings
(C) Breedlove had, five siblings,
(D) Breedlove had five siblings.
(E) Breedlove had five siblings:

ⒶⒷⒸ**Ⓓ**Ⓔ 3. In 1905, Breedlove moved to <u>Denver: where she invented a product called Madam Walkers'</u> Wonderful Hair Grower.
(A) Denver: where she invented a product called Madam Walkers'
(B) Denver; where she invented a product called Madam Walkers'
(C) Denver where she invented a product: called Madam Walkers
(D) Denver, where she invented a product called Madam Walker's
(E) Denver—where she invented: a product called Madam Walker's

ⒶⒷ**Ⓒ**ⒹⒺ 4. She moved to <u>New York in 1916 there, she got involved in civil rights activities'.</u>
(A) New York in 1916 there, she got involved in civil rights activities'.
(B) N.Y. in 1916, there: she got involved in civil rights activities.
(C) New York in 1916, and there she got involved in civil rights activities.
(D) New York in 1916 and she got involved in civil right's activities.
(E) New York in 1916: there, she got involved in civil rights activities

ⒶⒷⒸⒹ**Ⓔ** 5. When asked how she became a success, <u>Walker said—"I got my start by giving myself a start".</u>
(A) Walker said—"I got my start by giving myself a start".
(B) "Walker said: I got my start by giving myself a start".
(C) Walker said "I got my start by giving myself a start".
(D) "Walker said," I got my start by giving myself a start.
(E) Walker said, "I got my start by giving myself a start."

## B. Proofreading a Research Report

Use proofreading symbols to correct any punctuation errors in this introduction from a research report. Then answer the questions that follow. Answers will vary. Sample answers are shown.

| Proofreading Symbols | | | |
|---|---|---|---|
| ∧ | Add. | ⋎ | Delete. |
| ∧ (comma) | Add a comma. | / | Make lowercase. |
| ⊙ | Add a period. | ≡ | Capitalize. |

¹Consider the following quotation from Virginia Woolf's book, *A Room of One's Own*: "A woman must have money and a room of her own if she is to write fiction." ²This statement may seem obvious today. ³In the 1920s, however, most women did not have such things. ⁴In addition, literature written by women was not often considered important. ⁵Woolf argued that literature had been created by men and reflected men's needs (Grudin 56). ⁶Beliefs like these made Woolf an important figure in women's literature in the twentieth century.

**1.** How effective is the first part of the introduction?
The first part is effective. The author begins with an interesting quotation.

**2.** How clear and strong is the thesis, or claim?
The thesis is not very clear. Saying that she is important is very general.

**3.** What is one suggestion you would make to the author?
Make the thesis more specific. Perhaps the author could narrow it by previewing the main points that will be presented in the research report.

# Proper Nouns and Proper Adjectives

**Proper nouns** name specific people, places, things, or ideas. (See Lesson 7.1.) **Proper adjectives** are formed from proper nouns. (See Lesson 9.1.) Proper nouns and proper adjectives should begin with a capital letter.

| Type of Word | Examples |
|---|---|
| Names of specific people and animals | Albert Einstein, Lassie, J. K. Rowling |
| Languages and nationalities | Canadian, French, American, Mexican |
| Religions and religious writings | Buddhism, Christianity, Judaism, the Bible, the Koran, the Torah |
| Cities, states, regions, countries, and continents | Africa, Athens, Greece, China, Hawaii, the Northwest, Europe |
| Bodies of water and other geographical features | Grand Canyon, Nile River, Rocky Mountains, Blue Lake |
| Streets and highways | Ashland Avenue, Highway 70, Boxwood Road |
| Celestial bodies | Mars, Jupiter, Big Dipper, Milky Way |
| Titles used before or instead of a person's name | President Lincoln, General Patton, Uncle Ted, Judge Katherine Lee |
| Proper adjectives | British accent, Asian food, Shakespearean plays, Persian rug |

**WRITING HINT**

Do not capitalize words such as *north*, *south*, and *southwest* when they refer to compass directions. Capitalize these words only when they refer to a region or section.

The afternoon sun was in our eyes as we hiked west.

Fishing is an important industry in the Northwest.

# EXERCISE 1 Correcting Capitalization

Add a proofreading symbol (≡) under all letters that should be capitalized in the following sentences.

**EXAMPLE**   odessa is the fourth largest city in ukraine.

1. port huron is the easternmost point on land in the state of michigan.

2. The new england area includes Maine, new Hampshire, vermont, Massachusetts, rhode Island, and Connecticut.

3. The presbyterian minister gave an hour-long sermon.

**Remember**

Do not capitalize a common noun that refers to a proper noun.

The lake near my house is Lake Ontario.

**4.** Many people enjoy <u>b</u>ritish plays.

**5.** The effects of global warming can be felt from <u>a</u>ntarctica to many <u>s</u>outh American cities.

## EXERCISE 2 Proofreading an Article

Insert or delete capital letters as needed in the following article. To indicate a capital letter, use the symbol (≡). To indicate lowercase, use a slash (/).

**HiNT**

One word shows a family relationship. Capitalize it only if it is used as a name.

my aunt **A**unt Eileen

FRANCIS SCOTT KEY.

**Writing Model**

¹<u>f</u>rancis <u>s</u>cott <u>k</u>ey was the son of <u>j</u>ohn <u>r</u>oss <u>k</u>ey. ²He went to <u>S</u>chool at <u>st</u>. <u>j</u>ohn's and practiced law for a time with his uncle in <u>f</u>rederick <u>c</u>ity, Maryland. ³The <u>b</u>ritish invaded <u>w</u>ashington in 1814. ⁴One of Key's friends was captured by the <u>b</u>ritish. ⁵With the help of <u>p</u>resident <u>m</u>adison, Key rescued his friend. ⁶Key witnessed the attack on <u>b</u>altimore. ⁷When the fighting stopped, he looked to see if the <u>a</u>merican flag still flew. ⁸It did. ⁹Key was so moved that he wrote the song, "The Star-Spangled Banner." ¹⁰In a short time, people all over the <u>u</u>nited <u>s</u>tates knew the song. ¹¹A <u>M</u>onument to Key stands in <u>s</u>an <u>f</u>rancisco's Golden Gate Park.

# Quotations and Titles

➡ When deciding which words to capitalize in a quotation, pay attention to where the speaker's words begin and end.

**1.** Capitalize the first letter of a direct quotation if it is a complete sentence.

> Jenny asked, "**W**ill the picnic be tomorrow?"

**2.** When the second part of a divided quotation is a new sentence, add a period after the interrupting expression (or speech tag), and begin the next sentence with a capital letter.

> "No," said Lizzie firmly. "**W**e have no way to get there."

**3.** When the second part of a divided quotation continues the sentence, begin it with a lowercase letter.

> "Please," pleaded Jenny, "**w**e've already bought the food."

> To review the use of quotation marks in quotations and titles of short works, see **Lesson 11.6.**

➡ Capitalize the first and last words in titles of works such as books, songs, stories, poems, paintings, or newspapers.

**1.** Capitalize all nouns, pronouns, adjectives, verbs, and adverbs.

> "**S**weet **M**usic **P**layed **S**oftly"      "**W**e **L**ost"

**2.** Capitalize prepositions that are part of a verb phrase.

> "Backing **U**p Your Disk"      "Fitting **I**n at Camp"

**3.** Capitalize the second word in a compound word if it is a noun or a proper adjective or if it is of equal importance to other words.

> "Cross-**R**eference Tools"      *Test-**T**aking Strategies*

**4.** Do not capitalize articles, coordinating conjunctions, or prepositions with fewer than five letters unless they are the first word.

> *Cat in the Hat*      *Beauty and the Beast*      "**A** Bad Day"

# Exercise 1 Proofreading Sentences

Insert or delete capital letters as needed in the sentences below. Use proofreading symbols to mark corrections. To indicate a capital letter, use three underscores (≡). To indicate lowercase, use a slash (/).

**EXAMPLE** "we should talk," the coach explained, "about the game on Saturday."

1. "We've been practicing a lot," Angie said. "are we ready?"

2. The coach smiled. "yes, but you must keep your focus."

3. "What tips do you have," Daisy asked, "To improve our focus?"

4. "Do stretches and breathing exercises right before the game," she advised, "So that you are relaxed."

5. "Above all, stay confident," The coach said.

# Exercise 2 Rewriting Titles

Rewrite the following imaginary titles, making sure to capitalize them correctly.

1. "Setting up Your Computer"
"Setting Up Your Computer"

2. *The Time of our Lives*
*The Time of Our Lives*

3. "The Man survives"
"The Man Survives"

4. *Bringing in the money*
*Bringing In the Money*

5. "Let me Be Free"
"Let Me Be Free"

6. *Captain Of The Tigers*
*Captain of the Tigers*

7. *James And The cowboy*
*James and the Cowboy*

8. *Dancer in blue*
*Dancer in Blue*

9. *The Philadelphia daily News*
*The Philadelphia Daily News*

10. "Bears win Championship"
"Bears Win Championship"

# Exercise 3 Writing a Paragraph

Write a paragraph of at least five sentences. In your paragraph, briefly explain why you like a particular animal, hobby, or item of clothing. Include at least one direct quotation, and check your paragraph for correct capitalization.

Answers will vary. See sample answer in Answer Key at www.grammarforwriting.com.

# Other Capitalization Rules

Remember to capitalize the first word in every sentence and the pronoun *I*. The chart below shows other words that should be capitalized.

| Rule | Examples |
|---|---|
| Days, months, and holidays (but not seasons) | April, Labor Day, Thanksgiving, Tuesday, winter, summer |
| Historical events, documents, and periods | Civil War, Middle Ages, Declaration of Independence, Industrial Revolution |
| Monuments and buildings | Eiffel Tower, Golden Gate Bridge, Lincoln Memorial, Statue of Liberty |
| Organizations, teams, businesses, and brand names | Girl Scouts of America, New England Patriots, University of Illinois, Foodee Mart, Raisin Bites |
| Awards | Nobel Peace Prize, Pulitzer Prize, Purple Heart, World Cup |
| Governmental agencies | Congress, House of Representatives, Peace Corps, Senate, Supreme Court |
| Most abbreviations | Mr., Ms., Mrs., Jr., Sr., FBI, Ave., St., N.J., P.O. Box |
| First word in the greeting and closing of a letter | Dear Paula, My dear friend, Yours truly, |

**Remember**

In proper nouns that consist of more than one word, do not capitalize short words, such as *a, an, and, the,* or prepositions of fewer than five letters.

War **of** 1812

# EXERCISE 1 Correcting Capitalization Errors

Use proofreading marks to insert or delete capital letters as needed in the sentences below. If a sentence is correct, write *C*.

**EXAMPLE**   Pilgrim settlers wrote the mayflower compact in 1620.

**1.** In the United States, thanksgiving is celebrated on the fourth thursday in november.

**2.** In Canada, thanksgiving is celebrated in the Fall, on the second monday in october.

3. On july 8, 1776, the liberty bell rang out from the tower of independence hall.

4. The bell called the Citizens of Philadelphia to the first public reading of the declaration of independence.

5. You and i visited harvard university, our nation's oldest Institution of higher learning, last Summer.

6. My teacher, mr. Mehta, explained that the U.S. congress is made up of two bodies.

7. The congressional medal of honor was first issued during the civil war.

8. The statue of liberty was named a national Monument on october 15, 1924.

9. The California gold rush happened during the 1800s.

10. Many people moved to California during that time.ᶜ

**Working Together**

# EXERCISE 2 Writing Sentences

On a separate sheet of paper, write a one- or two-sentence response to each numbered question below. Ask a partner to help you proofread your sentences for correct use of capital letters.
Answers will vary. Sample answers are shown.

1. **What is an organization you would like to join? Why?**
I wish to be a member of the Patriots, our school's track team, because I love to run.

2. **What historical event would you like to know more about? Why?**
I would like to learn more about the Vietnam War. I am not sure how or why it started.

3. **Which building or monument would you like to visit? Why?**
I would enjoy visiting the Eiffel Tower. Climbing up it and getting a good view of Paris would be a thrill.

4. **What is your least favorite season? Why?**
My least favorite season is spring because that's when my allergies get really bad.

5. **What made-up award do you think you deserve? Why?**
I deserve the Barney's Best Friend Award. Barney is my dog, and I play with him and walk him every day.

# Spelling Rules

Learning some common spelling rules can help you become a better speller.

▶ Write *i* before *e* except after *c*, or when it sounds like a long *a* as in *neighbor* and *weigh*.

    bel**ie**ve      p**ie**ce      rec**ei**ve      v**ei**n      **ei**ght

▶ When you add a **prefix** to the beginning of a word, do not change the spelling of the word.

    *un-* + reliable = **un**reliable      *mis-* + spell = **mis**spell

▶ A **suffix** is added to the end of a base word. Learn the following rules:

1. If a word ends in *-y* preceded by a consonant, change the *-y* to *i* before adding a suffix.

       empty + *-ness* = empt**i**ness      busy + *-er* = bus**i**er

   *Exception*: Keep the *-y* when adding *-ing*. (empt**ying,** bus**ying**)

2. If a word ends in *-y* preceded by a vowel, keep the *-y*.

       joy + *-ous* = joy**ous**      employ + *-ment* = employ**ment**

3. Drop the final silent *-e* when you add a suffix that begins with a vowel.

       desire + *-able* = desir**able**      move + *-ing* = mov**ing**

   *Exception*: Keep the final silent *-e* if the word ends in *-ge* or *-ce* and the suffix begins with *a* or *o*. (courag**eous,** notic**eable**)

4. Keep the final silent *-e* when you add a suffix that begins with a consonant.

       advance + *-ment* = advance**ment**      care + *-less* = care**less**

5. For one-syllable words that end in a single consonant preceded by a single vowel, double the consonant before adding a suffix that starts with a vowel.

       flat + *-est* = flat**test**      swim + *-ing* = swim**ming**

## Common Prefixes

| | |
|---|---|
| *mis-* | (bad) |
| *pre-* | (before) |
| *re-* | (again) |
| *sub-* | (below) |
| *super-* | (above) |

## Common Suffixes

| | |
|---|---|
| *-able* | (capable of being) |
| *-ate, -fy* | (make, become) |
| *-er, -or* | (a person who) |
| *-less* | (without) |
| *-ous, -ful* | (full of) |

**R**emember

Almost every rule has exceptions. The best way to avoid spelling errors is to check a dictionary or use spell-check.

# EXERCISE 1  Using Prefixes and Suffixes

Spell each of the following words, adding the prefix or suffix. You may consult a dictionary.

**1.** wise + *-dom*
wisdom

**2.** notice + *-able*
noticeable

**3.** love + *-ing*
loving

**4.** pay + *-ment*
payment

**5.** heavy + *-ness*
heaviness

**6.** *pre-* + writing
prewriting

**7.** hit + *-ing*
hitting

**8.** *dis-* + approve
disapprove

**9.** hurry + *-ed*
hurried

**10.** plate + *-ful*
plateful

**11.** hop + *-ing*
hopping

**12.** *im-* + mortal
immortal

**13.** mystery + *-ous*
mysterious

**14.** spin + *-ing*
spinning

**15.** pretty + *-er*
prettier

# EXERCISE 2 Proofreading Sentences

If a sentence contains a misspelled word, underline it, and write the correct spelling. If a sentence has no spelling errors, write *C*.

**EXAMPLE**   The plane <u>droped</u> quickly. *dropped*

**1.** Someone's briefcase spilled open. c

**2.** The plane was <u>circleing</u> back to try to land. circling

**3.** I <u>retreived</u> my backpack from the aisle. retrieved

**4.** I was <u>hopeing</u> we would land soon.   hoping

**5.** My seatmate seemed to be the most <u>worryed</u> of anyone.
worried

**6.** I wanted to <u>recieve</u> more information from the pilot. receive

**7.** As the engine noise grew odder, my knees were <u>shakeing</u>.
shaking

**8.** I <u>tryed</u> to make jokes and seem courageous. tried

**9.** The <u>happyest</u> moment came when we finally touched down.
happiest

**10.** We were so relieved to land safely. c

# EXERCISE 3 Analyzing Your Writing

Find a draft of a paper you are currently working on. Use a dictionary to check it for any spelling errors. List any words you misspelled, and identify which, if any, of the rules in this lesson apply. Answers will vary.

**Remember**

Some spelling errors occur when you use the wrong word. Be careful to use **homophones** correctly. They are words that sound the same but have different spellings and meanings.

passed/past
peace/piece
threw/through

See page 293 for other commonly confused words.

# Plural Nouns

Refer to the chart below for help in forming **plural nouns.**

| Noun Type | Rule | Examples |
|---|---|---|
| **Most singular nouns** | Add -s. | cell — cell**s** |
| **Nouns that end in a consonant + -o** | Add -es. | echo — echo**es**<br>hero — hero**es** |
| **Nouns that end in a vowel + -o** | Add -s. | duo — duo**s**<br>radio — radio**s** |
| **Nouns that end in -s, -sh, -ch, -x, or -z** | Add -es. | match — match**es**<br>pass — pass**es**<br>wish — wish**es** |
| **Nouns that end in a consonant + -y** | Change the -y to i, and add -es. | city — cit**ies**<br>story — stor**ies**<br>worry — worr**ies** |
| **Nouns that end in a vowel + -y** | Add -s. | toy — toy**s**<br>valley — valley**s** |
| **Most nouns that end in -fe or -f** | Change the -f to v, and add -s or -es. | life — li**ves**<br>calf — cal**ves** |
| **Some nouns that end in -f** | Add -s. | chief — chief**s**<br>belief — belief**s** |
| **Compound nouns** | Make the most important word plural. | brother-in-law — brother**s**-in-law |

**R**emember

Be sure not to confuse possessive nouns that end in -s with plural nouns.

his **sister's** coat [coat of his sister]

his two **sisters** [more than one sister]

See **Lesson 7.2** for more about plural and possessive nouns.

➠ The plurals of some nouns are formed in irregular ways.

man — men        mouse — mice        person — people

➠ The singular and plural forms of some words are the same.

deer        moose        sheep        series

**ONLINE PRACTICE**
www.grammarforwriting.com

## EXERCISE 1  Writing with Plurals

Form the plural of each of the nouns below. Then write a sentence using the plural of each noun.

Sentences will vary. See sample answers in Answer Key at www.grammarforwriting.com.

**R**emember

Check your sentences for subject-verb agreement. Plural subjects take plural verbs. See **Chapter 10** for more practice with subject-verb agreement.

**EXAMPLE**   baby

*babies—The babies at the zoo are my favorites.*

**1.** life
lives

**2.** turkey
turkeys

**3.** church
churches

**4.** mouse
mice

**5.** craft
crafts

**6.** potato
potatoes

**7.** gate
gates

**8.** tomato
tomatoes

**9.** child
children

**10.** great-aunt
great-aunts

**11.** solo
solos

**12.** gulf
gulfs

**13.** studio
studios

**14.** sheep
sheep

**15.** gym
gyms

**16.** ferry
ferries

**17.** mix
mixes

**18.** piano
pianos

**19.** cheese
cheeses

**20.** half
halves

## EXERCISE 2  Proofreading for Plural Nouns

Read the following student paragraph. Find and correct the eight misspelled plural nouns. If you are unsure, use a dictionary.

**Writing Model**

¹My family saw ~~wolfs~~ (wolves) and ~~deers~~ (deer) this summer when we camped at a national park. ²I wish we had seen some monkeys or giraffes! ³Three young ~~childs~~ (children) came with us, and they had the best time of their lives. ⁴We are city ~~peoples~~ (people) and do not often see ~~animal's~~ (animals) other than birds, dogs, or cats. ⁵Away from thousands of ~~womens~~ (women) and ~~mans~~ (men), life was so much fun in the park. ⁶I want to take as many camping ~~journies~~ (journeys) as possible.

# Business Letter

**Business letters** are formal letters to a business or individual requesting a particular action. Business letters can have a variety of purposes.

## Purposes of a Business Letter

- to make a complaint and request action
- to request a change
- to apply for a job
- to make a recommendation

When you write a business letter, remember to include the following features.

## Key Features

- clearly stated purpose and relevant details
- concise formal language and precise words
- logical order
- all parts of a business letter
- correct capitalization, punctuation, and spelling

## ASSIGNMENT

**TASK:** Write a one- to two-page **business letter** to make a complaint and request action.

**PURPOSE:** to inform and persuade

**AUDIENCE:** a business

**KEY INSTRUCTIONS:** Write at least three paragraphs in the body of your letter.

**State Your Purpose** Your **purpose** is your reason for writing. In this case, your purpose is to make a complaint and request an action. Without a clearly stated purpose, the recipient of your letter will not understand why you are writing. State your purpose at the beginning of your letter.

UNCLEAR   Two weeks ago, I purchased a music player from your Web site. I usually buy all of my electronics online, but I'm unsure if I should in the future.

CLEAR   I am writing to make a complaint about a purchase I made from your company two weeks ago. I would like to be reimbursed for the cost of my purchase.

**Write Clear Paragraphs** If you want a business to take your letter seriously, stay focused on your purpose. Do this by creating **paragraph unity,** or including only relevant details in your paragraphs. As the model below illustrates, unnecessary details are distracting and make it difficult for the recipient to understand your request or take action on it.

For more help with improving paragraph unity, see **Lesson 4.2.**

### Writing Model

Cut unnecessary details.

Give specific information.

State your request directly.

¹I am unhappy with the music player that I purchased from your Web site. ²~~This is unusual, because I'm easy to please.~~ ³The player can store only half the amount of information that your Web site claimed it could. ⁴The color of the player is also not what I requested. ⁵Your company offers a money-back guarantee, and I would like a refund of my money. ⁶~~This experience will not prevent me from shopping online in the future.~~

**Be Clear and Formal** Make sure that you use **precise language.** Avoid words that do not clearly express your meaning.

VAGUE     I will accept **whatever solution** will fix this situation.

PRECISE   I will accept **reimbursement or an exchange** for the correct player.

Also, since you are writing to a business, use **formal language** in your letter. Formal language is free of contractions, slang, and abbreviations. For more help with precise and formal language, see Lessons 2.6 and 2.7.

INFORMAL  I'd hoped to receive the music player ASAP! But, it took forever to get here.

FORMAL    I had hoped to receive the music player promptly. Unfortunately, the package arrived several weeks later.

**How It Should Look** Follow the format below.

4341 Granite Street
Lansing, MI 48901
December 8, 2012

**Heading:** your address plus the date

Mr. Robert Curtis
1989 West Chesterfield Lane
Chicago, IL 60618

**Inside Address:** your recipient's name and address

Dear Mr. Curtis:

**Greeting:** the beginning of your letter

I am writing to make a complaint about a purchase I made from your company two weeks ago.

**Body:** states your purpose and gives details

Sincerely,

**Closing:** a formal phrase that ends your letter

Chandra Beck

**Signature:** your whole name

## CONNECTING
### Writing & Grammar

Include a colon after the greeting. Include a comma in four parts of your letter:

- between the city and state in the heading
- between the day and year in the heading
- between the city and state in the inside address
- after the closing

For more about commas and colons, see **Lessons 11.3, 11.4,** and **11.5.**

## WRITING CHECKLIST
### Did you...

✔ clearly state your purpose?

✔ include only relevant details?

✔ include all the parts of a business letter?

✔ state what action you would like the business to take?

✔ use a colon in the greeting?

✔ add a comma in four parts of the letter?

▶ **Check Your Draft** ▶ Use the Writing Checklist on the left to review your letter. Note one writer's business letter below.

### Writing Model

4341 Granite Street
Lansing, MI 48901
December 8, 2012

Mr. Robert Curtis
1989 West Chesterfield Lane
Chicago, IL 60618

Dear Mr. Curtis:

¹I am writing to make a complaint about a purchase I made from your company two weeks ago. ²I would like to be reimbursed for the cost of my purchase.

³I am unhappy with the music player that I ordered from your Web site. ⁴The player can store only half the amount of information that your Web site claimed it could. ⁵The color of the player is also not what I requested. ⁶Your company offers a money-back guarantee. ⁷I believe I am covered by this guarantee. ⁸I will accept reimbursement or an exchange for the correct player.

⁹Please contact me by e-mail with any questions you might have. ¹⁰Also, let me know as soon as you have made a decision regarding my complaint. ¹¹Thank you.

Sincerely,
**Chandra Beck**
Chandra Beck

Clear purpose and request

Relevant details

Formal language

# Chapter Review

## A. Practice Test

Read the draft and questions below carefully. The questions ask you to choose the best revision for sentences or parts of the draft. Fill in the corresponding circle for your answer choice.

**(1)** Marlee matlin was born in 1965 in a chicago Suburb. **(2)** She could hear when she was born, but she became deaf after liveing through a serious case of the measles when she was 18 month's old. **(3)** "When I was young, I knew I was deaf. I couldn't accept it, Matlin once told *People* magazine. **(4)** Matlin became interested in acting as a child and performed in shows with the children's theater for the deaf at chicago's center for deafness. **(5)** At just 22 years old, she won an academy award for her role as Sarah Norman in *Children Of A Lesser God*. **(6)** When speaking about her disability, Matlin said, "The real handicap of deaffness is not in the ear, but in the mind. **(7)** We can achieve much more if we focus on our abilitys rather than our perceived disabilitys."

Ⓐ Ⓑ Ⓒ ● Ⓔ **1.** Which words in sentence 1 should be capitalized?
    (A) Marlee, Matlin, Chicago, Suburb
    (B) Matlin, Chicago, Suburb
    (C) Marlee, Matlin, Suburb
    (D) Marlee, Matlin, Chicago
    (E) Marlee, Matlin, born

**TEST-TAKING TIP**

When answering multiple-choice questions, be sure to read each question carefully. Pay special attention to negative words and key words such as *all* and *except*. These words can change the meaning of the question, so they can also change what you should be looking for in the correct answer.

Ⓐ⬤ⒸⒹⒺ **2.** Which words in sentence 2 are misspelled?
    (A) born, month's
    (B) liveing, month's
    (C) liveing, serious
    (D) case, liveing, measles
    (E) when, month's

⬤ⒷⒸⒹⒺ **3.** Choose the correct way to punctuate and capitalize the quotation in sentence 3.
    (A) "When I was young, I knew I was deaf. I couldn't accept it," Matlin once told *People* magazine.
    (B) "When I was young, I knew I was deaf". "I couldn't accept it." Matlin once told *People* Magazine.
    (C) "When I was young, I knew I was deaf, I couldn't accept it, Matlin once told *People* magazine."
    (D) "When I was young, I knew I was deaf. I couldn't accept it, "Matlin once told *people* magazine."
    (E) When I was young, I knew I was deaf. I couldn't accept it," matlin once told *People* magazine.

ⒶⒷⒸ⬤Ⓔ **4.** Which capitalization rule is followed correctly in sentences 4 and 5?
    (A) Capitalize words in a title.
    (B) Capitalize names of organizations.
    (C) Capitalize names of awards.
    (D) Capitalize names of people.
    (E) Capitalize names of cities.

⬤ⒷⒸⒹⒺ **5.** Which words are misspelled in sentences 6 and 7?
    (A) deaffness, abilitys, disabilitys
    (B) abilitys, disabilitys, perceived
    (C) deaffness, achieve
    (D) perceived, achieve
    (E) deaffness, achieve, perceived

## B. Identifying Capitalization Rules

Use proofreading symbols to correct capitalization errors in the following sentences. Then write the rules you followed to make the corrections.

**Proofreading Symbols**

≡ Capitalize.

/ Make lowercase.

**1.** Isaac Bashevis Singer grew up in a poor jewish neighborhood in warsaw, poland. Capitalize religions, cities, and countries.

**2.** In 1917, the hardships of world war I separated his family.
Capitalize historical events.

**3.** Singer's first novel published in english was *the family moskat*.
Capitalize languages; capitalize first and last words and nouns in titles.

**4.** "The wastebasket," Singer once said, "Is the writer's best friend."
Don't capitalize the second part of a divided quotation unless it begins a new sentence.

**5.** Singer joined the national institute of arts and letters in 1964 and won the nobel prize in 1978. Capitalize names of organizations; capitalize awards.

## C. Choosing the Correct Spelling

For each item below, underline the word in parentheses that is spelled correctly.

**1.** As I rode by Megan's house, I saw a (moveing, <u>moving</u>) van out in front.

**2.** "I didn't hear that you were leaving," I said. "How could you break up our (<u>friendship</u>, freindship)?"

**3.** "I'm not leaving," Megan (<u>replied</u>, replyed). "We just got a new (<u>piece</u>, peice) of furniture."

**4.** The delivery men pulled the (heavyest, <u>heaviest</u>) sofa ever out of the truck and carried it through Megan's front door.

**5.** "Put it right here," her mother said. "You've been so (helpfull, <u>helpful</u>)."

## D. Forming Plurals

Complete each sentence below. In the blank, write the correct plural form of the word in parentheses.

**1.** My favorite Thanksgiving food is my mom's garlic mashed <u>potatoes</u>. (potato)

**2.** My aunt makes a delicious pie with fresh <u>peaches</u>. (peach)

**3.** We have dinner with a few other neighborhood <u>families</u>. (family)

**4.** We decorate the table with autumn <u>leaves</u>. (leaf)

**5.** Some of our neighbors eat dinner on their <u>patios</u>. (patio)

## E. Editing a Business Letter

Read the draft of a business letter below.

See answer in Answer Key at www.grammarforwriting.com.

- Rewrite the letter on a separate sheet of paper.
- Correct any errors in capitalization, spelling, and punctuation. Use a dictionary if necessary.
- Then, on a separate sheet of paper, answer the questions below.

ms. Bobbie Kleinfeld
silver arrow summer camp
P.O. Box 32
whispering pines, MA, 01267

Dear Ms. Kleinfeld,

[1]I am writeing to thank you for the great time I had at your Camp when i came for my interview last week. [2]the campground's are the niceest I have seen anywhere, and the peak of mount Greylock riseing in the distance is a wonderful sight.

[3]I passed my swiming test last month, and I am now qualifyed to work as a junior lifeguard. [4]I would love the opportunity to be a counselor at silver Arrow this Summer. [5]I have filled out your emploiment application carfully, and I hope to hear from you soon.

Sincerely
Stephanie Jackson
Stephanie Jackson

Students' answers will vary. Sample answers are shown below.

1. What features of a good business letter does this draft have?

2. What are two suggestions you would give to the writer to improve her letter?

1. The draft has a clearly stated purpose, a clear order, and all the parts of a business letter except for the heading. Also the language is precise and formal, and there are no irrelevant details.

2. I would suggest that the writer add a heading and do a much more careful job proofreading for distracting errors.

Copyright © 2014 by William H. Sadlier, Inc. All rights reserved.

290  Chapter 12 • Capitalization and Spelling

Chapter Review

# Frequently Misspelled Words

| | | | |
|---|---|---|---|
| abbreviate | brief | decision | exceed |
| accidentally | bulletin | definite | existence |
| achievement | business | dependent | experience |
| all right | cafeteria | description | familiar |
| analyze | calendar | desirable | fascinating |
| anonymous | campaign | despair | favorite |
| answer | cancel | development | February |
| apologize | candidate | dictionary | foreign |
| appearance | caught | different | fragile |
| appreciate | cemetery | disappear | generally |
| appropriate | certain | disappoint | genius |
| argument | changeable | discipline | government |
| athlete | characteristic | dissatisfied | grammar |
| attendance | clothing | eighth | guarantee |
| awkward | colonel | eligible | guard |
| beautiful | column | embarrass | height |
| because | committee | enthusiastic | humorous |
| beginning | courageous | environment | immediately |
| believe | criticize | especially | independent |
| bicycle | curiosity | exaggerate | irritable |

| | | | |
|---|---|---|---|
| jewelry | nuclear | pursue | success |
| judgment | nuisance | realize | surprise |
| knowledge | obstacle | receipt | syllable |
| laboratory | occasionally | receive | sympathy |
| leisure | opinion | recognize | symptom |
| library | opportunity | recommend | temperature |
| license | outrageous | reference | thorough |
| lightning | parallel | rehearse | throughout |
| literature | particularly | repetition | tomorrow |
| loneliness | people | restaurant | traffic |
| mathematics | permanent | rhythm | tragedy |
| minimum | persuade | ridiculous | truly |
| mischievous | pleasant | sandwich | Tuesday |
| misspell | pneumonia | schedule | unnecessary |
| necessary | possess | scissors | usable |
| neighbor | possibility | separate | usually |
| nickel | prejudice | similar | vacuum |
| niece | privilege | sincerely | various |
| ninety | probably | souvenir | vicinity |
| noticeable | psychology | specifically | weird |

# Commonly Confused Words

▶ **accept, except** *Accept* is a verb that means "to receive" or "to agree to something." *Except* is a preposition that means "but."

Melinda will **accept** the offer.

She liked all of the features of the house **except** the basement.

▶ **affect, effect** *Affect* is usually a verb that means "to influence." When *effect* is used as a noun, it means "the result of an action."

The storm will **affect** the school outing.

The **effects** will probably be a cancellation and several disappointed students.

▶ **all ready, already** *All ready* is a phrase that means "completely ready." *Already* is an adverb that means "before now."

Julio's family is **all ready** for the family portrait.

The photographer **already** has the studio set up.

▶ **all right** *All right* is always spelled as two words.

Is it **all right** if I go to Carmen's house?

▶ **borrow, lend** The verbs *borrow* and *lend* are opposites. *Borrow* means "to take something temporarily for later return." *Lend* means "to give something temporarily."

My friend asked if he could **borrow** my new video game.

I will **lend** it to him this week.

▶ **bring, take** These verbs are opposites. Use *bring* to refer to an action toward or with the speaker. Use *take* to refer to an action away from the speaker.

**Bring** a pencil to class.

**Take** your jacket to the coat room.

**capital, capitol** *Capital* is usually a noun that refers to a city. Use the word *capitol* to refer to a building where the state government meets.

Springfield is the **capital** of Illinois.

News reporters gathered in front of the **capitol** building.

**desert, dessert** *Desert* can be a noun that means "a hot, dry area of land." It can also be a verb that means "to abandon." The noun *dessert* is a sweet treat.

The tourists will **desert** the **desert** if the heat is unbearable.

A peach with whipped cream is a refreshing **dessert**.

**fewer, less** Use *fewer* to refer to nouns that can be counted. Use *less* to refer to nouns that can't be counted.

**Fewer** viruses affected the computer.

**Less** space was needed on the desk.

**good, well** *Good* is always an adjective. *Well* can be an adjective or an adverb. As an adjective, *well* refers to health. As an adverb, *well* means "done in a satisfactory way."

Dr. Johnson is a **good** doctor.

If I don't feel **well,** I see him. He does his job **well**.

**it's, its** *It's* is a contraction for "it is." *Its* is a possessive pronoun.

**It's** time to take the dog to the vet.

**Its** shots are due.

**lay, lie** *Lay* means "to place." *Lie* means "to recline."

**Lay** the book on the shelf.

If you **lie** down to read, you'll probably fall asleep.

⏸▶ **lead, led** *Lead* (pronounced with a long *e* as in *bead*) is usually a present tense verb that means "to guide." *Led* is the past tense of *lead*.

> Can you **lead** us through the corn maze?

> The last time I **led** us, we got lost.

⏸▶ **loose, lose, loss** *Loose,* an adjective, means "free or not tied up." *Lose,* a verb, means "to misplace." *Loss* is a noun that means "something or someone that was lost."

> The cockatoo got **loose**.

> The owner cannot **lose** his prized bird.

> It would be a terrible **loss**.

⏸▶ **passed, past** *Passed* is the past tense of the verb *pass,* and it means "went by" or "succeeded." *Past* can be an adjective that means "of a previous time." As a noun, *past* means "a previous time."

> When I **passed** Mr. Young's classroom, I shouted that I **passed** my English test.

> I had spent the **past** two weeks studying for it.

> I spent more time than I had in the **past**.

⏸▶ **peace, piece** *Peace* means "a state of calm or stillness." *Piece* means "a part of something."

> The early morning hours were full of **peace**.

> I wrote a poem on a **piece** of paper.

⏸▶ **principal, principle** A *principal* is a person in charge of a school. A *principle* is a belief.

> Our school **principal** is a strong leader.

> He has a **principle** of honesty.

➡ **their, there, they're** *Their* is a possessive pronoun. *There* is a pronoun used to introduce a sentence. *They're* is a contraction for "they are."

Where should runners do **their** stretches?

**There** are tons of runners in this marathon.

**They're** determined to win.

➡ **to, too, two** *To*, a preposition, means "in the direction of." *Too*, an adverb, means "also" or "very." *Two* is the number 2.

Bring a friend **to** the party.

You can bring your brother, **too**.

Don't arrive **too** early.

**Two** bands will play.

➡ **whose, who's** *Whose* is an interrogative pronoun. *Who's* is a contraction for "who is."

Do you know **whose** phone this is?

**Who's** calling?

➡ **your, you're** *Your* is a possessive pronoun. *You're* is a contraction for "you are."

Finish **your** homework on Friday so **you're** not worried about it all weekend.

# Index

## A

*a, an,* 201
abbreviations, 247–248, 277
   state, 247
abstract nouns, 157
*accept, except,* 293
acronyms, 247
*Across the Centuries,* 92
action verbs, 145, 181
active voice, 44, 189, 196
address, abbreviations for, 247
adjective(s). *See also* adverb(s);
  modifiers
   articles as, 201
   comma to separate, 249
   defined, 201
   degrees of comparison in, 203
   distinguishing between
    adverbs and, 205
   infinitives as, 191
   participles as, 191
   predicate, 147, 201, 205
   proper, 202, 273
   use of, 205
adjective phrases, 211
adverb(s). *See also* adjective(s);
  modifiers
   defined, 201
   degrees of comparison in, 203
   distinguishing between
    adjectives and, 205
   ending of, with *-ly,* 201
   infinitives as, 191
   use of, 205
adverb phrases, 211
*affect, effect,* 293
agreement
   pronoun-antecedent,
    161, 165
   subject-verb, 143, 227,
    229, 282
   collective nouns and, 235
   with compound subjects, 231
   with compound subjects and
    verbs, 143
   with indefinite pronouns
    and, 235
   with inverted subjects, 233
   phrases between subject and
    verb and, 229
*Alice's Adventures in Wonderland,*
  by Lewis Carroll, 83

*all ready, already,* 293
*all right,* 293
anecdotes
   in conclusion, 123
   as evidence, 170
   as supporting details, 92
antecedent, 161, 162, 167, 175
   pronoun agreement with,
    161, 165
apostrophe(s)
   in contractions, 257
   in forming plurals, 257
   in possessive nouns, 159
   to show omitted letters or
    numbers, 257
   to show possession, 257
appositive phrases, 77
   commas to set off, 77
argument. *See* persuasive essay
articles as adjectives, 201
audience, 10, 11, 54
audio presentations, 21
autobiographical writing, 22–28
   drafting in, 25
   editing and proofreading
    in, 28
   key features of, 22
   prewriting in, 23–24
   publishing and presenting
    in, 28
   revising in, 26–27
awards, capitalizing, 277

## B

*be,* forms of, 147, 186
*The Big Sea,* by Langston
  Hughes, 27
block method organization, 129
blog, posting work in, 85
body, 12
   in book review, 218
   in compare-contrast
    essay, 131
   in essays, 113, 120–121
   in persuasive essay, 172
   in research report, 264
   in writing response, 239
book review, 215–221
   drafting in, 218
   editing and proofreading for,
    220–221
   key features of, 215

   prewriting for, 216–217
   publishing and presenting
    in, 221
   revising of, 219
books, italicizing title for, 71
*borrow, lend,* 293
brainstorming, 9, 23, 81,
  127, 194
brand names, capitalizing, 277
*bring, take,* 293
buildings, capitalizing, 277
businesses, capitalizing, 277
business letters, 283–286
   colon after greeting in, 253
   formal language in, 285
   key features of, 283
   parts of, 284–285
   purposes of, 283, 284

## C

calendar items, abbreviating, 247
*Call Me María,* by Judith Ortiz
  Cofer, 211
*capital, capitol,* 294
capitalization
   of abbreviations, 277
   of awards, 277
   changing, in correcting
    sentence fragments, 138
   of days, months, and
    holidays, 277
   of first word in greeting and
    closing of letter, 277
   of first words in quotations,
    255, 275
   of first words in sentence, 137
   of governmental
    agencies, 277
   of historical events,
    documents, and
    periods, 277
   of monuments and
    buildings, 277
   of organizations, teams,
    businesses, and brand
    names, 277
   of proper adjectives, 273
   of proper nouns, 28, 157, 158
   in split quotation, 275
   of titles of works, 275
*capitol, capital,* 294
cause and effect, 121
   transition to show, 99, 121

characters, creating, in story, 80
checklists
    editing and proofreading, 17, 28, 85, 132, 174, 267
    revising, 14
    topic, 9
    writing, 55, 107, 152, 196, 240, 286
chronological order, 24, 81, 96, 121, 195
    in autobiographical writing, 22, 24
    in narrative paragraph, 101
    in stories, 79
citation, in-text, 266
*City of the Beasts,* by Isabel Allende, 212
claim, 52, 53, 115–118, 169, 170
clause(s)
    commas with, 251
    defined, 69
    independent, 69
    subordinate, 33, 69, 137
    words that begin, 66
clichés, avoiding using, 47
climax, 79, 81
coherence, in paragraphs, 96, 121
collective nouns, 157
    subject-verb agreement and, 235
colons
    after greeting in business letter, 253, 285
    before formal or long quotation, 253
    between hour and minutes, 253
    to introduce list of items, 253
combining sentences
    compound parts, 75
    compound subjects and verbs in, 143
    key words and phrases in, 77
    parallel structure in, 41–43
commas
    after greeting in friendly letter or before short quotation, 253
    after introductory phrase, 78, 99, 137
    after mild interjection, 213
    after opening transition, 99
    after speech tag, 25
    after transitional phrase, 99, 105

    avoiding use of, between compound subject or compound verbs, 75
    in business letters, 285
    in compound sentences, 36, 72, 75, 249, 254
    defined, 249
    position with quotation marks, 255
    to separate date in sentence, 251
    to separate direct quotation from rest of sentence, 251
    to separate two or more adjectives, 249
    in series, 41, 249, 250
    to set off appositives, 77, 251
    to set off interrupters, 251
    to set off introductory group of words, 209, 251
    to set off parenthetical expressions, 251
    to set off speech tags, 255, 267
    to set off subordinate clause, 67, 70, 137, 251
common nouns, 157
comparative degree, 203
compare-contrast essay, 126–132
    drafting for, 129
    editing and proofreading for, 132
    key features of, 126
    prewriting for, 127–128
    publishing and presenting for, 132
    revising for, 130–131
comparison(s), 121, 129, 203
comparison and/or contrast of pattern of organization, 121
complete predicate, 137, 139
complete subject, 137, 139
complex sentences, 73
compound-complex sentences, 73
compound direct object, 145
compound noun, 157
compound parts, 75
compound predicate adjectives, 147
compound predicate nominatives, 147
compound prepositions, 211
compound sentences, 72, 75, 84
    comma in forming, 36, 72, 75, 249, 254

    semicolon in forming, 72, 75, 253
compound subjects, 75, 143, 231, 240
    subject-verb agreement and, 231
compound verbs, 38, 75, 143
compound words
    capitalization in, 275
    hyphens in joining, 259
computer
    drafting on, 18
    editing and proofreading on, 18
    spell-checking on, 18
conciseness, 44, 151
concluding sentence, 113
conclusions, 12
    in book review, 218
    in compare-contrast essay, 131
    in essays, 113, 123–124
    in persuasive essay, 172
    in research report, 264
    in writing prompt response, 239
concrete noun, 157
conflicts, 24
    brainstorming for, 81
    external, 24, 81
    internal, 24, 81
conjunctions, 213
    coordinating, 36, 72, 75, 213
    correlative, 213
    subordinating, 69, 70
*Connecting Writing and Grammar,* 25, 28, 41, 53, 67, 70, 75, 77, 82, 99, 105, 118, 124, 132, 137, 141, 150, 152, 175, 189, 191, 196, 209, 218, 220, 240, 251, 285
connotations of words, 151
contractions
    apostrophe in, 257
    subject-verb agreement and, 233
contrasts, transition to show, 121, 129
controlling idea, 115
coordinating conjunctions, 213
    in compound sentences, 72, 75
    in correcting run-on sentences, 36
correlative conjunctions, 213
counterarguments, 171
    tone in responding to, 171

**D**

dashes
    length of, 260
    to set off explanation, 259
    to show break in
      thought, 259
dates, commas to separate parts
  of, 251
days, capitalizing, 277
declarative sentence, 61
    period at end of, 137, 245
degrees of comparison, 203
    irregular, 203
demonstrative pronouns, 161
denotations of words, 151
dependent clauses. *See*
  subordinate clauses
descriptive writing, 101, 104–107
    key features of, 104
*desert, dessert,* 294
"Design Flaws," by Bill Bryson, 119
details
    adding, 39, 64, 191
    gathering, 11, 23, 128
    organizing, 10, 24, 81, 96
    sensory, 39, 82, 92, 101,
      106–107
    supporting, 92
    vivid, 27
diagrams. *See* graphic organizers
dialogue, 82
    adding comma after speech
      tag in, 25
    bringing stories to life
      with, 25
    quotation marks in, 82
    sentence fragments in, 33
dictionary, 47
    abbreviations in, 247
    checking spelling in, 279
    compound nouns in, 157
    irregular verbs in, 185
differences, transition to show, 99
direct address, commas with, 251
direct objects, 145, 148
    for action verbs, 181
    gerund as, 191
    object pronoun as, 163
direct quotations
    capitalization in, 255, 275
    commas with, 251
    quotation marks with, 124,
      255, 267
double comparison, 203
double negatives, 207

drafting, 12–13
    in autobiographical
      writing, 25
    of book review, 218
    of compare-contrast
      essay, 129
    defined, 12
    of persuasive essay, 172
    of research report, 264
    of stories, 82
    of thesis statement, 262
dynamic character, 80

**E**

editing and proofreading, 17–19
    of autobiographical writing,
      28
    of book review, 220–221
    checklist for, 17, 28, 85, 132,
      174, 267
    of compare-contrast
      essay, 132
    defined, 17
    of persuasive essay, 174–175
    of research paper, 267–268
    of story, 85
editorials, 175
*effect, affect,* 293
elaboration, 92
e-mail, 221
    colon after greeting in, 253
end marks, 61, 137
    defined, 245
    exclamation point as,
      137, 245
    period as, 245
    question mark as, 245
English
    formal, 50–51
    informal, 50–51
*Esperanza Rising,* by Pam Muñoz
  Ryan, 66
essays
    body in, 113, 120–121
    coherence of, 121
    compare-contrast, 126–132
    conclusion in, 113, 123–124
    expository, 113
    how-to, 20
    introduction in, 113, 117–118
    parts of, 113
    persuasive, 20, 113, 169–175
    thesis statement in,
      115–116, 117
essay tests, 116
evidence

    stating, 170, 217
    supporting reasons with, 53
examples
    as evidence, 170
    as supporting details, 92
    transitions to show, 99
*except, accept,* 293
exclamation point
    after interjection, 213
    as end mark, 137, 245
    following abbreviation at end
      of sentence, 248
    position with quotation
      marks, 255
exclamatory sentence, 61, 84
exposition, 79, 81
expository writing, 101–102
    instructions as, 193
    parts of, 113
external conflict, 24, 81

**F**

facts
    as evidence, 170
    as supporting details, 92
falling action, 79, 81
family relationships,
  capitalization of words that
  show, 274
feedback, in peer review, 26
*fewer, less,* 294
first-person point of view, 24, 82
    in autobiographical
      writing, 22
formal English, 50–51
formal language, 285
freewriting in prewriting, 9, 127
future perfect tense, 187
future tense, 187

**G**

gerund phrases, 191
gerunds, 191
gestures, using, 55
*good, well,* 294
governmental agencies,
  capitalizing, 277
graphic organizers, 127
    Argument Organizer as, 52
    in brainstorming, 127, 194
    Character Chart as, 80, 128
    Inverted Pyramid, 10, 127
    listing details in, 24
    Sequence Chart as, 10, 24, 195
    Timeline as, 24
    Venn diagram as, 116, 126, 239

Web as, 104, 217
graphics in presentations, 21
greeting, in business letter, 253

# H

hard-to-find subjects, 141
helping verbs, 70, 181, 187
    common, 139, 181, 227
    with past tense, 184
historical events, documents, and
    periods, capitalizing, 277
holidays, capitalizing, 277
homophones, 280
how-to essay, 20
hyphens
    compound adjectives with, 259
    to divide words, 259
    to join compounds, 259–260
    length of, 260
    numbers with, 259

# I

ideas
    and content, 14
    claim, 115
    controlling, 115
imagery, 106–107
imaginary setting, 80
*I'm a Stranger Here Myself,* by Bill
    Bryson, 119
imperative sentences, 61
    period at end of, 137, 245
implied main idea, 91
importance, order of, 97
    transition to show, 121
impression, 25
indefinite pronouns, 161, 165
    plural, 165, 235
    showing ownership with, 257
    singular, 165, 235
    subject-verb agreement and,
    235
independent clauses, 69
    in complex sentence, 73
    in simple sentence, 72
infinitive phrases, 191
infinitives, 191
informal English, 50–51
information
    checking accuracy of, 220
    transition to show, 121
informative/explanatory writing,
    126–132, 150–152, 193–196,
    261–268
informative paragraphs, 101–102
    topic sentences in, 91

initials, 247
instructions, 193–196
    active voice in, 196
    key features of, 193
    transitions in, 195
interjections, 213, 245
internal conflict, 24, 81
Internet
    posting of report on, 268
    in sharing essay, 132
interrogative sentence, 61
    question mark at end of,
    137, 245
interrupters, setting off with
    commas, 251
in-text citation, 266
introduction, 12
    in book review, 218
    in compare-contrast essay,
    131
    in essay, 113, 117–118, 123
    length of, 117
    linking to conclusions, 123
    in persuasive essay, 172
    in research report, 264
    in writing prompt
    response, 239
introductory phrase, comma
    after, 78, 137, 251
Inverted Pyramid, 10, 127
inverted sentences, 141, 233
    subject-verb agreement
    in, 233
irregular degrees of
    comparison, 203
irregular verbs, 183, 185
italics, 71
*it's, its,* 294

# L

language
    formal, 285
    precise, 47, 54
*lay, lie,* 294
*lead, led,* 295
*lend, borrow,* 293
*less, fewer,* 294
letters. *See also* business letters
    apostrophes with, 257
linking verbs, 145, 147, 181
    common, 147, 181
    predicate adjectives and,
    201, 205
    predicate nominative after, 163
    subject complement for,
    147, 181

lists
    colon to introduce, 253
    numbered, 195
    in prewriting, 217
literary analysis, 237–240
*Literary Model,* 27, 42, 64, 66, 83,
    92, 94, 99, 119, 146, 171, 181,
    189, 211, 212
location, transition to show,
    99, 121
logical order, 97
*loose, lose, loss,* 295

# M

main clauses. *See* independent
    clauses
main idea, 91
    implied, 91
    supporting, 92
main verb, 181
misplaced modifiers, 209
    avoiding, 220
    fixing, 209
modifiers. *See also* adjective(s);
    adverb(s)
    defined, 209, 220
    misplaced, 209, 220
months, capitalizing, 277
monuments, capitalizing, 277
mood, 80
movie titles, italicizing, 71

# N

names
    initials with, 247
    proper, 142
    titles with, 247
narrative writing, 101
    chronological order in, 101
    conflict in, 24
negatives, double, 207
negative words, 207
nonessential appositives, commas
    with, 251
nonessential clauses, commas
    with, 251
notes, taking, 263
noun(s), 157
    abstract, 157
    collective, 157
    common, 157
    compound, 157
    concrete, 157
    defined, 157
    as direct object, 145
    gerund as, 191

infinitive as, 191
plural, 159, 228, 258, 281
possessive, 159
as predicate nominative, 147
proper, 28, 157, 273
numbers
  apostrophes to form plurals
    of, 257
  apostrophes to show left
    out, 257

**O**

object pronouns, 163
objects
  direct, 145, 148, 163, 181, 191
  of preposition, 163, 166,
    191, 211
  of prepositional phrase, 166
online dictionary, 18
opinion, offering, 123
opposition, making room for, 171
oral presentation, 20
organization in revising checklist,
  14
organization in writing prompt
  response, 239
organization pattern, 121
  cause and effect of, 121
  chronological, 22, 24, 79, 81,
    96, 121, 195
  comparison and/or contrast
    of, 121
  of importance, 97, 99, 121
  logical, 97
  spatial, 96, 121
organizations
  abbreviations for, 247
  capitalizing names of, 277
outline, 172, 264
ownership, apostrophe to show,
  257

**P**

paragraphs
  being specific in, 106
  change of speakers in, 256
  clarity of, 105
  coherence in, 96
  descriptive, 101, 104–107
  expository, 101–102
  informative, 101–102
  main idea in, 91
  narrative, 101
  parts of, 91–92
  patterns of organization in,
    96–97

persuasive, 102
  supporting detail in, 92
  topic sentence in, 91
  types of, 101–102
  unity in, 94, 105, 284
parallel structure (parallelism),
  41–43
  as persuasive technique, 54, 171
paraphrase, 150, 263
parentheses, 259
parenthetical expressions, setting
  off with commas, 251
participial phrases, 191
participles, 191
  past, 183
  present, 183
parts of speech. *See also*
  adjective(s); adverb(s);
  conjunctions; interjections;
  noun(s); preposition(s);
  pronoun(s); verb(s)
  defined, 157
*passed, past*, 295
passive voice, 44, 189, 196
past as principal parts of verb,
  183
past participle as principal parts
  of verb, 183
past perfect tense, 187
past tense, 187
  avoid helping verb with, 184
*peace, piece*, 295
peer review, 15, 26
perfect tense, 187
periods
  as end mark, 137, 245
  at end of abbreviations, 247
  with quotation marks, 255
personal pronouns
  use as objects, 163
  use as subjects, 163
  use in sentence, 161
persuasive speeches, 52–55
  key features of, 52
persuasive techniques, 54–55
persuasive writing, 20, 102,
  169–175
  drafting of, 172
  editing and proofreading of,
    174–175
  key features of, 169
  prewriting, 170–171
  publishing and presenting of,
    175
  revising in, 173
photographs

in making presentations, 21,
  28
phrases, 69
  adjective, 211
  adverb, 211
  appositive, 77
  between subject and verb, 229
  commas with, 251
  gerund, 191
  infinitive, 191
  participial, 191
  prepositional, 163, 211, 212,
    229
  verb, 139, 181, 227
*piece, peace*, 295
*The Pigman & Me*, by Paul Zindel,
  64
*A Place Called Ugly*, by Avi, 42
plagiarism, 266
plot
  defined, 81
  parts of, 81
  in stories, 79
plot diagram, 79
plural nouns, 159, 228, 258, 281
  apostrophes in, 257
plural subjects, 227
plural verbs, 227
poems, 20
point by point organization, 129
point of view, 82
  first-person, 24, 82
  third-person limited, 82
  third-person omniscient, 82
portfolio, writing, 21
position, taking in persuasive
  speech, 53
positive degree of comparison, 203
possession, apostrophes with, 257
possessive nouns, 159
possessive pronouns, 161
precise language, 47, 54, 285
predicate
  complete, 137, 139
  simple, 139
predicate adjectives, 147
  compound, 147
  linking verb and, 201, 205
predicate nominative, 147, 148,
  163
  subject pronoun as, 163
predicate noun, gerund as, 191
prefixes, 279
preposition(s)

capitalization of, in verb phrase, 275
common, 211, 229
compound, 211
defined, 211
object of, 163, 211
prepositional phrases, 163, 211
defined, 229
object of, 166
position of, in sentence, 212
present as principal parts of verb, 183
presentations, 20–21. *See also* publishing and presenting
present participle
forming, 185
as principal parts of verb, 183
present tense, 187, 190
in writing about literary works, 218
prewriting, 9–11
analyzing audience in, 10, 11
in autobiographical writing, 23–24
for book review, 216–217
brainstorming in, 9, 23, 127, 194
choosing purpose in, 10, 11
choosing topic in, 10, 23, 105, 170, 262
for compare-contrast essay, 127–128
defined, 9
freewriting in, 9, 127
gathering details in, 23, 128
gathering sources in, 263
narrowing subject in, 9, 127
organizing details in, 10, 11, 24
for persuasive essay, 170–171
research in, 127
of research paper, 262–263
stating reasons and evidence, 170
for stories, 80–81
taking notes in, 263
Web in, 9, 27
primary sources, 263
principal parts
of irregular verbs, 185
of verbs, 183
*principal, principle,* 295
pronoun(s)
agreement with antecedent, 165
antecedent for, 161, 162
avoiding errors with, 175
defined, 161, 175
demonstrative, 161
as direct object, 145
indefinite, 161, 165, 235
object, 163
personal, 161, 163
possessive, 161
as predicate nominative, 147
subject, 163
types of, 161
pronoun reference, 167
proofreading. *See also* editing and proofreading
symbols in, 17–18
proper adjectives, 202
capital letter for, 273
proper names, 142
proper nouns, 28, 157
capital letter for, 28, 158, 273
publishing and presenting, 20–21
for autobiographical writing, 28
for book review, 221
for compare-contrast essay, 132
for persuasive essay, 175
for research report, 268
for story, 85
punctuation. *See also specific mark*
changing, in correcting sentence fragments, 138
purpose, in writing, 10, 11, 284

**Q**
question(s), 84
ending conclusion with, 123
revising, 26, 83, 130, 173, 265
rhetorical, 54, 171
question marks
as end mark, 245
following abbreviation at end of sentence, 248
with quotation marks, 255
quotation(s), 263
direct, 124, 267
ending conclusion with, 123
as evidence, 170
as supporting details, 92
quotation marks
defined, 255
for direct quotations, 124, 267
enclosing dialogue in, 82
question mark or exclamation point with, 245
for titles of short works, 255

**R**
realistic setting, 80
*Real-World Writing,* 15, 39, 47, 106
reasons, 170, 217
*Reflect on Your Writing,* 28, 85, 132, 175, 221, 268
regular verbs, 183
repetition, 54, 171
research in prewriting, 127
research reports, 20, 261–268
drafting of, 264
editing and proofreading of, 267–268
key features, 261
prewriting of, 262–263
publishing and presenting of, 268
revising of, 265–266
Works Cited in, 266
resolution, 79, 81
revising, 14–16
in autobiographical writing, 26–27
of book review, 219
checklist for, 14
for compare-contrast essay, 130–131
peer review in, 15
in persuasive essay, 173
questions for, 26, 83, 130, 173, 265
in research report, 265–266
of stories, 83–84
thesis statements, 115
in writing process, 14–16
rhetorical questions, 54, 171
rising action, 79, 81
run-on sentences, 36–38

**S**
secondary sources, 263
semicolons
in compound sentences, 36, 72, 75, 253
in series, 253
sensory details, 39, 82, 106–107
in descriptive paragraph, 101
as supporting details, 92
sentence(s)
adding details to, 39–40, 64, 96
capitalization in, 137

changing word order in, 76
combining short, 118
commas after transition in compound, 254
complete, 139
complete predicate in, 137, 139
complete subject in, 137, 139
complex, 73, 84
compound, 72, 75, 84
compound subjects in, 231
concluding, 113
coordinating conjunction in, 36, 72, 75, 213
correlative conjunction in, 213
declarative, 61, 245
defined, 137
end punctuation in, 137, 245
exclamatory, 61, 84, 245
imperative, 61, 245
interrogative, 61, 245
inverted, 141, 233
kinds of, 61
parallel structure in, 41–43
patterns of organization, 96–97
simple, 72, 84
subordinating conjunction or clause in, 69, 70
supporting, 113
topic, 91, 94, 113, 120
varying, 63, 66–67, 72–73, 84
sentence fluency, 14
sentence fragments, 69, 137
correcting, 33, 34, 53, 137, 138, 152
defined, 33
in dialogue, 33
identifying, 34
in persuasive speeches, 171
Sequence Chart, 10, 24, 195
series
commas in, 41, 249, 250
semicolons in, 253
setting, 80
similarities, transition to show, 99
simple predicate, 139
simple sentences, 72, 84
simple subject, 139
singular subject, 227
*The Skin I'm In,* by Sharon G. Flake, 181
slang, 50

*Something Wicked's in Those Woods,* by Marisa Montes, 99
sources, 263
spatial order, 96, 121
speech, 52–55
key features of, 52
persuasive, 52–55, 175
practicing, 54–55
speech tags, 25, 255
commas to set off, 255, 267
spell-check, 18
spelling rules, 279
with comparisons, 203
*i* before *e* except after *c,* 279
for irregular verbs, 183
for plural nouns, 281
when adding prefix, 279
when adding suffix, 279
state abbreviations, 247
statements, thesis, 115–116, 117, 120, 128, 170, 216, 238, 262
static character, 80
*Step by Step,* 123, 145, 229
stories, 20, 79–85
conflict in, 81
dialogue in, 25, 82
drafting, 82
editing and proofreading of, 85
key features of, 79
mood of, 80
plot in, 79, 81
prewriting, 80–81
publishing and presenting of, 85
revising of, 83–84
theme in, 81
study notes, purpose of, 149
style, formal, 52, 126, 129, 169, 171, 237
subject, 227
agreement with verb, 143, 227, 229, 240, 282
complete, 137, 139
compound, 75, 143, 231, 240
defined, 139
finding, 140
gerunds as, 191
hard-to-find, 141
phrases between verb and, 229
plural, 227
simple, 139
singular, 227
subject pronoun as, 163

understood, 61, 141
subject complements, 147
linking verb need for, 147
for linking verbs, 181
predicate adjective as, 147
predicate nominative as, 147
subject pronouns, 163
subordinate clauses, 33, 69, 137
in complex sentence, 73
using comma after, 67, 137
words that begin, 66
subordinating conjunctions, 69, 70
suffixes, 279
summary, 149–152, 263
conciseness in, 151
in conclusion, 123
including essential information in, 150
key features of, 149
superlative degree, 203
supporting details, 92
in Venn diagram, 239
supporting sentences, 113
symbols, proofreading, 17–18
synonyms, 47
in thesaurus, 25, 47, 49, 151

**T**
*take, bring,* 293
*Tangerine,* by Edward Bloor, 189
teams, capitalizing names of, 277
technology, 20, 85, 132, 221, 261–268
terms, defining unknown, 195
tests, essay, 116
*Test-Taking Tip,* 36, 86, 116, 148, 163, 176, 214, 241, 269, 287
*the,* 201
*their, there, they're,* 296
theme, 81
thesaurus, 151
synonyms in, 25, 47, 49
thesis statements, 115–116
body paragraphs and, 120
for book review, 216
in compare-contrast essay, 128
drafting, 262
for essay, 117
for essay test, 116
in persuasive essay, 170
in prewriting, 128
revising, 115
for writing prompt

response, 238
*they're, their, there,* 296
third-person limited, 82
third-person omniscient, 82
time(s)
    abbreviations for, 247
    colon in, 253
    transition to show, 99, 121
Timelines, 24
title(s)
    giving, to paper, 20
    with names, 247
titles of works
    capitalization of, 275
    italicizing, 71
    quotation marks with, 255
*to, too, two,* 296
tone, 171
topic
    checklist for, 9
    choosing, 23, 105, 170, 262
    narrowing of, 9, 127
topic sentence, 94, 113
    for body paragraphs, 120
    in research report, 264
    stating of main idea in, 91
traits of good writing, 14, 17
transitions
    adding comma after, 99, 105
    common, 66
    in compound sentence, 254
    in instruction, 195
    in persuasive essay, 172
    to show cause and effect,
      99, 121
    to show comparisons, 121,
      129, 239
    to show contrasts, 121,
      129, 239
    to show examples, 99
    to show importance, 121
    to show information, 121
    to show location, 99, 121
    to show order of
      importance, 99
    to show organization, 96, 264
    to show similarities and
      differences, 99
    to show time, 24, 99, 121

**U**
underlining. *See* italics
understood subject, 61, 141
unity, in paragraphs, 94, 105,
120, 284

**V**
Venn diagrams
    brainstorming with, 127
    as graphic organizers, 116,
      126, 239
verb(s), 139, 181–192, 227
    action, 145, 181
    active voice for, 44, 189
    agreement with subject, 143,
      227, 229, 240, 282
    compound, 38, 75, 143
    helping, 70, 139, 181, 187
    irregular, 183, 185
    linking, 145, 147, 181
    main, 181
    passive voice for, 44, 189
    plural, 227
    present tense, 190
    principal parts of, 183
    regular, 183
verbals, 191
verb phrases, 139, 181, 227
    capitalization in, 275
verb tenses, 187
video recording, 55
visuals, 21, 195
voice
    active, 44, 189, 196
    monitoring your, 55
    passive, 44, 189, 196
    in revising checklist, 14

**W**
Web, 9, 104, 217
*well, good,* 294
"What Is an American?" by
    Harold Ickes, 171
*Where Will This Shoe Take You?
A Walk Through the History of
Footwear,* by Laurie Lawlor, 94
*whose, who's,* 296
word(s)
    connotations of, 151
    denotations of, 151
    negative, 207
word choice, 47, 106, 151
    in revising checklist, 14
wordiness
    avoiding, 44, 45, 189
Works Cited, 266
*A Wrinkle in Time,* by Madeleine
    L'Engle, 146

writer's block, 12
writer's workshops
    autobiographical writing,
      22–28
    book review, 215–221
    compare-contrast essay,
      126–132
    persuasive essay, 169–175
    research report, 261–268
    story, 79–85
*Write What You Think,* 35, 68,
    103, 140, 158, 184, 236, 252
writing
    avoiding wordiness in, 44, 45
    checklists for, 55, 107, 152,
      196, 240, 286
writing applications
    business letter, 283–286
    descriptive paragraph,
      104–107
    instructions, 193–196
    speech, 52–55
    summary, 149–152
    writing prompt response,
      237–240
writing conventions, 14
*Writing Hint,* 14, 20, 24, 33, 45,
    54, 72, 80, 81, 83, 91, 96, 115,
    117, 120, 125, 151, 165, 167,
    170, 171, 172, 174, 183, 195,
    201, 207, 216, 231, 239, 245,
    253, 263, 273
*Writing Model,* 13, 16, 18, 25, 55,
    82, 84, 85, 96, 97, 101, 102,
    107, 129, 130, 131, 152, 172,
    173, 174, 194, 195, 196, 218,
    219, 221, 228, 234, 238, 239,
    240, 264, 268, 274, 282,
    284, 286
writing portfolio, 21
writing process, 9–21
    editing and proofreading in,
      17–19
    prewriting in, 9–11
    publishing and presenting in,
      20–21
    revising in, 14–16
writing prompt response,
    237–240

**Y**
years
    apostrophes with, 257
    commas with, 251
*you,* as subject, 61
*your, you're,* 296